HISTORY AS IT I

SYRIA

DESCENT INTO THE ABYSS

The ♦INDEPENDENT

Mango Media
Miami
in collaboration with
The Independent

Independent Print Limited

Copyright © 2016 The Independent. All rights reserved.
This material may not be published, broadcast, rewritten or redistributed.

Published by Mango Media, Inc.
www.mangomedia.us

No part of this publication may be reproduced, distributed or transmitted in any form or by any means, without prior written permission.

This is a work of non-fiction adapted from articles and content by journalists of The Independent and published with permission.

SYRIA *Descent Into The Abyss*
ISBN: 978-1-63353-370-7

"Western Intervention in Syria would make matters worse."

– Patrick Cockburn, April 2011

Table of Contents

Spring 2011: It Begins

PROTESTS SWEEP THROUGH SYRIA AS TROOPS OPEN FIRE 1

DESPERATE ASSAD TRIES TO BLUNT UPRISING WITH NEW PROMISES OF REFORM 2

SHOTS FIRED AS PROTESTERS TAKE TO THE STREETS AGAIN 5

WESTERN INTERVENTION IN SYRIA WOULD MAKE MATTERS WORSE 6

OUT OF SYRIA'S DARKNESS COME TALES OF TERROR 9

AS TANKS LINE THE STREETS, SYRIANS STAND FIRM TO DEFY BRUTAL REGIME 12

Summer 2011: Armed Insurrection

THE PEOPLE VS THE PRESIDENT 15

'THEY SHOT PEOPLE WHO WERE TRYING TO GET AWAY' 17

THEY CAME AT DAWN, AND KILLED IN COLD BLOOD 20

THE NEW FOCUS OF SYRIA'S CRACKDOWN HAS SEEN SIMILAR BLOODSHED BEFORE 23

IT'S HIS FAST-DISAPPEARING BILLIONS THAT WILL WORRY ASSAD, NOT WORDS FROM WASHINGTON 25

Autumn 2011: Dying For Assad

'WE ARE ALL READY TO BE MARTYRED FOR SYRIA AND OUR PRESIDENT' 27

SYRIA SLIPS TOWARDS SECTARIAN WAR 29

WHAT THE KILLING OF GADDAFI MEANS TO SYRIA 31

COMPARED WITH SYRIA, THE FALL OF LIBYA WAS A PIECE OF CAKE 34

Winter 2012: Conflict Goes International

ONLY A CRAZY LEADER KILLS HIS OWN PEOPLE, SAYS ASSAD 37

SYRIA'S SECTARIAN WAR GOES INTERNATIONAL AS FOREIGN FIGHTERS AND ARMS POUR INTO COUNTRY 38

JOURNALISTS KILLED IN SYRIA ROCKET STRIKE 'WERE TARGETED' 40

ASSAD OPENS NEW FRONT IN WAR ON HIS PEOPLE 42

'WE ARE NOT AFRAID OF ASSAD ANY LONGER. BUT WHY MUST MORE PEOPLE DIE?' 44

'I HAVE TO HELP MY FAMILY, BUT I DID NOT WANT TO SHOOT MY OWN PEOPLE' 47

Spring 2012: 'Cleaning'

THE REGIME CALLS IT 'CLEANING', BUT THE DIRTY TRUTH IS PLAIN TO SEE 51

THE FEARFUL REALITIES KEEPING THE ASSAD REGIME IN POWER 52

SYRIA IS TOO FAR STEEPED IN BLOOD FOR RESOLUTION BY NEGOTIATION 56

AS THE BODIES CONTINUE TO MOUNT UP, A PEOPLE ON EDGE PREPARE FOR CIVIL WAR 57

THE WEST IS HORRIFIED BY CHILDREN'S SLAUGHTER NOW. SOON WE'LL FORGET 59

HAGUE SENT PACKING BY RUSSIA AS ANNAN PEACE PLAN CRUMBLES 60

Summer 2012: Inconvenient Truth

WESTERN AGREEMENT 'COULD LEAVE SYRIA IN ASSAD'S HANDS FOR TWO MORE YEARS' 63

SYRIAN WAR OF LIES AND HYPOCRISY 66

SYRIA'S ANCIENT TREASURES PULVERISED 68

UN LEAVES SYRIA TO ITS BLOODY FATE 72

Autumn 2012: Divided State

ANOTHER WEEK IN THE VIOLENT, MURDEROUS AND DIVIDED WORLD OF SYRIA 75

SYRIA'S ROAD FROM JIHAD TO PRISON 77

'THE FINAL STRAW': TURKEY AUTHORISES ATTACK ON SYRIA 81

HOW REBELS WERE SOLD EXPLODING RIFLES - BY A BRITON NAMED 'EMILE' 83

'WE LEFT HOMS BECAUSE THEY WERE TRYING TO KILL US. THEY WANTED TO KILL US BECAUSE WE ARE CHRISTIANS' 85

Winter 2013: Horror Upon Horror

SYRIA: THE DESCENT INTO HOLY WAR 91

PERSECUTION OF THE CHRISTIANS 95

SYRIAN REGIME CAPTURES AL-QA'IDA CHIEF'S BROTHER ON 'AID MISSION' 97

SYRIA'S CARNAGE IS NOT IN DISPUTE. BUT THE NUMBERS ARE IMPOSSIBLE TO QUANTIFY 99

NEW FEARS ON SYRIA'S CHEMICAL WEAPONS 101

Spring 2013: Barbaric Beyond Belief

WEST HAS NEVER UNDERSTOOD SYRIA - JUST TAKE A LOOK AT THE HISTORY BOOKS 103

CONFLICT IN SYRIA CREATES NEW WAVE OF BRITISH JIHADISTS 105

IRAQI AL-QA'IDA DECLARES TAKEOVER OF LEADING SYRIAN REBEL FACTION 107

A BARBARIC WAR THROWS UP A HORROR STORY THAT MAKES VILLAINS OF ALL 109

HISTORY LESSONS THE WEST REFUSES TO LEARN 111

THE DAY I MET THE CANNIBAL COMMANDER'S BRIGADE 114

Summer 2013: The Media Is Getting It Wrong

WAR WITHOUT END IN A LAND AWASH WITH ARMS 117

BRITISH JIHADI ONE OF THREE WESTERNERS KILLED IN BATTLE WITH SYRIAN REGIME 120

FOREIGN MEDIA PORTRAYALS OF THE CONFLICT IN SYRIA ARE DANGEROUSLY INACCURATE 122

VIOLENCE IS ONE THING, BUT WHAT CAUSES REAL TERROR IS THE THREAT OF KIDNAPPING 125

SYRIA CONFLICT: THE DARKEST DAY YET? 128

Autumn 2013: Hopes For A Hollywood Ending

ONCE WASHINGTON MADE THE MIDDLE EAST TREMBLE - NOW NO ONE THERE TAKES IT SERIOUSLY 131

VIOLENCE BURSTS IN TO SHATTER CHRISTIANS' MOUNTAIN REFUGE 133

CUT! OBAMA'S HOPES FOR A HOLLYWOOD ENDING IN SYRIA WERE ALWAYS GOING TO END IN TRAGEDY 135

AS THE WEST LOOKS AWAY, THE ISLAMISTS CLAIM SYRIA'S REBELLION FOR THEMSELVES 138

Winter 2014: Destroying The Past Too

THE ROAD FROM IRAQ TO DAMASCUS 143

WEST SUSPENDS AID FOR ISLAMIST REBELS IN SYRIA 146

THE SYRIAN REBELS HAVE TAKEN ICONOCLASM TO NEW DEPTHS, WITH THEIR DESTRUCTION OF SHRINES, STATUES AND EVEN A TREE - BUT TO WHAT END? 147

GRAVEDIGGERS STAY BUSY IN SYRIA AS PEACE TALKS END IN FAILURE . 149

THE REBEL STRONGHOLD IN THE SKIES 151

THE BATTLE FOR HOMS 153

Spring 2014: Damascus To Homs
SYRIA'S ROAD TO HELL 157

SYRIA'S SECULAR UPRISING HAS BEEN HIJACKED BY JIHADISTS...................162

FOREIGN JIHADIS IN SYRIA PLEDGE THEIR OWN 9/11......................................166

Summer 2014: ISIS Takes Over
DEATH ZONE: THE SYRIAN INDUSTRIAL ESTATE TURNED INTO A SUICIDE FORTRESS BY AL-QA'IDA 171

ISIS MAKES ITS MOVE...173

THE SYRIAN 'MODERATES' WHO AREN'T SO MODERATE IN IRAQ 176

ISIS MARCHES FURTHER INTO SYRIA 178

AIR STRIKES? TALK OF GOD? OBAMA IS FOLLOWING THE JIHADISTS' SCRIPT...180

Autumn 2014: Breeding ISIS
FROM DAMASCUS TO LATAKIA, A TOUR OF A NATION CONVULSED 183

ASSAD'S LETTER TO AMERICA 187

SYRIAN ARMY LEADERS SLAUGHTERED 189

DESTROYED, THE SHRINE TO VICTIMS OF ARMENIAN GENOCIDE...............191

'NO ONE IS BORN A TERRORIST. THE ISLAMIC COUNTRIES HAVE HELPED TO BREED ISIS' 194

Winter 2015: ISIS Digs In
WEST IS WRONG AGAIN IN FIGHT AGAINST TERROR...197

FOR CENTURIES, EVERY SYRIAN HAD A RIGHT OF PASSAGE TO LEBANON. NOT ANY MORE 200

'WE CANNOT PUT SOLDIERS EVERYWHERE ON THE SYRIAN BORDER'.....202

HOW SYRIA LOST ITS HUMANITY 205

Spring 2015: Defeating ISIS
'THE BEATING WENT ON AND ON. I KNEW I MUST FIGHT BUT I BEGAN TO PASS OUT' 211

THE KURDISH FORCES WITH A LESSON IN HOW TO DEFEAT ISIS 215

KURDS COUNT THE COST OF BATTLING ISIS 218

THE ROAD TO RAQQA..221

Summer 2015: No End To The Slaughter
MY SOLDIER'S BROTHER WAS BEHEADED FAR AWAY IN IDLIB. THEY VIDEOED IT AND SENT THE RECORDING TO HIS PHONE HERE 225

SLAUGHTER IN THE SACRED CITY OF PALMYRA: THE STORIES OF THE SURVIVORS..228

NUSRA PLAYS THE NICE GUY, BUT IS AS NASTY AS ISIS 232

TURKEY DUPED THE US, AND ISIS REAPS REWARDS..235

Autumn 2015: No Good Guys Left

DESOLATION, RUINS, DANGER: SYRIA'S KURDS HAVE LITTLE CHOICE BUT TO FLEE 239

IF JIHADIST FORCES CAPTURE THIS VITAL HIGHWAY, MORE AND MORE DESPERATE PEOPLE WILL FLEE SYRIA 241

RUSSIAN AIR STRIKES DESTROY ISIS TARGETS, BUT REBELS CLAIM MANY CIVILIAN DEATHS...244

SYRIA'S 'MODERATES' HAVE DISAPPEARED... AND THERE ARE NO GOOD GUYS LEFT 246

PREFACE

This remarkable anthology of reportage chronicles more than four years of spiralling violence and despair in Syria: atrocity heaped upon atrocity, misery upon misery, and all - so far - to no avail. No faction is without blood on its hands; no crime, from torture to poison gas, has been deemed taboo. The dead are too numerous to count: the UN mid-2014 figure of 190,000 is one of the more conservative estimates. As for the living, close to 3 million refugees have fled Syria, with millions more internally displaced.

How did we come to this? There is no better way to answer this question than to revisit The Independent's published accounts of the unfolding tragedy. Spearheaded by peerless and profoundly experienced correspondents such as Patrick Cockburn, Robert Fisk, Kim Sengupta, our coverage has led the world in its fearlessness and insight.

Syria's tragedy is not yet over. Perhaps it has not even reached its final act. One day, however, historians will ask themselves how an ancient and proud civilisation was reduced to ruins, a century-old regional settlement reduced to irrelevance and a generation of innocent civilians condemned to live in a vicious, desolate war-zone. When they do so, the testimony and analysis in this volume could provide a valuable starting-point.

Spring 2011

It Begins

PROTESTS SWEEP THROUGH SYRIA AS TROOPS OPEN FIRE
By Patrick Cockburn
26 March 2011

Syrian troops opened fire on demonstrators yesterday as protests swept the country on an unprecedented scale with tens of thousands challenging the rule of the Assad family. In the southern city of Deraa, where the protest movement started a week ago, troops shot at demonstrators who set fire to a statue of the late President Hafez al-Assad, whose son Bashar has ruled Syria since 2000. Demonstrators first demanded reform of the regime, but increasingly call for a revolution.

In the town of Sanamein, near Deraa, security forces are reported to have killed 20 people after Friday prayers yesterday as they protested against the regime and killings by the security services.

In Hama, north of Damascus, people ran through the streets shouting "freedom is ringing out!" - a slogan used in popular uprisings in the Arab world over the past three months.

Police with batons reacted harshly and swiftly in breaking up small demonstrations in the capital Damascus including one in the ancient Umayyad Mosque. Dozens of people who chanted slogans in support of the people of Deraa were dragged away by police. In Tel, near Damascus, a thousand people rallied, calling the Assad family "thieves" and there were rallies in most other Syrian cities.

The focus of the Arab uprising has switched to Syria over the past week after police arrested a dozen children in Deraa for writing anti-government graffiti on a wall.

Security services have tried to crush the protesters by force, killing 37 of them in a mosque on Wednesday. State television made the unlikely claim that the mosque was the headquarters of a kidnap gang and showed machine guns leaning against a wall and a table with neat bundles of bank notes on it.

The protests are the biggest domestic challenge to the Assad family since the early 1980s, when President Hafez al-Assad crushed a Sunni revolt centred on Hama where some 10,000 people were reputedly killed in 1982. The current protests are secular in tone, but Deraa and Hama are Sunni strongholds resentful of the influence of the Alawites, a Shia sect, to which many members of the ruling elite belong.

The government showed some restraint early yesterday during the funerals in Deraa of those killed by the security forces, but later there was the sound of gunfire. The police had dismantled many checkpoints and were at first trying to keep a low profile. Journalists were escorted out of the city.

Witnesses said that 50,000 people had rallied in Assad Square in Deraa chanting "Freedom! Freedom!" as they waved Syrian flags and olive branches.

Bashar al-Assad has offered concessions to the protesters such as ending the state of emergency that has existed since 1963, greater press freedom and promising a pay rise to public employees. Previously he had expressed confidence that the protests would not spread to Syria from Tunisia and Egypt, apparently believing that his family's nationalist credentials and confrontations with Israel and the US would immunise Syria from unrest.

The Baath party has held power in Syria since 1963. The government said that all those arrested in Deraa since the start of the protests had been released, but at the same time a human rights agitator, Mazen Darwish, was arrested.

DESPERATE ASSAD TRIES TO BLUNT UPRISING WITH NEW PROMISES OF REFORM
By Patrick Cockburn
28 March 2011

President Bashar al-Assad is facing the greatest challenge to his family's rule over Syria since his father took power 40 years ago, as protests sweep through the country.

Yesterday the government deployed the army for the first time, in the main port of Latakia. Authorities admitted that 12 people had been killed and 200 wounded over a two-day period in the north-western city, but said all who died had been members of the security forces or their attackers.

Speculation was growing last night that President Assad would announce widespread political reforms in a bid to bring the disturbances under control. His adviser, Bouthaina Shaaban, told Al Jazeera that the emergency law in existence since 1963 and hated by Syrian reformists for the far- reaching powers it gives to security services would be lifted, but did not give a timetable.

In another bid to placate protesters, authorities released the political activist Diana Jawabra and 15 others. They had been arrested for taking part in a silent protest demanding the release of a dozen schoolchildren, detained for writing anti-regime graffiti.

While Mr Assad may offer concessions such as ending emergency law, releasing prisoners, giving the press greater freedom and legalising political parties other than the ruling Baath party, such changes are unlikely to be seen as credible as long as the same people run the army and the security forces. And the ever-creeping death toll is increasing calls for an end to the regime.

The crisis that is threatening to overturn the Syrian government has erupted suddenly over the past week, initially provoked by the security forces in the southern city of Deraa arresting the graffiti-scrawling children. Their detention provoked demonstrations that were met with live fire, and the funerals of the dead turned into vast political rallies.

Human Rights Watch says 61 people have been killed in Deraa and surrounding towns and villages.

The threat to Mr Assad is the greatest the Baathist regime has ever experienced, and it has in the past always responded to dissent with repression. During the Muslim Brotherhood guerrilla war in 1976-82 Mr Assad's father, Hafez al-Assad, crushed the rebellion in the city of Hama by killing an estimated 10,000 people.

Baath party veterans may consider their best hope of staying in power at this time is to avoid making concessions, which, they believe, will only be interpreted as weakness and lead to additional demands.

Mr Assad, a British-educated eye doctor, is widely respected in Syria but his popularity is likely to slump as he fails to speak or respond adequately to the present crisis.

His spokesmen have made contradictory statements on the release of prisoners and other issues, putting in doubt the regime's seriousness in making reforms.

They have also released unlikely explanations of the killing of protesters, claiming that demonstrators opened fire first or were foreign infiltrators. These are often directly contradicted by videos taken by mobile phone and shown on YouTube or by satellite television stations such as al-Jazeera whose correspondents entered Deraa.

In the capital, Damascus, pro-government rallies, with supporters waving Syrian flags and posters of Mr Assad, have taken over main squares and threatened to storm the al-Jazeera offices.

The anti-government protests are fuelled by the demand for political and civil liberty but Syrians, who spend half their income on food according to UN figures, are also suffering from high prices, unemployment and corruption.

Some 30 per cent of the 22 million population are below the poverty line. The government is short of money because of declining oil revenues but has tried to reduce economic discontent by cutting duties and taxes on food and other staples.

The US Secretary of State, Hillary Clinton, yesterday drew a clear distinction between Syria and Libya, ruling out involvement in Damascus' affairs.

"Each of these situations is unique," she told CBS News. "Certainly we deplore the violence in Syria... What's been happening there the last few weeks is deeply concerning, but there's a difference between calling out aircraft and indiscriminately strafing and bombing your own cities [as in Libya], than police actions which frankly have exceeded the use of force that any of us would want to see."

In Latakia, the state news agency said "armed elements roamed the streets, occupied the rooftops of some buildings and opened fire randomly, terrorising people". Troops have now moved into the city, which is majority Sunni Muslim but its hinterland is largely populated by Allawites, the Shia Muslim sect to which much of Syria's ruling elite belongs.

SHOTS FIRED AS PROTESTERS TAKE TO THE STREETS AGAIN
By Patrick Cockburn
31 March 2011

Within hours of President Bashar al-Assad's speech yesterday, 100 or more people went out on to the streets of the port city of Latakia in protest, shouting "Freedom!" Residents said they heard shots fired in the old al- Sleibeh district of the city as security forces confronted the demonstrators.

Opposition groups are calling for more protests after Friday prayers tomorrow, while the government will intensify security measures to stop further demonstrations.

Mr Assad's speech offered few concessions. He has not satisfied the protesters' demands or given the impression that the grip on power he and his family hold of himself and his family is weakening.

In his first response to the crisis, Mr Assad said there was "a major conspiracy" against Syria directed from outside the country, though he did not spell out who he believed was behind the plot. The opposition had expected him to introduce reforms, such as ending the state of emergency that has existed since 1963. "We don't seek battles but, if a battle is imposed on us today, we welcome it," the President said in a televised speech. Among those he blamed for provoking the violence were satellite television channels.

It may be that there are serious divisions in the leadership about how to respond to the protests. Mr Assad's adviser, Bouthaina Shaaban, said last week that a committee had been formed to study a series of reforms, including lifting emergency laws. Even so, the security apparatus is unlikely to be restrained by the exact letter of the law.

If the Syrian regime is seriously weakened by the present turmoil, and unable to bring it under control, there will be a radical change in the balance of power in the Middle East. The losers will be Iran, since Syria is its one reliable ally in the Arab world; Hezbollah in Lebanon, which relies on Syrian backing; and Hamas in Gaza, which has been able to use Damascus as a headquarters. Israel and the US, at least in the short term, will be the winners.

Mr Assad did concede that the Syrian people "have demands that have not been met", adding: "If we stay without reform we are on the course of destruction." But he appears to be thinking of incremental change to the way the regime operates and not to any reduction in its authority. He claimed that some protesters had been "duped" into the streets, while others' legitimate demands would be met.

WESTERN INTERVENTION IN SYRIA WOULD MAKE MATTERS WORSE
By Patrick Cockburn
27 April 2011

The Syrian army is moving to crush in blood the protesters calling for democracy and the overthrow of President Bashar al-Assad and his regime. Unburied bodies lie in the streets of Deraa, the city in the south which has been at the centre of the popular revolt.

Will the government succeed? The chances for the moment look evenly balanced, with almost everything depending on whether or not demonstrators continue to march and rally all over Syria despite the savage repression. There is also the possibility of divisions in the army, though less so than in many other Arab countries.

The uprising against police states, both republican and monarchical, in the Arab world is entering its fifth month without a decisive victory by either the powers-that-be or the protesters. In Tunisia and Egypt the political and military elite felt that, if they got rid of their geriatric leaders along with their families and cronies, they might prevent radical changes in the political and social status quo. In Bahrain the monarchy, aided by Saudi Arabia and other Sunni Gulf states, destroyed the pro-democracy movement and is terrorising its supporters.

Syria is going down the same road as Bahrain. At the end of last week President Assad and his inner circle appear to have decided that such limited concessions as they were willing to make were only being interpreted as weakness. They gave orders to their security forces to shoot unarmed demonstrators and stamp out all signs of dissent on the streets.

Repression in Syria may work for the moment. The government has a core of support based on the Alawite minority, to which the Assad family and top military and political members of the regime belong. There are others who work for the state and fear change, as well as Christian and Druze minorities who do not believe opposition claims to be non-sectarian.

Overall, however, the police states in the Arab world, which have seemed so immovable for the past 35 years, are fighting to survive. Before about 1975 there was an era of army coups d'etat, but these stopped as ferocious multi- layered security agencies turned military dictatorships into police states.

East European intelligence agencies gave fraternal advice on how this could be done.

There was more to total state control than just keeping the army in its barracks. Censorship of all forms of media was pervasive, as was control of all non-state agencies such as trade unions and political parties. Only the mosque retained some autonomy, which explains why opposition to autocracy so often took an Islamic form.

By this year the old ingredients of repression had lost something of their potency. Torturers and executioners still retained their ability to frighten. But regimes had lost their control over information and communications thanks to the internet, satellite television and even the humble mobile phone. One member of the Syrian opposition points out that when 20,000 people in Hama were slaughtered by the forces of President Hafez al-Assad in 1982 there was not a single picture of even one of the bodies. Today pictures of the dead and wounded in Deraa and elsewhere in Syria are transmitted to the rest of the world within seconds of being taken.

Of course governments can counter-attack and close down mobile-phone networks and ban journalists from operating in Syria. But 100 satellite phones distributed by an opposition Syrian businessman make total control of information almost impossible to establish. The role of the internet in the Arab awakening has been well-publicised, but that of satellite stations, notably Al Jazeera, is underplayed. The US has every reason to be embarrassed by this since Washington spent years claiming that Al Jazeera's criticism of US policy in Iraq after the invasion showed it must be linked to al-Qa'ida. An Al Jazeera cameraman was held in Guantanamo for six years so that US interrogators could find out more about the television station.

Britain, France and Italy have called for sanctions against Syria. But they should not do more because intrusive foreign intervention is likely to prove counter-productive. There are already signs of this in Libya. Justifiable action against impending massacre turns into imperial intervention. NATO air strikes against Colonel Gaddafi's tanks advancing on Benghazi have escalated into an air war, aided by foreign advisers on the ground, with the purpose of overthrowing the regime. In such an offensive the Libyan rebels, whatever their popular support and skill in media relations, may play only a walk-on part.

It is worth recalling that most Afghans were pleased when the Taliban collapsed in 2001 and most Iraqis were glad to see the back of Saddam Hussein in 2003. But it did not follow that the opponents of autocracy were united, had real support or were less corrupt or more competent than their predecessors. Nor were Afghans or Iraqis prepared to see foreign armies determine who should hold power in their countries.

People whom Western states claim they are trying to aid for humanitarian reasons are understandably sceptical about how altruistic their motives really are. Their suspicions will only be confirmed by documents published by The Independent giving details of talks between the British government and BP and Royal Dutch Shell in 2002 on how to avoid US companies excluding them from exploiting Iraqi oil reserves.

There is a further reason why Britain and other foreign states should limit their involvement in the conflicts now raging in the Arab world. It is true that the struggle is primarily between popular protests or uprisings against vicious autocracies. But these crises have at least some aspects of a civil war: there are tribes which support Colonel Gaddafi and there are Syrians who believe that the opposition is more sectarian and Sunni-dominated than is evident from their human-rights agenda.

It is right for Britain and its allies to protest at the butchery in Syria, though their criticism might carry more weight had they been equally vocal about torture, disappearances and killings in Bahrain. But this humanitarian zeal easily becomes a cover for wider intervention, because retreat is humiliating and therefore politically impossible, and the field cannot be left open to other competing interventionist powers. The outside world can mitigate, but should not try to change, what is happening in Syria.

OUT OF SYRIA'S DARKNESS COME TALES OF TERROR
By Robert Fisk
29 April 2011

In Damascus, the posters - in their tens of thousands around the streets - read: "Anxious or calm, you must obey the law." But pictures of President Bashar al-Assad and his father Hafez have been taken down, by the security police no less, in case they inflame Syrians.

There are thieves with steel-tipped rubber coshes on the Damascus airport road at night, and in the terminal the cops ask arriving passengers to declare iPods and laptops. In the village of Hala outside Deraa, Muslim inhabitants told their Christian neighbours to join the demonstrations against the regime - or leave.

Out of the darkness of Syria come such tales.

And they are true. Syrians arriving in Lebanon are bringing the most specific details of what is going on inside their country, of Fifth Brigade soldiers fighting the armed units of Maher Assad's Fourth Brigade outside Deraa, of random killings around Damascus by the ever-growing armed bands of Shabiha ("the mafia") from the Alawite mountains, of massive stocking up of food. One woman has just left her mother in the capital with 10 kilos of pasta, 10 kilos of rice, five kilos of sugar, box after box of drinking water.

In Deraa - surrounded, without electricity or water or supplies - the price of bread has risen 500 per cent and men are smuggling food into the city over the fields at night.

But it is the killings which terrify the people. Are they committed by the Shabiha from the port city of Lattakia - created by the Assad family in the 70s to control smuggling and protection rackets - or by the secret police to sow a fear that might break the uprising against Assad? Or by the murderers who thrive amid anarchy and lawlessness? Three men carrying sacks of vegetables outside Damascus at night were confronted by armed men last week. They refused to stop. So they were executed.

The Syrian government is appealing to the minorities - to the Christians and the Kurds - to stay loyal to the authorities; minorities have always been safe in Syria, and many have stayed away from protests against the regime. But in the village of Hala, Christian shops are shut as their owners contemplate what are clearly sectarian demands to join in the uprising against Assad. In an attempt to rid Syria of "foreign" influence, the ministry of education has ordered a number of schools to end all English teaching - even banning the names of schools in French and English from school uniforms. Even the kindergarten where the President's two young children are educated has been subject to the prohibitions.

There are bright lights, of course, not least among the brave men and women who are using the internet and Facebook to keep open the flow of information from Syria. The Independent can reveal that a system of committees has been set up across the cities of Syria, usually comprising only 10 or 12 friends who have known and trusted each other for years.

Each of them enlists 10 of their own friends - and they persuade 10 more each - to furnish information and pictures. Many were put in touch with each other via the cyber kings of Beirut - many of them also Syrian - and thus "circles of trust" have spread at the cost of the secret police snooping that has been part of Syrian life for four decades.

Thus there now exist - in Damascus alone - "The Co-ordination of Douma", "The Co-ordination of al-Maydan" (in the centre of the city), "The Co- ordination of Daraya", "The Co-ordination of Harasta" and others. Some of them are trying to penetrate the mukhabarat secret police, to get the brutal cops to work for them on the grounds that - come the end of the Assad regime, if that end ever comes - they will be spared the trials and revenge punishments to come. One Beirut blogger says that several of the cops have already declared themselves for the uprising - but are unwilling to trust them in case it is a trap to discover the identity of those behind the committees.

Yet Syrians in Lebanon say that the Syrian security police - often appointed through graft rather than any technical or detective abilities - simply do not understand the technology that is being used against them. One Syrian security official sent three Facebook posts. The first said: "God, Syria and Bashar al-Assad or nothing." The second read: "It's the time to declare war for Allah." The third announced: "The legacy of God on earth is an Islamic Republic."

"The fool was obviously supporting Bashar - but then wanted to frighten people by suggesting Islamists would take over a post-Assad Syria," one of the Syrian bloggers in Beirut says. "But he didn't realise that we could tell at once that they all came from the same Facebook page!" The same man in Beirut found himself under interrogation by

Syrian state security police several weeks ago. "He was a senior officer - but he didn't even know what Google was." Many of the Syrians sending information out of their country are anxious that exaggerations and rumours will damage the credibility of their reports. For this reason, they are trying to avoid dispatches which cannot be verified; that two Iranian snipers, for example, have arrived to help the security police; that one man was actually interrogated by two Iranians - a friend suspects that the cops were from the north and spoke in the Kurdish language, which the detainee misidentified as Iranian.

More serious - and true - is the report that Khaled Sid Mohand, an Algerian journalist working for France Culture and Le Monde, was arrested in Damascus on 9 April and has disappeared into a security prison. A released detainee says that he saw Mohand in Security Section 255 in Baghdad Street in the capital some days later. But this story may not be correct. Diplomats have been unable to see the missing journalist.

There are also reports that two young European women working for a Western embassy were arrested and gagged when they left a party at 3am several days ago, and only released several hours later after interrogation. "It means that there is no longer any immunity for foreigners," a Syrian citizen said yesterday. "We heard that a North American had also been taken from his home and questioned by armed men."

Especially intriguing - because there are many apparent witnesses of this episode - is a report that Syrian Fourth Brigade troops in Deraa dumped dozens of weapons in the main square of the city in front of the Omari mosque, telling civilians that they could take them to defend themselves. Suspecting that they were supposed to carry them in demonstrations and then be shot as "terrorists", the people took the weapons to the nearest military base and gave them back to the soldiers.

The rumours of army defections continue, however, including splits in the Fifth Brigade at Deraa, whose commander's name can now be confirmed as General Mohamed Saleh al-Rifai. According to Syrians arriving in Lebanon, the highways are used by hundreds of packed military trucks although the streets of most cities - including Damascus - are virtually empty at night.

Shops are closing early, gunfire is often heard, checkpoints at night are often manned by armed men in civilian clothes. Darkness indeed.

AS TANKS LINE THE STREETS, SYRIANS STAND FIRM TO DEFY BRUTAL REGIME
By Khalid Ali and Kim Sengupta
7 May 2011

Thousands of protesters faced the guns of the Syrian regime yesterday undeterred by a ferocious crackdown and a campaign of intimidation that has failed to quell popular discontent against the rule of President Bashar al- Assad.

Security forces opened fire on marches in several cities killing at least 21 protesters, according to rights activists, continuing the brutal crackdown that has left more than 550 people dead since widespread civil unrest began in March.

The Syrian regime has arrested up to 500 people a day in a new drive to crackdown on the protest movement, according to diplomatic sources, with more than 7,000 being held in a network of secret prisons. The upsurge in detentions, taking place across the country, has been going on for the last week and is seen as an attempt to prevent the organising or co-ordinating of demonstrations.

Tanks ringed the southern city of Deraa yesterday, where the protests began and has been the scene of a major military offensive by the regime to try to prevent any major shows of defiance. The city has been the scene of a wave of arrests with local residents claiming that virtually all males over the age of 15 had been taken away in raids by security forces.

Despite the crackdown, protests were held in dozens of cities and towns across the country, with many of the protests broken up by regime forces. Video downloaded to YouTube purported to show a demonstration in Hama with protesters running down a main street and hurling stones. Loud screams could be heard as the sound of machine-gun fire started and people fled for cover.

A second video, supposedly from the central city of Homs and filmed from behind a curtain inside a home, showed two army snipers on a rooftop taking aim at unseen targets below. Neither of the videos could be verified.

"We were chanting, peaceful, peaceful, and we didn't even throw a stone at the security forces," a witness told The Associated Press and claimed that there were 10,000 people on the streets in the city. "But they waited for us to reach the main square and then they opened fire on us."

Security forces yesterday targeted leaders of the opposition. They dragged off Riad Seif, a prominent figure from a rally in the Midan district of Damascus. Mr Seif, 64, and suffering from cancer, has spent a total of eight years on charges of "weakening national morale" for demanding democratic reforms and freedom of expression in his homeland, and came out of jail following his latest sentence last year. His daughter, Jumana Seif, said "My father was shoved into a bus with other protestors who were detained during the demonstration near the al-Hassan mosque."

Elsewhere in Damascus there were reports of shootings in two eastern suburbs while demonstrators also reportedly took to the streets in Moadamiyah and Daraya - two towns close to the capital which have seen brutal army crackdowns in recent weeks. Security forces cordoned off Douma, to the east of Damascus, and allowed nobody to enter or leave.

Another witness said that he had seen tanks being transported by train to Homs, while in the north-western city of Baniyas thousands of people, many carrying olive branches and Syrian flags, chanted for the fall of the regime.

"The protests have spread more than any we have seen in the past seven weeks," said Wissam Tarif, executive director of Middle East human rights organisation Insan. "We had counted uprisings in 108 towns and villages across the country. We have seen intimidation. There have been snipers, and a strategy of building a wall of fear. A lot of people are scared, so it's amazing that people are coming out."

A spokesman for the National Initiative for Change, an umbrella group for opposition figures inside Syria, claimed that yesterday's protests indicate that the pro-reform movement was becoming too big for the government to cope with. The protests have escalated steadily since they were triggered by the arrests of 15 schoolchildren for spraying anti-regime graffiti in Deraa.

Summer 2011

Armed Insurrection

THE PEOPLE VS THE PRESIDENT
By Robert Fisk
8 June 2011

Syria's revolt against the rule of President Bashar al-Assad is turning into an armed insurrection, with previously peaceful demonstrators taking up arms to fight their own army and the "shabiha" - meaning "the ghosts", in English - of Alawi militiamen who have been killing and torturing those resisting the regime's rule.

Even more serious for Assad's still-powerful supporters, there is growing evidence that individual Syrian soldiers are revolting against his forces. The whole edifice of Assad's Alawi dictatorship is now in the gravest of danger.

In 1980, Assad's father, Hafez, faced an armed uprising in the central city of Hama, which was put down by the Special Forces of Hafez's brother Rifaat - who is currently living, for the benefit of war crimes investigators, in central London - at a cost of up to 20,000 lives. But the armed revolt today is now spreading across all of Syria, a far-mightier crisis and one infinitely more difficult to suppress. No wonder Syrian state television has been showing the funerals of up to 120 members of the security services from just one location, the northern town of Jisr al-Shughour.

The first evidence of civilians turning to weapons to defend their families came from Deraa, the city where the bloody story of the Syrian uprising first began after intelligence officers arrested and tortured to death a 13-year-old boy. Syrians arriving in Beirut told me the male citizens of Deraa had grown tired of following the example of peaceful Tunisian and Egyptian protesters - an understandable emotion since people in those countries suffered nothing like the brutal suppression meted out by Assad's soldiers and militiamen - and were now sometimes "shooting back" for the sake of "dignity" and to protect their wives and children.

Bashar and his cynical brother Maher - the present-day equivalent of the outrageous Rifaat - may now be gambling on the old dictator's saw that their regime must be defended against armed Islamists supported by al-Qa'ida, a lie which was perpetrated by Muammar Gaddafi and the now-exiled leaders Ali Abdullah Saleh of Yemen and Ben Ali of Tunisia and Hosni Mubarak of Egypt and the still-on-the-throne al-Khalifas of Bahrain.

The few al-Qa'ida cells in the Arab world may wish this to be true, but the Arab revolt is about the one phenomenon in the Middle East uncontaminated by "Islamism". Only the Israelis and the Americans may be tempted to believe otherwise.

Al Jazeera television yesterday aired extraordinary footage of a junior Syrian officer calling upon his comrades to refuse to continue massacring civilians in Syria. Identified as Lt Abdul-Razak Tlas, from the town of Rastan, he said he had joined the army "to fight the Israeli enemy", but found himself witnessing a massacre of his own people in the town of Sanamein. "After what we've seen from crimes in Deraa and all over Syria, I am unable to continue with the Syrian Arab army," he announced. "I urge the army, and I say: 'Is the army here to steal and protect the Assad family?' I call upon all honourable officers to tell their soldiers about the real picture, use your conscience... if you are not honourable, stay with Assad."

Differentiating rumour from fact in Syria is getting easier by the week. More Syrians are reaching the safety of Lebanon and Turkey to tell their individual stories of torture and cruelty in security police barracks and in plain-clothes police cells. Some are still using the telephone from Syria itself - one to describe explosions in Jisr al-Shughour and of bodies being tossed into the river from which the town takes its name.

For well over a month, I have been watching Syrian television's nightly news and at least half the broadcasts have included funerals of dead soldiers. Now Syria itself declares that 120 have been killed in one incident, an incredible loss for an army that was supposed to instill horror into the minds of the country's protesters. But then the supposedly invincible Syrian army often showed itself woefully unable to suppress Lebanese militias during the country's 1975-90 civil war. An entire battalion of Syrian Special Forces troops was driven out of east Beirut, for example, by a ragtag group of Christian militias who would have been crushed by any serious professional army.

If you wish to destroy unarmed civilians, you shoot them down in the street and then shoot down the funeral mourners and then shoot down the mourners of the dead mourners - which is exactly what Assad's gunmen have been doing - but when the resistors shoot back, the Syrian army has shown a quite different response: torture for their prisoners and fear in the face of the enemy.

But if the armed insurrection takes hold, then it is also the 11 per cent Alawi community - once the frontier force of the French mandate against the Sunnis and now the prop of Assad against the poorer Sunnis - which is at threat. So appalled is the Assad regime at its enemies that it has been encouraging Palestinians to try to cross the frontier wire on Israeli-occupied Golan. The Israelis say this is to divert world attention from the massacres in Syria - and they are absolutely right.

The Damascus government's Tishrin newspaper has been suggesting that 600,000 Palestinians may soon try to "go home" to the lands of Palestine from which the Israelis drove them in 1948, a nightmare the Israelis would prefer not to think about - but not as great a nightmare as that now facing the people and their oppressors in Syria itself.

'THEY SHOT PEOPLE WHO WERE TRYING TO GET AWAY'
By Kim Sengupta and Justin Vela
14 June 2011

The haunting memories of savage violence and loss are fresh in their minds. Now, with the vengeful forces of the regime closing in, the terrified and exhausted stream of the dispossessed fleeing Syria's strife await an uncertain fate. More than 10,000 people have headed for the Turkish border in an attempt to escape the onslaught unleashed by Bashar al-Assad. They were living in squalor with little food and water and no shelter. But they were prepared to suffer that to reach a place of relative safety away from the tanks, artillery and helicopter gunships, and the death they bring.

It is not known just how long this respite will last. The regime's forces are less than 15km away, and yesterday Damascus announced that the current offensive in Idlib province, which saw the storming of

Jisr al-Shughour - a city which had become a symbol of militant opposition - will continue to roll on until the "criminal gangs" are crushed.

The Independent met some of these victims of a war waged on them by their own state by crossing over from Turkey across valleys and ridges on a smugglers' route. Our guides were young men carrying in meagre supplies by hand: bottles of water and loaves of bread. This is the only aid of any kind getting through to a humanitarian crisis which worsens by the day.

The tales we heard were harrowing - of indiscriminate shootings and casual killings, of hurried burials and burning houses. One needs to be cautious of these accounts because they can be embellished. But there was a sense of bewilderment among those huddled together about what has happened.

There was also the sight of the very young and elderly swathed in bandages. On a sloping hillside were a series of graves of those who, lacking medical help, had succumbed to their injuries.

Among the crowd were soldiers who had changed sides. They acknowledged serving a repressive regime without question. But they had stopped doing so, they insisted, because of the vicious nature of the current military operations. Surrounded by people who have suffered at the hands of their fellow troops, the soldiers were nervous. Ismail Sher Saleh, a 25-year-old former sergeant of infantry, had deserted just before troops of the 4th Armoured Division led by the President's brother, Lt-Colonel Maher al- Assad, had launched their attack on Jisr al-Shughour.

"They could kill me if they caught me," he said, twisting a black-and-white checked keffiyeh [scarf] in his fingers. "It could be the Mukhabarat [secret police] or even people I had served with. Some terrible things are being done: I have seen people getting shot for no reason. They would kill me because they would consider me a traitor and because I know what they had done."

Cradling three-year-old Sabia in her arms, Halima Um Qais traced her finger along the three sticking plasters on her daughter's forehead. "Something large exploded near our house and she was cut by metal which came through the air. We are poor people, farmers - I do not know why they wanted to bomb us," she said. "We are going to try to take her to a hospital. We are worried because it is in the head and it could be serious."

The family is among the hundreds who are crossing into Turkey every day. Officials have put the figure so far at around 6,000, although many more have slipped in. The wounded are taken for treatment, but the rest are sent immediately to holding centres. The number of these camps has increased from one to three in seven days, with a fourth one under construction, away from contact with local people and, more specifically, the media.

Turkey's Prime Minister, Recep Tayyip Erdogan, whose party won national elections held two days ago, has watched the chaos in Syria with growing alarm. He has called on President Assad, with whom he had built up strong links, to rein in his troops, and has denounced the "barbaric" actions still being taken.

On Sunday evening, while receiving a congratulatory telephone call from David Cameron, he gave his backing to a proposed Anglo-French resolution at the United Nations condemning the actions of the Syrian regime.

Meanwhile, Turkish troops at the border have stopped the media from venturing into Syria - The Independent had to take a detour to avoid patrols and reach families strung out along a river valley. There was suspicion in the camp, rumours of intelligence agents sent to collect information and seek out targets for future reckoning. A tall man with a bulge under his blue jacket scrutinised the identity card of our Turkish guide and questioned me about our journey. "Please excuse us," he said. "We have to be careful about spies. The [regime's] soldiers are not very far back. They may come this way; I am looking after security."

There had been reports that some of the "refugees" had come armed with Kalashnikov rifles and rocket-propelled grenade launchers, which would give credence to claims from Damascus of armed groups moving among the protesters. "No, we are just ordinary people," said the security man. Was he carrying a pistol? "No absolutely not," he shook his head.

The vast majority of those present were sleeping under trees offering scant cover from the rain; a few have managed to drive pick-up trucks cross- country and use the trailer to sleep; others have built makeshift tents out of rags and plastic sheeting. A small well could not cope with the demands of the growing numbers. A pond with floating rubbish and the waters of the river, with animals wallowing in the shallows, was being used for washing and drinking.

"I know this is bad, but we are alive" said Siraz Abdullah, a 19-year-old student from a village near Jisra al-Shughour. "We have nothing left there. We had big guns used [against us] and then there were helicopters. They were flying low, so they could see they were shooting at people. They shot people who were not fighting but trying to get away. I saw two men getting hit as they were running away."

There were repeated claims that fighters from the Shabiha, a militia from the Alawite community to which the Assad family and country's élite belong, had taken part in atrocities. Mohammed Hafiz, a carpenter from a hamlet south of Jisra al-Shughour, said: "They were not the army, but they came just afterwards. These men were very aggressive: they enjoyed shooting people.

"They went up on rooftops and shot at demonstrations. No one knew who sent them. We found out that they were this militia everyone was frightened of. It was they who started the real trouble by firing on a funeral." Ahmed ibn Abdurrahman was too tired to carry on. Sitting with his wife and brother on a rug laid on the dust, he sighed, "I need to go home. I have a house and I want to go back to that." Mr Abdurrahman's home was in Maarat al-Numan. A military spokesman in Damascus announced that city will be "dealt with" in the next few days.

THEY CAME AT DAWN, AND KILLED IN COLD BLOOD
By Kim Sengupta
19 June 2011

The houses looked abandoned, windows and doors locked, a broken shutter clattering in the wind. Then, one by one, they began to appear from their hiding places, mainly women and children, a few elderly people. The residents of this village had learned to their cost that being caught unawares in this violent conflict could have lethal consequences.

The raid by the secret police - the Mukhabarat - and the Shabbiha militia had come at dawn. The killings had been cold-blooded and quick, three men shot dead as, barely awake, they tried desperately to get away. A search for others had proved fruitless; they had fled the day before. The damage to homes vented the frustration of the gunmen at missing their quarries.

"They were working from a list. But they made mistakes. One of them was the wrong person. They did not even have the right name of the man they killed," said Qais al-Baidi, gesturing towards the graves on a sloping hillside. "But none of them deserved this. They were not terrorists. They had just taken part in some demonstrations. These Assad people are vicious. They have no pity. They like killing."

The three killings were among the many that had followed the ferocious onslaught launched by Bashar al-Assad against the uprising. Two centres of opposition in the north of the country had been taken after bloody clashes, Jisr al-Shughour early in the week, Maaret al-Numan falling on Friday. This village was among a cluster that had been subjected, according to a regime commander, to a "cleaning-up" operation.

The offensive had led to a terrified exodus of much of the local population, with 12,000 huddled in squalid conditions on the Syrian side of the border. Another 10,000 had made it across to Turkey, only to be herded into holding centres, locked away from the outside world, the government in Ankara making it clear that these people will be sent back at an opportune time.

The locals in the Turkish province of Hatay and the international media have been kept away from the dispossessed families. The Turkish government insists they are "guests", as accepting they are refugees could lead to legal obligations towards them. But Angelina Jolie, Hollywood actress and UN goodwill ambassador, was taken to see one of the centres after expressing a wish to help to alleviate the suffering of Syria. A banner put up by the Turkish authorities at the entrance to the camp read "Goodness Angel of the World, Welcome".

Away from the focus of celebrity attention, there is little help for those stuck at the frontier. The vast majority sleep under trees; a few have managed to drive pick-up trucks cross-country and sleep in the trailer; others have built makeshift tents out of rags and plastic sheeting. A pond with floating rubbish and water from the river were being used for washing and drinking. Some of the injured had perished without adequate medical help, and their funerals were held where they had died.

The only "aid" for a humanitarian crisis worsening by the day had been meagre supplies such as bottles of water and bread smuggled in by groups of young men travelling on foot across steep ridges, along the same path taken by The IoS. Relief organisations have not been allowed access by either the Syrians or the Turks. But the border camp offer relative safety from the savagery of a state waging war on its own people.

Hania Um Jaffar, whose 22-year-old nephew, Khalid Abdullah, was one of those killed, was convinced that the journey there was the only choice. "We had hidden in the fields the day before when we saw helicopters flying over us. But they went away and we thought it had passed. But then they came later on foot. They did not come into our home, but went to others, to the one where Khalid was staying. He was shot many times.

"I don't want anyone else in my family to die. Surely that is what will happen if we stay here. My sons have gone to the mountains, and another nephew has done the same. They cannot come back to take us to Turkey. That is too dangerous for them. We have to make our own way there."

The tiny community remaining in the dozen houses were running out of food. Bassem Mohammed Ibrahim, a 68-year-old farmer, spread his hands. "[The regime forces] did not burn the crops here like they have done in other places. But the only men left here now are old ones like me. We cannot work the fields by ourselves. Our farms will be ruined. But if we stay here, I don't think we will survive."

The journey to the border, however, is fraught with risk. The secret police and the Shabbiha, drawn from the community to which President Assad and the Syrian elite belong, had ambushed families, forcing some to turn back. A small group of opposition fighters provide protection along the route. "But we only have a few of these," said Habib Ali Hussein, holding up his Kalashnikov assault rifle. "Assad has tanks, artillery, helicopters."

Until two weeks ago Mr Hussein was part of those forces as a lieutenant in the army. He deserted, he said, sickened by the violence meted out to unarmed civilians.

"They were shooting people who were refusing to follow orders. That is what happened at Jisr al-Shughour. I am from that area, and my people were being attacked. So I got my family away and then I left. We haven't got the weapons to go forward. All we are doing is defending."

At the border camp, Isha al-Diri, a medical assistant from Jisr al-Shughour, had been administering treatment as best he could. "The seriously injured have been taken to Turkey. But some died before that could happen. The problem here is that we haven't got enough medicine."

Rawat Khalifa had come seeking cough medicine for his six-year-old daughter. "It is the damp; a lot of the young ones are ill. We shall have to go to Turkey if they get any worse. We cannot take risks with their lives.

"We have not crossed over so far because we are Syrians. We want to stay in our own country. But we are afraid to go back home. We are afraid that our own leaders will try to kill us."

Yesterday, Syrian troops arrived with tanks at Bdama, 12 miles from the Turkish border. Dozens were arrested and houses burned, according to eyewitnesses. The area had been considered key for passing food and supplies to people who have fled the violence in their villages, but have yet to cross the border into Turkey.

THE NEW FOCUS OF SYRIA'S CRACKDOWN HAS SEEN SIMILAR BLOODSHED BEFORE
By Robert Fisk
6 July 2011

History comes full circle in Syria. In February 1982, President Hafez al- Assad's army stormed into the ancient cities to end an Islamist uprising. They killed at least 10,000 men, women and children, possibly 20,000. Some of the men were members of the armed Muslim Brotherhood.

Almost all the dead were Sunni Muslims, although even senior members of the Baath party were executed if they had the fatal word Hamwi - a citizen from Hama - on their identity cards. "Death a thousand times to the hired Muslim Brothers, who linked themselves to the enemies of the homeland," Assad said after the slaughter.

Years later a retired Dutch diplomat, Nikolaos Van Dam, wrote a detailed study of the Baath party and its Alawi leadership, The Struggle for Power in Syria, and stated presciently of the Hama massacre, that "the massive repression... may very well have sown the seeds of future strife and revenge". Never a truer word - and if the activists' estimate that there were 250,000 citizens on the streets of Hama at the weekend to demand the end of the Assad family's rule is correct, then the seeds of future strife were indeed planted in the historic city's soil 29 years ago.

I remember Hama's first siege, when I managed to enter the city by driving down the international highway and getting right in among the Syrian tanks - which were shelling the most beautiful mosque in Hama - because two army officers asked my driver to drop them off beside the river Orontes, where their units were fighting the brotherhood. The soldiers gave me and my driver tea as we took in this terrible scene.

The fighting had gone on for 16 days; girl suicide killers were taking military lives by exploding hand grenades next to them when they were taken prisoner. I only had a few minutes to see all this. Rifaat al-Assad's defence forces in their drab pink uniforms sat on their tanks. Some of them had been badly wounded - they had bandages on their arms. A woman refugee got into my car with her child, but when I tried to give it food, she snatched it and scoffed the lot. She was starving. These, of course, were the parents of the weekend's demonstrators. Perhaps the hungry child was on the streets of Hama three days ago.

The situation was similar yesterday, after 500 troops surged into the city, wounding at least 20 after opening fire. But it's not an Islamic uprising this time - the insurgents of Hama were killing the families of Baath party members in 1982 - but the very name of the city sounds like a tolling bell in the history of the Assads' rule. In those days, Assad let the press into Damascus - which is how I drove to see friends in Aleppo and return via Hama - but this time the regime has simply closed the frontier to almost all reporters.

In 1982, there was no YouTube, no Twitter, there were no mobile phones. Not a single photograph of the dead was ever published. Some of Syria's tanks now appear to be brand new imports from Russia. The problem is that the people's technology is new too.

IT'S HIS FAST-DISAPPEARING BILLIONS THAT WILL WORRY ASSAD, NOT WORDS FROM WASHINGTON
By Robert Fisk
19 August 2011

Obama roars. World trembles. If only.

Obama says Assad must "step aside". Do we really think Damascus trembles? Or is going to? Indeed, the titan of the White House only dared to go this far after condemnation of Bashar al-Assad by Saudi Arabia, Qatar, Kuwait, Turkey, Jordan, the Palestinian Authority, the EU and Uncle Tom Cobley and all (except, of course, Israel - another story). The terrible triplets - Cameron, Sarkozy and Merkel - did their mimicking act a few minutes later.

But truly, are new sanctions against Assad "and his cronies" - I enjoyed the "cronies" bit, a good old 1665 word as I'm sure Madame Clinton realised, although she was principally referring to Bashar's businessman cousin Rami Makhlouf - anything more than the usual Obama hogwash? If "strong economic sanctions" mean a mere freeze on petroleum products of Syrian origin, the fact remains that Syria can scarcely produce enough oil for itself, let alone for export. A Swedish government agency recently concluded that Syria was largely unaffected by the world economic crisis - because it didn't really have an economy.

Of course, in the fantasy of Damascus - where Bashar appears to live in the same "sea of quietness" in which the Egyptian writer Mohamed Heikel believes all dictators breathe - the world goes on as usual. UN Secretary General Ban Ki-moon - another earth-trembler if ever there was one - no sooner demands an "immediate" end to "all military operations and mass arrests", than dear old Bashar tells him that "military and police action" has stopped.

Well, blow me down, as the Syrian population must now be saying. So what were all those reports coming in yesterday from Syria, of widespread gunfire in Latakia, of troops looting private property in the city, of a man arrested in his hospital bed in Zabadani, of snipers still on the rooftops of government buildings in Deir el-Zour? Crimes against humanity? Needless to say, the Syrian government knows nothing about this.

Besides, hasn't Gaddafi been accused of "crimes against humanity"? Wasn't he supposed to have "stepped aside" six months ago? And isn't Gaddafi - a little more fragile now, of course - still in Tripoli? And this is after months of NATO bombardment, something that Bashar has nothing to worry about.

Well, well, well.

Bashar will also have noticed a weird mantra adopted by the Great Roarer of Washington. Repeatedly, Assad was told by Obama to "step aside" - never "step down" - and to "get out of the way", whatever that means. Intriguingly, Madame Clinton used the phrase "step down" yesterday afternoon - and then immediately corrected herself to "step aside".

The Great and the Good don't use these phrases by chance. The implication still seems to be that "step aside" might allow Bashar to stay in Syria but let others take over, rather go on the run with a war crimes tribunal hanging over his head. Which is what, I suspect, yesterday's roaring was all about.

The real fear for Bashar is not oil sanctions but banks - especially the £12bn in foreign reserves that existed in Syria's Central Bank in February, a sum which is now being depleted by around £50m a week. In May, Syria's foreign minister - the mighty (physically) Walid Moallem - asked Baghdad for cheap Iraqi oil. Nearly 10 per cent of Syria's banking deposits disappeared in the first four months of 2011; £1.8bn was withdrawn, some of it ending up in Lebanese banks.

All in all, then, a nasty economic climate in which to go on bashing your own people. So who cares what Obama says? Certainly not the Syrians, which is why they are now trying to set up a "High Commission for Leading the Revolution" to co-ordinate protesters in the country's provinces.

This will indeed also worry Assad, who will have to send his spooks out to identify members of this "high commission" (which sounds unhappily like a colonial name) so they can spend some rest-and-recreation in the Latakia sports stadium under friendly interrogation from the state security police.

Autumn 2011

Dying for Assad

'WE ARE ALL READY TO BE MARTYRED FOR SYRIA AND OUR PRESIDENT'
By Robert Fisk
26 October 2011

Sergeant Jassem Abdul-Raheem Shehadi and Private Ahmed Khalaf Adalli of the Syrian Army were sent to their graves yesterday with the send-off their families would have wished for; coffins draped with the Syrian flag, trumpets and drums and wreaths held by their comrades, and the presence of their commanding officer. There was a Last Post, Chopin's funeral march - mixed with ululating staff at the Tishreen Hospital to which their remains had been transferred - and then the nine-hour journey by ambulance to their hometown, Raka. Shehadi was 19, Adalli was 20. And their uncles swore they had died for President Bashar al-Assad.

They were shot dead in Deraa - by snipers, according to their commanding officer, Major Walid Hatim. "By terrorists," he said several times. Assad's opponents might have no sympathy with these dead soldiers - nor Amnesty, nor Human Rights Watch, nor the United Nations, who say 3,000 civilians have been killed by Syrian security forces, nor the Americans, nor the British et al - but those two coffins suggested that there is more than one story to the Syrian Revolution. Syrian officers told me yesterday that 1,150 soldiers have been killed in Syria in the past seven months, an extraordinary death toll for regular Syrian troops if correct. On Zawi mountain near Idlib, Major Hatim said, 30 Syrian soldiers had been killed in an ambush. Mazjera was the word he used. A massacre.

Shehadi and Adalli were based in Deraa, where the opposition to Assad began. Shehadi was there for six months, Adalli for four. It was a sign of the times that Major Hatim arrived at the Damascus funeral in civilian clothes. Why was he not wearing his uniform, I asked? "It is easier," he replied.

Because of the dangers driving from Deraa? "Maybe," he replied. That, too, told its own story. Both the dead soldiers had lost their fathers years ago and their two uncles had travelled here from Raka to escort the bodies home.

They were from poor families, they said. The boys and their uncles had been looking after their mothers.

Shehadi's uncle, Salim Abdullah, in a brown abaya and drawing heavily on a cigarette, was on the edge of tears. "My nephew had three brothers and two sisters, and they are very poor," he said. "His mother Arash will now have to be looked after by us. Those killers have killed the hope of our family. He was the youngest boy."

Behind Salim Shehadi, Syrian troops stood in full battledress as the coffins were brought from the hospital mortuary. All Syria's military dead leave from the gloomy portals of the Tishreen Hospital, a vast concrete building in the suburbs of Damascus. Even the ambulance driver prostrated himself in tears over his vehicle.

Syrian television had a crew at the hospital, along with the ever loyal Syrian Arab News Agency, but it was highly unusual for a foreign reporter to be invited to this ceremony, let alone to speak to Syrian officers. Major Hatim explained to me that the two soldiers were killed in a planned ambush; the sniper was firing from between two houses. There was a strange confluence in this description. Opponents of Assad often claim that it is they that are fired on by snipers using the cover of buildings.

But few people in Syria now doubt that, however peaceful - and yet bloody - the anti-government demonstrations in Homs and Hama are, the Syrian Army has become a major target. Needless to say, Major Hatim, a 25-year army veteran, was also a supporter of the President.

Hatim talked of Syria's "resistance" on the part of the Palestinians, that soldiers sometimes had to die for their country, that their enemy is Israel. There is much talk in Damascus of a "foreign hand" behind the killings in Syria, although the Major admitted that, in this case, "unfortunately the killers are Syrian".

But Salim Shehadi wanted to say more. "I hope you will be honest and tell the truth," he said. "Tell the truth about the killing of Syrian people. The hand of terrorists took my nephew. We are all ready to be martyred for Syria and for our President Assad." It sounded too pat, this little speech from a grieving man, and a reporter must ask if this was a set-up. Yet the military had only four minutes before I arrived for the funeral, and I doubt if they could have coaxed this poor man to say these words.

Perhaps, up in distant Raka, they believe these words of loyalty - Abdullah Hilmi, Adalli's uncle, an older man in a brown robe, said much the same - and certainly Major Hatim believed what he said. But what of those YouTube pictures, of the shooting of demonstrators and mourners at funerals – no danger of that at this funeral yesterday - and the 3,000 civilian dead of which the UN now talks?

I suppose that, until we Western journalists can investigate without government restrictions, it's a YouTube picture against the word of two poor men in peasants' clothes.

SYRIA SLIPS TOWARDS SECTARIAN WAR
By Robert Fisk
27 October 2011

So there was the reporter from Syrian television asking what I thought of the situation in Syria, and there was I saying that you can no longer infantilise Arabs, that the uprisings/revolts/revolutions/unrest in the Arab world were all different; but that dictatorship didn't work, that if there were - if - a serious new constitution, pluralist political parties and real and genuine free elections, Syria might just climb out of its tragedy but that the government was running out of time, fast.

We shall see if this gets on air on Saturday (readers will be kept informed) but outside in the street another pro-Assad demonstration was starting, 10,000 then 50,000 - it might have reached 200,000 by midday - and there was no Saddam-style trucking of the people to the Omayad Square, no mukhabarat intelligence presence and the only soldiers were standing with their families. How does one report a pro-government demo during the Arab Awakening? There were veiled women, old men, thousands of children with "Syria" written on their faces. Most held Syrian flags, some held the flags of Russia and China.

Were they coerced? I don't think so - not by the Assad government, at least. Some played football games in the parks round the square. Others signed their names - Muslim and Christian - on a banner decorated with the branches of a massive Syrian tree. But if they were coerced, it was by stories from further north. I spoke to 12 men and women. Five spoke of relatives in the army killed in Homs. And the news from Homs was very bad. I had dinner on Tuesday night with an old friend. His 62-year-old cousin, a retired engineer, had given water to some soldiers in Homs. Next morning, armed men knocked at his front door and shot him dead. He was a Christian.

Of course, the Assad government had been warning of a sectarian war. Of course, the Assad government has set itself up as the only sure protector of minorities. Of course, the Assad government had claimed that Islamists and "terrorists" were behind the street opposition to the regime. It's also clear that the brutality of the Syrian security forces in Deraa and Homs and other cities against unarmed protesters has been a scandal, which those in the government privately acknowledge.

But it's also transparent that the struggle in Syria now cuts through the centre of the country and that many armed men now oppose the army. Indeed, I have been told that Homs slips - for hours at a time - out of government control. Damascenes travelling to the northern city of Aleppo can take the bus. But now more than ever, they are flying to avoid the dangerous road between Hama and Aleppo. These are the reasons, I suspect, why so many thousands came to demonstrate in Damascus yesterday. They are frightened.

Foreign journalists are not allowed to travel to Homs - a serious error by the regime - where Sunnis, Alawites and Christians live close together amid Armenians, Circassians and other groups. A sectarian war may well be in the cynical interests of any regime fighting for its life. But unless everyone I've met is lying (which I don't believe), this is now a growing reality in central Syria. Against this, no Russian or Chinese vetoes in the United Nations are of any use.

A delegation from the Arab League - that pathetic and most useless of Arab institutions - was due to arrive in Damascus yesterday afternoon. To what effect? Are they supposed to send a "peace" force? Two days ago, Mohamed Kadour, the Dean of the Petrochemicals Faculty at Homs University, was kidnapped in return for the freeing of detainees. He was released a day later. Whether imprisoned men were released, we don't know. But it has happened before. In Idlib, so they say, everyone is armed. And the weapons - so they say - are coming from Lebanon.

Ask who the armed men are in central Syria and you receive a spread of replies: Bedouin who smuggle drugs to Saudi Arabia, army defectors, "Islamists" from Iraq, "people who just think there is no other way to get rid of the regime". Damascus is safe; bright lights and late-night shopping and restaurants and thousands wandering the streets. But Damascus is not the rest of Syria. It lives in a kind of bubble.

I got up yesterday after only an hour and a half of sleep - because outside my hotel, government workers were testing the deafening sound system for the demonstration. All night there were bursts of taped cheering and drums and cheers and trumpets. But did those crowds yesterday really need this false applause and fraudulent additions to their own demonstration? Officially, things are getting better in Syria. I doubt it.

If the UN figure of more than 3,000 civilian dead is correct and if the Syrian statistic of 1,150 military deaths are correct and if the deaths of the last three days - perhaps another 50 - are true, then up to 4,200 Syrians have been killed in seven months. And that's enough to frighten anyone.

WHAT THE KILLING OF GADDAFI MEANS TO SYRIA
By Robert Fisk
29 October 2011

Two days before Gaddafi was murdered, I was reading the morning newspapers in Beirut and discovered a remarkable story on most front pages. At the time, the mad ex-emperor of Libya was still hiding in Sirte, but there was this quotation by the US Secretary of State, La Clinton, speaking in Tripoli itself. "We hope he can be captured or killed soon," she said, "so that you don't have to fear him any longer." This was so extraordinary that I underlined La Clinton's words and clipped the article from one of the front pages. (My archives are on paper.) "We hope he can be captured or killed soon." Then bingo. NATO bombs his runaway convoy and the old boy is hauled wounded from a sewage pipe and done away with.

Now in an age when America routinely assassinates its enemies, La Clinton's words were remarkable because they at last acknowledged the truth.

Normally, the State Department or the White House churned out the usual nonsense about how Gaddafi or Bin Laden or whoever must be "brought to justice" - and we all know what that means. But this week, the whole business turned much darker. Asked about his personal reaction, Obama the Good said that no one wanted to meet such an end, but that Gaddafi's death should be a lesson "to all dictators around the world". And we all knew what that meant. Principally, the message was to Bashar al-Assad of Syria. Maybe, ran the subtext, they would meet the same sticky end.

So now here I am in Damascus and I've been asking Syrians what they made of the whole business. Whenever I said Gaddafi was a crackpot, they would wholeheartedly agree. But when I spoke to a very senior government official who works directly for the Syrian leadership, he spoke in slightly different terms. "We don't accept any comparisons," he said. "But the seriousness of Gaddafi's killing is that in the West in the future, they are going to say: 'See how the Libyans behave? See how the Arabs behave? See how Muslims behave?' This will be used against Islam. It was humiliating for the Libyans more than it was for Gaddafi, and that is why I fear it will be used against all of us. This is my real concern."

On Syrian television this week, I made the point that Gaddafi was insane and that - whatever else you thought of him - Assad was not. This was met (naturally) by vigorous agreement from the presenter. But wait. I promised to tell readers what happened to the programme. Well, two days ago, quite by chance, I bumped into the journalist who had interviewed me. Alas, he said, he thought the translation and subtitles wouldn't be ready for Saturday night's broadcast. Maybe we could do another interview later. Back to that old saw, I guess: we shall see.

In any event, I was made very much aware by her own personal assistant how "deeply hurt" Bashar al-Assad's wife Asma was at a report in The Independent a couple of weeks ago which suggested that she was indifferent to the plight of civilian opponents of the regime killed by the security forces. The story - not by me - quoted an aid official in Damascus who was present at a meeting with the First Lady, saying that - when asked about the casualties - "there was no reaction".

Needless to say, this report was gobbled up by the Arab media, including al- Jazeera, Assad's most hated TV station. Now Asma al-Assad's assistant has just given me the Syrian Arab Red Crescent's own official Arabic-language account of the meeting. It makes interesting reading. SARC volunteers told the president's wife that they received better treatment from the army "which has a clear leadership" than they did from the intelligence services at the checkpoints across Syria - they said the "muhabarrat" intelligence "enjoys no leadership or clear principles, at least from our point of view" - and that vehicles from the Ministry of Health are sometimes misused by "parties without control and this has created a situation of fear among citizens". Mrs Assad was told how difficult it was for the SARC to work in dangerous areas and to move the wounded.

"Mrs Asma [sic] showed her understanding of the difficulties our volunteers are going through," the SARC report says, "and expressed her deep admiration for their efforts in serving humanity and individual people... and promised to convey some of their demands to the authorities." Mrs Assad's visit was "informal" and the discussions "friendly".

In the days that followed, the SARC report continued, the behaviour of "security checkpoints" towards their volunteers improved. A subsequent report in the weekly Syria Today quotes Mrs Assad as telling the Red Crescent volunteers that they "must remain neutral and independent during this time, focusing solely on humanitarian needs".

So there you have it. Certainly not indifferent - but hardly a ringing condemnation of human rights abuses. Of course, I can see Asma al-Assad's problem. Had she spoken out directly against the killing of protesters, of course, the world's press and television would not have said that Mrs Assad stood up for human rights. The headlines would have been political, and would have read: "Syrian President attacked by wife." The truth, I fear, is that once war begins, you just can't win. Even if you are the wife of the president.

COMPARED WITH SYRIA, THE FALL OF LIBYA WAS A PIECE OF CAKE
By Patrick Cockburn
20 November 2011

President Bashar al-Assad's enemies are closing in for the kill. The Arab League is suspending Syria, and Turkey, once a close ally, is leading the pack in seeking to displace the government that has ruled for 40 years. Arab leaders are talking to West European states about deploying the same mix of political, military and economic sanctions against Syria that was used in Libya.

This final assault is already producing convulsions across the Middle East and beyond, because the outcome of the struggle will have an explosive impact on the entire region. By comparison, the overthrow of Colonel Muammar Gaddafi was a marginal event. Complex though these developments are, the media's coverage has been misleadingly simple-minded and one-dimensional, giving the impression that all we are witnessing is a heroic uprising by the Syrian masses against a brutal Baathist police state.

This is certainly one aspect of the crisis. Brutal repression is continuous. Death squads roam the streets. Foreign journalists, banned from Syria and reliant on information from the opposition, report this. But manipulation of the media by the opposition is also made easy by the lack of information from the country. Opposition claims, such as one last week that an air force intelligence centre near Damascus had been stormed, are credulously accepted and published, although other accounts suggest that all that happened was that the building was hit by rocket-propelled grenades that scorched its paintwork.

The line-up of the Syrian government's opponents should make it clear to anybody that there is more at stake here than Arab and international concern for human rights. The lead is being taken by Saudi Arabia - its repressive regime one of the few absolute monarchies left on the planet. In March, it sent 1,500 troops into Bahrain to crush protests very similar to those in Syria. Unstinting support was given by the Saudis to the Bahraini authorities as they tortured distinguished hospital consultants whose only crime was to treat injured protesters. Is it really conceivable that Saudi Arabia should be primarily motivated by humanitarian concerns?

A more convincing motive for international involvement is the decades-old but escalating struggle against Iran by the US, its NATO allies, Israel and the Sunni states of the Middle East. But the last few years have shown the limits of effective action against Iran, short of war, which, for all the bluster from Washington and Tel Aviv, they are wary of fighting. But Syria is a different matter. "If you can't beat Iran, the second best option is to break Syria," says the Iraqi political scientist Ghassan Attiyah, who points out the absurdity of Saudi Arabia presenting itself as a defender of human and democratic rights in the Middle East.

The US has been carefully keeping in the background, although one senior Arab official says that Damascus had sent emissaries to talk to the Americans to see if Washington would ease up on the campaign against it. The US price was that Syria must break with Iran, but the Syrians were dubious about what exactly they would get in return for giving up their sole ally. "We are being asked to jump into a swimming pool with no water in it," they said.

The struggle for Syria is the latest arena for the sectarian conflict between Sunni and Shia. Its modern origins lie in the Iranian revolution of 1979, deepened during the Iran-Iraq war of 1980-88, and reached new depths of hatred in Iraq during the Shia-Sunni civil war in 2005-07.

In 2005, Iraq became the first Arab state since the Fatimids in Egypt in the 12th century to have a predominantly Shia government. In Lebanon, the Shia political-military Hezbollah movement became the leading political player and withstood an Israeli military assault in 2006. In post- Taliban Afghanistan, the Hazara, a Shia ethnic group which was once oppressed as virtual serfs, grew in political and economic strength.

The Arab Spring at first seemed to work in favour of the Shia and Iran by deposing some of their most notable opponents, such as President Hosni Mubarak of Egypt. The 70 per cent Shia majority in Bahrain demanded democratic rights in February and March, only to be brutally repressed. Those tortured say their torturers continually demanded they confess to links to Iran. Underlining the sectarian nature of the repression, the Bahraini authorities demolished Shia mosques and desecrated the graves of Shia holy men.

The gathering alliance against the Assad government is both anti-Iranian and anti-Shia. It is based on the correct assumption that the fall of the present regime will be a blow to both. The Alawites, the heteredox Shia sect to which 12 per cent of Syrians belong, dominate the ruling elite. A senior Middle East diplomat says: "The Alawites have decided they must do or die with Assad." The Christians and Druze likewise do not expect much mercy from a triumphant Sunni regime, while Hezbollah will be weakened in Lebanon and Syria's 30-year alliance with Iran will end. Not surprisingly, the Iranians see the assault on Syria primarily as an anti-Shia and anti-Iranian counter-revolution wearing a human rights mask.

How will Iran and Iraq, the two most important Shia states, respond to the growing likelihood of the fall of the government in Damascus? The Iranians will do all they can to prop it up, but already suspect this may not be enough. Consequently, they will respond to the loss of their Syrian ally by increasing their influence in Iraq. "They will do everything to hold Iraq as their last line of defence," Dr Attiyah says, "but the country will become a battleground."

Baghdad has its own reasons for fearing the outcome of the crisis in Syria. The Sunni minority in Iraq, politically marginalised by the Shia and Kurds, will be strengthened if a Sunni regime takes over next door in Damascus. The withdrawal of the last US troops at the end of the year means that Washington has less reason to defend the Prime Minister, Nouri al-Maliki. The Iraqi leader should be under no illusion about the hostility of his Sunni neighbours.

The fall of the government in Syria will not be confined to one country, as happened in Libya. It will throw the whole Middle East into turmoil. Turkish leaders say privately they have been given a free hand by the US and Britain to do what they want. But the Saudis have no wish to see Turkey become the champions of the Muslim world. The battle for Syria is already producing fresh rivalries and the seeds of future conflicts.

Winter 2012

Conflict Goes International

ONLY A CRAZY LEADER KILLS HIS OWN PEOPLE, SAYS ASSAD
By Kim Sengupta
8 December 2011

President Bashar al-Assad has declared that only a "crazy" leader kills citizens of his own country and those who have died in Syria since the start of the protests were supporters, rather than opponents, of his regime.

Around 4,000 people have died since the start of the protests and Syria faces the threat of sanctions from the Arab League and punitive measures from the wider international community. But Assad insisted yesterday his loyal followers were the real victims.

"We don't kill our people," he said in an interview on ABC, above. "No government in the world kills its people, unless it's led by a crazy person. Most of the people that have been killed are supporters of the government, not the vice versa... There is a difference between having a policy to crack down and having some mistakes committed by some officials." Asked whether he regretted the strife which has engulfed Syria, he said he had done his best to "protect the people".

US Assistant Secretary of State Jeffrey Feltman dismissed the Syrian leader's claims, stating: "Assad and his clique should stop the killing, stop the torture, stop the jailing. We want to use all of the tools that are available to the international community to change what is happening in Syria by peaceful means."

But a senior western European diplomat warned yesterday that the absence of senior government defection so far meant Western countries pushing for change "could be in it for the long haul".

SYRIA'S SECTARIAN WAR GOES INTERNATIONAL AS FOREIGN FIGHTERS AND ARMS POUR INTO COUNTRY
By Kim Sengupta
20 February 2012

The attack at night was sudden and fierce, mortar rounds followed by machine-gun fire. There was panic among some of the inexperienced Syrian rebel fighters. But Sadoun al-Husseini had seen it all before.

Mr Husseini got his combat experience in Iraq, fighting first against American forces and then as a member of the "Anbar Awakening", when Sunni nationalists turned their guns against foreign fighters affiliated with al-Qa'ida.

His presence inside Syria, where an overwhelmingly Sunni uprising is taking place against Bashar al-Assad's Alawite-dominated establishment, can be interpreted as an example of the country's civil war turning into an international sectarian conflict, a source of great unease in the region. Or it could be, as the 36-year-old engineer from the Iraqi city of Ramadi insisted, an expression of solidarity with oppressed brethren sharing a common heritage.

What it does illustrate is a reversal of roles between two countries. For years after the US-led invasion of Iraq, weapons and fighters slipped in across the border from Syria. Now the roles are being reversed with the flow coming the other way, although the numbers involved remain unclear.

Ayman al-Zawahiri, Osama bin Laden's successor as head of al-Qa'ida, declared this month that it was the duty of all Muslims to take part in jihad in Syria. The organisation's Iraqi arm was, according to some American officials, responsible for recent bombings in Damascus and one in Aleppo. A message on the website of al-Qa'ida in Iraq said: "A lot of people fought side-by-side with the Islamic state of Iraq and it is good news to hear about the arrival of Iraqi fighters to help their brethren in Syria."

Mr Husseini had already been into Syria through Iraq's Anbar province. He maintained that his visit to the Idlib area, a circuitous route through Turkey, was part of a humanitarian mission. He got caught up in violence, he said, when regime forces attacked a village.

Speaking to The Independent inside Syria, he said: "Our Syrian brothers are fighting their own war. I am not involved. But it is the duty of all true Muslims to help people in this struggle. We are just trying to work out what help is needed. People in Iraq and other countries are seeing the suffering that is taking place and I am working with a group that is giving support - but it is all peaceful."

Mr Husseini acknowledged some arms may be coming across the Iraqi border. "This is something I have heard," he said. "There are plenty of guns, rocket-propelled grenades, other things one can buy in Iraq. So some businessmen are maybe doing this."

He did not want to reveal details of the group he is working with for "security reasons". But he said: "We are the same family. There may be a lot of refugees coming into Iraq and we must look after them, just as the Syrians looked after us when people from Iraq had to escape there. Yes, I have heard all this talk of al-Qa'ida doing things in Syria. But that does not have the support of true Iraqis... this is propaganda, spread inside Iraq by people who want to damage solidarity with Syria."

The Shia-dominated Iraqi government has said it is taking urgent steps to stop arms going into Syria. The office of the Prime Minister, Nouri al-Maliki, said he held a meeting at the weekend "to work on closing all the gaps over the border with Syria, which terrorists and criminal gangs are using for all kinds of smuggling, including arms".

Yet the worry of sectarian strife spilling across the region continues to grow. Yesterday, in the southern Turkish city of Antakya, a demonstration took place in support of the Syrian regime by about 3,000 people, the vast majority of them Alawites, chanting: "We shall shed our blood for you, Assad."

Inside Syria, meanwhile, the official news agency, Sana, reported that gunmen killed a state prosecutor and a judge in Idlib province. They blamed "terrorists" - a catch-all phrase the regime uses to describe anyone opposed to President Assad's rule.

JOURNALISTS KILLED IN SYRIA ROCKET STRIKE 'WERE TARGETED'
By Kim Sengupta
23 February 2012

Marie Colvin, one of the pre-eminent war correspondents of her generation, was killed yesterday, along with an award-winning French photographer, Remi Ochlik, as they covered the siege of the Syrian city of Homs.

Two other journalists, including Paul Conroy, a photographer who also worked for The Sunday Times with Colvin, were injured when the house in which they were staying was hit by rockets. Fellow journalists, human rights activists and politicians condemned the killings amid claims that the regime of President Bashar al-Assad knew the building was being used by foreign media.

Colvin, 55, had written a powerful and poignant dispatch for her newspaper in which she described the suffering inflicted on the population of Homs, which has become a symbol of resistance during the Syrian uprising.

She had also appeared on a number of international broadcast networks, including the BBC and CNN, to accuse President Assad's forces of murder. She said the regime was peddling "complete and utter lies that they are only targeting terrorists". Describing what was happening as "absolutely sickening", she declared: "The Syrian army is simply shelling a city of cold, starving civilians." She also gave a charged description of watching a two- year-old die from a shrapnel wound.

Jean-Pierre Perrin, a reporter with the French newspaper Libération, was with Colvin in Homs last week. He claimed they were told that the Syrian army was "deliberately" planning to shell their makeshift press centre.

There were also unconfirmed reports that intercepted radio traffic between Syrian army officers contained threats to kill foreign journalists.

The Syrian ambassador to London, Dr Sami Khiyami, was summoned to the Foreign Office to be told the UK expects prompt arrangements to be made for the repatriation of the journalists' bodies and for the injured British photographer to be given medical treatment.

Colvin, an American who had worked for The Sunday Times since 1985, seamlessly used both steeliness and charm in pursuit of stories. She lost her left eye to shrapnel in 2001 while working in Sri Lanka.

When she was stopped at a checkpoint after the fall of Tripoli in Libya last year, she got past a particularly obdurate militia commander by browbeating him. But she won him over enough to have him ask for his picture to be taken with her. "You never know, we might need him on the way back," she pointed out.

She was fiercely proud of what the best kind of journalism could achieve. "You hear all this talk about the meaning of the media, the need for integrity etc," she said while discussing the Leveson Inquiry. "But isn't it quite simple? You just try to find out the truth of what's going on and report it the best way you can. And because we are kind of romantic, our sympathy goes towards the underdog."

Colvin was adamant, however, that it was necessary to relax at times on tough assignments. One night in Tunis, at the start of the Arab Spring, her reaction to journalists being refused a late drink was to tell the waiter: "If you don't serve us I warn you I will take off my eye patch." We were served with alacrity.

She could organise a party anywhere. I have fond memories of a dinner at the BBC house in Kabul, when she decided everyone was being far too serious. She got the furniture pulled back, the carpet lifted and got everyone up for not very refined but highly enthusiastic dancing.

As tributes poured in, Simon Kelner, chief executive of the Journalism Foundation and former editor of The Independent, said: "Marie Colvin embodied all the qualities required of a great journalist: bravery, integrity and a fearless desire to seek the truth. At a time when newspapers are under intense scrutiny, her work is a reminder of the fundamental purpose of journalism, and her death, along with the French photographer Remi Ochlik, represents a dark day indeed."

ASSAD OPENS NEW FRONT IN WAR ON HIS PEOPLE
By Kim Sengupta
23 February 2012

Syrian regime forces came in four pick-up trucks, some in uniform and others in civilian clothing - but all carrying guns. They found the man they sought working on a farm, there was shouting and then they shot him in the head.

"They dragged his body away and threw it into the back of one of the cars. One of the soldiers said they would have to dump it somewhere. They were so casual, it was as if they had just killed a stray dog," said 19-year-old Mohammed Hani. "This was not the first time this had happened, we have seen lots of people killed around here but now it's getting even worse."

This was just one death among many in this area during a violent and vengeful operation by the troops of Bashar al-Assad. Villages along the border between Syria and Turkey have been systematically cleansed in an apparent attempt to destroy supply routes vital for opposition safe havens.

With a death toll of around 80, Idlib province has experienced more people killed in the last 48 hours than Homs, the pre-eminent centre of resistance. That city has been subjected to continuous bombardment, which claimed the lives, among others, of journalists Marie Colvin and Remi Ochlik. In this region, many of the fatalities have been targeted executions, with the seeming aim of exterminating activists and crushing resistance.

Wassim Sabbagh, who is directing communications for the rebels in the Idlib border area, said: "What we saw in these attacks is the total disregard with which Bashar al-Assad holds the people of Syria. Regime forces have gone into these villages and killed people and destroyed homes just as a punishment for carrying out protests."

The Turkish hamlet of Hacipasa, straddling the frontier, is one of the bases used by the rebels. Bullets regularly stray from fire fights in adjoining fields and hills. Swirls of smoke rose yesterday from mortar rounds which, the revolutionaries claimed, were aimed at a community centre used by protesters in the Syrian village of Asmarin.

Mr Hani, who is Turkish, said: "We have families on both sides of the border and see what is happening. I was working in Libya and got stranded during the revolution. Terrible things happened there and now the same is happening here. We don't know how many were killed in the last two days."

According to the Syrian Network for Human Rights, 32 men, mostly young, were killed at the villages of Idita, Iblin and Bashon. Another dozen died at Darcush when an attack by regime troops began on Tuesday morning following a demonstration. A convoy including five members of the local campaign group who were arrested and being taken to nearby Jar Ash Shaghur was ambushed by revolutionaries.

"We failed to get the men free, but we have to rescue them, they are leaders of the revolution in this area," said Izzedin Hihano, the rebel commander in charge of defending the villages in this stretch of the border. "But, more than that, they will be killed. They will not die quickly, they will be tortured."

Commander Hihano, a former marble craftsman, is the head of the Martyr Hisham Haboub Group, named after a fallen rebel which has about 300 fighters in its ranks. "There are another 700 in this area. But we are very short of ammunition... that is the main problem."

Yesterday, Commander Hihano went back into Turkey, where he stays in a refugee camp, with the mission of buying ammunition.

The revolutionaries were able to bring their own injured, as well as some civilians, towards the border, thanks to subterfuge of the residents in one village. "Some of the wounded were saved. They pretended to hold a march in honour of Bashar al-Assad. The soldiers were surprised, but they went away to fight the revolutionaries," said Haitham al-Baid, who lives in Iblin.

"That created a passage and they could take wounded people out."

Commander Hihano said: "The fight will continue - we have no choice. But the priority is to get medical help. Assad has declared war on his own population, you have seen that, so it is up to us to protect the welfare of people."

'WE ARE NOT AFRAID OF ASSAD ANY LONGER. BUT WHY MUST MORE PEOPLE DIE?'
By Kim Sengupta
25 February 2012

The bodies were in a field, dumped during the night. They were men who had been arrested and taken away for interrogation after the forces of the Syrian regime began a vicious and vengeful sweep through this region.

The families in the village of Kurin have not been able to collect and bury their dead because they would be walking into a trap; any approach so far, they say, has been met with sniper fire. A force of rebel fighters who went to carry out the task twice had to retreat under fire from mortars.

Their commander, Abdul Haq, spread his hands in apology. "If we went any further there would be more killed, more for us to try and bring back. We feel we are failing our people, but we cannot match the weapons of the enemy."

Yesterday, as the savage strife continued, the Friends of Syria - America, Western Europe and the Arab countries - meeting in Tunis issued yet another ultimatum to Bashar al-Assad and announced that the opposition group, the Syrian National Council, would be recognised as the legitimate government by a number of states, including the UK.

None of this brings much relief in these killing grounds. The estimate of fatalities varies: according to the United Nations it is around 5,400, while activists say it is around 7,300. But it is a figure rising daily and, to those who have borne the losses, it seems little is being done to stop the murderous campaign.

Nor is there much enthusiasm for the Syrian National Council. Few in the rural areas have heard of it and many among those who have, including rebel fighters, view them as preaching revolution from a comfortable exile.

Here in Idlib province, in north-western Syria, The Independent found the reality is of troops and armour backed by the Alawite militia, the Shabiha, systematically going through the area, killing more people in the last four days than have fallen victim even in the terrible bombardment of Homs.

Almost every village and township has tales of being visited by organised violence. On the day that the eight bodies were found at Kurin, activists were being held at Azmarin, Idita, Iblin and Bashon, on occasions after being identified by informers.

Six were arrested at Darkush, including a 13-year-old boy and a schoolteacher. There "they had a list, they knew the ones they wanted" said Issa Mohammed, 22. "No one could go to help them because there were so many roadblocks. If anyone said anything they would be captured as well."

One needs to be cautious of these accounts in such a bloody conflict in which hurt and anger, as well as political expediency, can lead to embellished tales.

But here residents would come forward with names of those killed and detained, albeit with requests that the names of those still thought to be alive should not be made public because this may expedite their deaths and put relations and friends in harm's way.

Abd Jibilawe, from al-Janoudiyah, described how three friends have lost their lives so far, before adding quietly "and there was Ahmed Jibilawe who was my cousin and my best friend".

At a hamlet near Darkush, Hasina Um Samin was mourning her brother, Abu Khalid. "We are just poor people, we have not done anything bad," she said, huddled under a thin blanket at her home, unheated because of a lack of fuel. "Still they came and took him. We thought it must be a mistake, but we don't know where he is. We fear will not see him again."

There is little defence in Idlib against a state which is clearly waging a war on its own people. The revolutionaries here are mainly local men, with courage but no military training and woefully short of anything like adequate arms and ammunition. Witnessing their plight, one had wry memories of rebels in Libya firing thousands of rounds into the air, often in celebration of imaginary victories.

The Libyan revolution was, of course, facilitated by months of NATO bombing. The constant question here is why no military action has followed grandiose statements by the West. For the time being, however, the rebels would be grateful for supplies which would go some way towards enabling them to take on the regime.

Commander Haq, a 34-year-old mechanic, has around 50 fighters under his command, but not even one semi-automatic rifle between them. Instead they pass around 20 hunting rifles, shotguns and handguns and one set of body armour brought over by a soldier who defected.

As we sat at his base, a farm building in the hills above Darkush, pinned down by a burst of machine-gun fire flying overhead, he opened a rucksack containing cartridges. "This is what I've been sent. Perhaps the Syrian National Council can send us some proper guns and ammunition from all the international money they are getting. Look at these, how old they are. Some of these are rusting. Some of these are not even the right type for the guns we have."

At this point a Remington pump-action shotgun one of his men was using simply fell apart, possibly due to metal fatigue. Fortunately, no one was hurt, but the men were keen to show other examples of their antiquated armoury - a Soviet Star pistol proudly bearing the place of manufacture, CCCP, and the date, 1948. Britain, too had provided a little help for the Syrian revolution - a Webley revolver, circa the 1930s.

Later in the afternoon, during a break in the shooting, another commander, Abu Staif, came in proudly bearing the favoured tool of revolutionaries the world over, a Kalashnikov AK-47.

This one, the first for the group, was a regime-issue weapon. It had not been captured but bought from a member of the Shabiha. "It cost us $2,000 - even then we had to wait for almost two months," said Commander Staif. "The man who sold it to us stole it from another person from the Shabiha so the registration would not get back to him if Bashar's people capture it back.

"The Shabiha and the army are both corrupt, just like the rotten regime they serve. The soldiers are more corrupt. One officer offered to sell us his entire checkpoint with tanks, but he wanted more money than we could ever have. The Shabiha are more difficult because they are Alawites and they hate us."

The price of a Kalashnikov of similar vintage would probably be around

$300 in places like Afghanistan. The Syrian rebels insist paying so much is not an illustration of being flush with Qatari or Saudi largesse, but rather of having to turn to wherever they can.

Most of their funding, they claimed, came from donations raised by local communities. This, however, has suffered a setback because one of their main fund-raisers had been killed that morning at Jisr al-Shughour.

"They used an agent. He was sent to find out who were the organisers, and they came and shot him in front of his family," said Izzedin Hihano, a revolutionary from the town.

"For years, the Assads controlled us by fear. We are not afraid any longer. People would rather die than go back to that. But why must that happen? Why must more die? We need help quickly - we are desperate."

'I HAVE TO HELP MY FAMILY, BUT I DID NOT WANT TO SHOOT MY OWN PEOPLE'
By Kim Sengupta
28 February 2012

The protesters were unarmed, posing no threat, offering no provocation. When the order came to open fire, many among the security forces were shocked, a few refused. One of those was dragged out of the ranks, made to kneel on the roadside, and shot.

"His name was Abdullah al-Zinat, he was a young guy. He was picked out because he had been arguing the most with the officers, saying what was happening was wrong. That's what killed him," said Mohammed Zidan.

"I did not fire, we could fire up to 100 rounds without having to get permission. I did not do that, but I did not say anything either. I was afraid, others were afraid as well."

Four days after Mr Zinat's execution, Mr Zidan deserted from the police. Initially, he returned to his post after threats to his family and was briefly imprisoned, before finally escaping. Now he is with the revolutionaries. The 23-year-old is, however, one of a relatively small number of security personnel to defect so far, a handicap for the rebels who suffer acutely from a lack of military experience and weaponry. Furthermore, the ones who have gone over to the other side are often divided. The Free Syrian Army, for instance, operates separately from the Free Officers Group. Both bodies, in turn, are often disparaging of the hierarchy of the Syrian National Council, the opposition's main political organisation.

Mr Zidan did not want to speak to me at first at the rebel base in Idlib province. But then he decided that it was necessary to discuss the mentality and motivation of the soldiers and policemen engaged in this vicious conflict.

"They are saying that these men are killers and doing terrible things, this is what they are saying especially in other countries," he said. "But for most this was just a job, how could they know that all these things will happen when they started. They did not know that they would be told to attack fellow Syrians."

The quietly spoken young man with an anxious face, hastily covered up later with a checked keffiyeh (scarf) for the photograph, seemed to have had some worries about what may lie ahead when he joined the police a year ago.

"I joined the homicide branch because I thought I would not have to deal with things like demonstrations," he said. "We had seen on television what was going on in Egypt, things were starting in Libya, things starting here. I wanted the job because it was good money and I have to help my family, but I did not want to shoot my own people."

Mr Zidan left his home in Idlib City for a nine-month course in Aleppo. "They wanted us out on duty as soon as possible, I was concerned but I still thought I could be a detective."

However, after graduating, Mr Zidan was told he would have to defend the country against terrorists. He was posted to the town of Al-Qamishli near the Iraqi border, an area which was being used, said his superiors, to smuggle arms into the country.

"I don't know if that was happening. We were immediately put into units and sent out to arrest opposition people, some of them women, some of them old," he stated. "They were hurt when they were questioned. They were taken away to other places where even worse things happened, especially to the women. We were also told that we must break up any kind of marches. We were told we could open fire any time, a hundred rounds and then get permission for more, which was always given. Some people enjoyed that but many of us were very upset, some officers were upset as well."

Mr Zidan's first defection ended after the police in Idlib City told his family that they would suffer unless he gave himself up. "I was beaten, but it was not as bad as I thought it was going to be. I think at the time they were trying to keep as many of us as possible."

But the increasingly brutal treatment of protesters and the shooting of Mr Zinat convinced him that he could no longer serve the regime. He organised a call from home to say his mother was very ill and was given compassionate leave. "But after three days they said I must return. I had no choice but to run away and join the freedom fighters."

The security forces carried out their threat against his relations. "My father has now been arrested many times, he is an old man, but they have no respect," Mr Zidan shook his head. "I feel very worried, guilty. But I have made my choice, I have joined the people."

Spring 2012

'Cleaning'

THE REGIME CALLS IT 'CLEANING', BUT THE DIRTY TRUTH IS PLAIN TO SEE
By Robert Fisk
1 march 2012

So it's the "cleaning" of Baba Amr now, is it? "Tingheef" in Arabic. Did that anonymous Syrian government official really use that word to the AP yesterday? It's a chilling expression, one that always precedes a lot of killing. And the UN says it's 7,600 so far. The Israelis used the same word in English when they stormed into Lebanon in 1982 (total dead about 17,500). Five months earlier, when the Syrians were finishing off the Muslim insurgents of Hama, just north of Homs (more than 10,000, possibly 15,000 dead), they said they were "researching" the area, "searching", "investigating". The word they used was "bahagh".

It's a honey of a word for all armies when they're going to abandon human rights. The Brits used to like "mopping up" in the Second World War (approximately 60 million dead). So did the Russians. In the Warsaw Ghetto, the Germans referred to the "cleansing" of Jewish streets in 1944. The word was that of SS Major General Jürgen Stroop in his "police" report (50,000 dead). Cleaning, searching, mopping up, cleansing; massed killing washed of all responsibility. After you "clean" something, it doesn't smell any more.

No, the Syrians are not the Israelis, the Israelis are not the Brits and Russians, and the Syrians, Israelis, Brits and Russians are not the SS. But words do have an unhappy way of reflecting real intentions. The more you polish, search, wash, clean, cleanse, the less blood there should be on the ground. The defence brigades who crushed Hama 30 years ago were led by "Uncle" Rifaat Assad, his nephew, Bashar, is now President of Syria, his other nephew, Maher, is reputedly leading his 4th Brigade into Baba Amr.

Anyway, the tanks bombarded the Sunni district of Homs first, then the infantry - according to residents on the phone yesterday - started to move in. The "decisive month" had begun, according to another "anonymous" Syrian official. Every month in Syria, of course, has been a "decisive month". It's been that way for a year now. In September 1980, I remember, Saddam's gombeen men talked about the "decisive month" in the "Whirlwind War" - the invasion of Iran. The war lasted eight years (about 1.5 million dead).

Anyway, we'll see what Assad's squadrons are made of. Will his infantry defect when they have to batter their way into Homs? A real worry. Will the Free Syria Army fight to the death or run away to fight another day? And civilian casualties in Baba Amr?

If Assad's men win, we might hear a figure. The Assad version won't include Sunni "enemy" dead, any more than his antagonists are going to tell us how many Alawite and Christian "enemies" they've killed. Assad says he's fighting "terrorists". Rifaat said the same at Hama. The Israelis used the word a thousand times about the Palestinians. The Russians said the same about the Germans. Stroop said the same about the Jews.

Alas, all the perfumes of Arabia will not sweeten these little hands.

THE FEARFUL REALITIES KEEPING THE ASSAD REGIME IN POWER
By Robert Fisk
4 March 2012

In my 1912 Baedeker guide to Syria, a page and a half is devoted to the city of Homs. In tiny print, it says that, "in the plain to the southeast, you come across the village of Baba Amr. A visit to the arcaded bazaar is worthwhile - here you will find beautiful silks. To the north of Homs, on a square, there is an artillery barracks..." The bazaar has long since been demolished, though the barracks inevitably passed from Ottoman into French and ultimately into Baathist hands; for 27 days last month, this bastion has been visiting hell on what was once the village of Baba Amr.

Once a Roman city, where the crusaders committed their first act of cannibalism - eating their dead Muslim opponents - Homs was captured by Saladin in 1174. Under post-First World War French rule, the settlement became a centre of insurrection and, after independence, the very kernel of Baathist resistance to the first Syrian governments. By early 1964, there were battles in Homs between Sunnis and Alawi Shia. A year later, the young Baathist army commander of Homs, Lieutenant Colonel Mustafa Tlas, was arresting his pro-regime comrades. Is the city's history becoming a little clearer now?

As one of the Sunni nouveaux riches who would support the Alawi regime, Tlas became defence minister in Hafez al-Assad's Baathist government.

Under their post-1919 mandate, the French had created a unit of "Special Forces" in which the Alawis were given privileged positions; one of their strongholds was the military academy in Homs. One of the academy's most illustrious students under Hafez al-Assad's rule - graduating in 1994 - was his son Bashar. Bashar's uncle, Adnan Makhlouf, graduated second to him; Makhlouf is today regarded as the corrupting element in the Assad regime.

Later, Bashar would become a doctor at the military Tishreen Hospital in Damascus (where today most of the Syrian army's thousands of victims are taken for post-mortem examination before their funerals). Bashar did not forget Homs; his British-born Sunni wife came from a Homs family. One of his closest advisers, Bouthaina Shabaan, comes from Homs; even last year the city was too dangerous for her to visit her mother's grave on the anniversary of her death. Homs lies deep in the heart of all Syrians, Sunni and Alawite alike. Is it surprising that it should have been the Golgotha of the uprising? Or that the Syrian authorities should have determined that its recapture would break the back of the revolution? To the north, 30 years ago, Hafez Assad created more than 10,000 "martyrs" in Hama; last week, Homs became a little Hama, the city's martyrdom predicted by its past.

So why were we so surprised when the "Free Syrian Army" fled the city? Did we really expect the Assad regime to close up shop and run because a few hundred men with Kalashnikovs wanted to stage a miniature Warsaw uprising in Homs? Did we really believe that the deaths of women and children - and journalists - would prevent those who still claim the mantle of Arab nationalism from crushing the city?

When the West happily adopted the illusions of Nicolas Sarkozy, David Cameron and Hillary Clinton - and the Arab Gulf states whose demands for Syrian "democracy" are matched by their refusal to give this same democracy to their own people - the Syrians understood the hypocrisy.

Were the Saudis, now so keen to arm Syria's Sunni insurgents - along with Sunni Qatar - planning to surrender their feudal, princely Sunni power to their own citizens and to their Shia minority? Was the Emir of Qatar contemplating resignation? Among the lobbyists of Washington, among the illusionists at the Brookings Institution and the Rand Corporation and the Council on Foreign Relations and all the other US outfits that peddle New York Times editorials, Homs had become the new Benghazi, the start-line for the advance on Damascus.

It was the same old American dream: if a police state was ruthless, cynical and corrupt - and let us have no illusions about the Baathist apparatus and its panjandrum - then its opponents, however poorly armed, would win; because they were the good guys. The old clichés clanked into focus. The Baathists were Nazis; Bashar a mere cipher in the hands of his family; his wife, Asma, variously an Eva Braun, Marie Antoinette or Lady Macbeth. Upon this nonsense, the West and the Arabs built their hopes.

The more Sarkozy, Cameron and Clinton raged against Syria's atrocities, the more forceful they were in refusing all military help to the rebels. There were conditions to be met. The Syrian opposition had to unite before they could expect help. They had to speak with one voice - as if Gaddafi's opponents did anything like this before NATO decided to bomb him out of power. Sarkozy's hypocrisy was all too obvious to the Syrians. So anxious was he to boost his chances in the French presidential election that he deployed hundreds of diplomats and "experts" to "rescue" the French freelance journalist Edith Bouvier, hampering all the efforts of NGOs to bring her to safety. Not many months ago, this wretched man was cynically denouncing two male French journalists - foolhardy, he called them -- who had spent months in Taliban custody in Afghanistan.

French elections, Russian elections, Iranian elections, Syrian referendums - and, of course, US elections: it's amazing how much "democracy" can derail sane policies in the Middle East. Putin supports an Arab leader (Assad) who announces that he has done his best "to protect my people, so I don't feel I have anything to be blamed for...

you don't feel you're to blame when you don't kill your own people". I suppose that would be Putin's excuse after his army butchered the Chechens. As it happens, I don't remember Britain's PM saying this about Irish Catholics on Bloody Sunday in 1972 - but perhaps Northern Ireland's Catholics didn't count as Britain's "people"?

No, I'm not comparing like with like. Grozny, with which the wounded photographer Paul Conroy drew a memorable parallel on Friday, has more in common with Baba Amr than Derry. But there is a distressing habit of denouncing anyone who tries to talk reality. Those who claimed that the IRA would eventually find their way into politics and government in Northern Ireland - I was one - were routinely denounced as being "in cahoots with terrorists". When I said in a talk in Istanbul just before Christmas that the Assad regime would not collapse with the speed of other Arab dictatorships - that Christian and Alawite civilians were also being murdered - a young Syrian began shrieking at me, demanding to know "how much you are being paid by Assad's secret police"? Untrue, but understandable. The young man came from Deraa and had been tortured by Syria's mukhabarat.

The truth is that the Syrians occupied Lebanon for almost 30 years and, long after they left in 2005, we were still finding their political claws deep inside the red soil of Beirut. Their intelligence services were still in full operation, their power to kill undiminished, their Lebanese allies in the Beirut parliament. And if the Baathists could smother Lebanon in so powerful a sisterly embrace for so long, what makes anyone think they will relinquish Syria itself easily? As long as Assad can keep Damascus and Aleppo, he can survive.

After all, the sadistic ex-secret police boss Najibullah clung on as leader of Afghanistan for years when all he could do was fly between Kabul and Kandahar. It might be said that, with all Obama's horses and all Obama's men on his side, this is pretty much all Hamid Karzai - with his cruel secret police, his regime's corruption, his bogus elections - can do today. But that is not a comparison to commend itself to Washington, Paris, London, Doha or Riyadh, or even Istanbul.

So what of Bashar Assad? There are those who believe that he really still wants to go down in history as the man who gave Syria its freedom.

Preposterous, of course. The problem is that even if this is true, there are those for whom any profound political change becomes a threat to their power and to their lives. The security police generals and the Baathist paramilitaries will fight to the death for Assad, loyal to a man, because - even if they don't admire him - they know that his overthrow means their own deaths. But if Assad were to indicate that he intended to "overthrow" himself - if the referendum and the new constitution and all the "democratic" changes he talks about became real - these notorious men would feel both fear and fury. Why, in this case, should they any longer remain loyal?

No, Bashar Assad is not a cipher. He is taking the decisions. But his father, Hafez, came to power in 1970 in a "corrective" revolution; "corrections" can always be made again. In the name of Baathism. In the name of Arab nationalism. In the name of crushing the al-Qa'ida-Zionist-Islamist-terrorist enemy. In the name of history.

SYRIA IS TOO FAR STEEPED IN BLOOD FOR RESOLUTION BY NEGOTIATION
By Patrick Cockburn
10 April 2012

In Northern Ireland it used to be called "the politics of the last atrocity", when the latest act of violence and the retaliation it provoked dictated the direction of day-to-day politics. Syria has travelled far in this direction, its towns convulsed by mini-civil wars too bitter and bloodstained to end by mediation.

It is this which is making it so difficult for Kofi Annan, joint envoy for the UN and Arab League, to succeed in his mission. The Syrian government has demanded guarantees from the militiamen it is fighting that they will abide by a ceasefire. This is unlikely to happen given the total distrust between the two sides and with the insurgents fearful of risking torture and execution.

The skirmish on the Syrian-Turkish border is an example of the problems facing any attempt to end the fighting. Anti-government forces attacked a Syrian government checkpoint near the frontier, killed six soldiers and were then shot at as they retreated across the frontier, with bullets hitting dwellings in a nearby refugee camp.

Could this provoke Turkish intervention in the shape of a safe haven for refugees? Ankara has so far been unwilling to risk an all-out conflict. Both sides are playing to the gallery, the insurgents trying to publicise any action by the Syrian army that might goad foreign powers into action. Mr Assad needs to make a show of moderation to keep Russia and China on side.

So far it is the differences between Libya and Syria which are most striking. In Syria, NATO countries want an excuse not to do anything radical, while in Libya they were looking for a justification to intervene. And without direct action by foreign powers, the only alternative for the Free Syrian Army is to wage an escalating guerrilla war against Bashar al-Assad's government which is unlikely to bring about a collapse of the regime.

Mr Assad's options are also limited. He and his government have survived a year of pressure. During fighting in and around Homs, the Syrian army showed that it could crush any insurgent band.

But the government's brutality, including torture, summary executions and artillery bombardments of civilian areas, means it is always creating fresh enemies.

Diplomats say Mr Assad's senior officials are in a confident, and possibly an over-confident, mood. They may have stopped the tide of insurgency, but they will be unable to reverse it. Concessions made last spring might have had an impact, but since then too much blood has been spilled.

AS THE BODIES CONTINUE TO MOUNT UP, A PEOPLE ON EDGE PREPARE FOR CIVIL WAR
By Patrick Cockburn
28 May 2012

In Damascus there are small but menacing signs of abnormality. Soldiers prevent all but military and security personnel entering certain streets.

Heavy goods vehicles are being stopped on the outskirts of the capital because of fear of suicide bombs.

The massacre of the children of Houla and their parents has deepened the sense of crisis here, though many Syrians are becoming inured to violence. Unlike the rest of the world, which focuses on Syria only intermittently when there is some particularly gruesome outrage, people here may be losing their sense of shock after seeing 13,000 die in the last 15 months, according to the latest estimates.

But the most frightening indication that something is wrong is the emptiness, the absence of people and vehicles in previously crowded streets. Many stay at home fixated by a crisis they largely see unfolding on television and online. In the hotel where I am staying in Damascus, I am the only guest.

The government itself often feels curiously absent, perhaps because its attention is elsewhere. Decision-making in Syria was always slow because so many decisions had to be taken at the top but now it is worse.

"I sense that lower-ranking officials do not want to take decisions themselves because they might be countermanded by harder-line officials above them," said a diplomat. At the same time, massacres like Houla, if carried out by Alawite militia men, suggest a leadership not quite in control of its own forces.

The mood is edgy. One person, in the space of a few minutes, shifted from claiming he had total confidence in the happy future of the Syrian people to expressing grim forbodings about the possibility of civil war.

"Why do you foreigners harp on about differences between our minorities?" an anti-government human rights activist asked me in exasperation yesterday. "The French said we would fight each other when they left Syria, but nothing happened. We Syrians stick together whatever governments say about our divisions."

A quarter of an hour later, the same man, a Christian from the city of Hama in central Syria, not far from where the Houla massacre took place, was gloomily wondering about the prospect of sectarian conflict. He explained that Houla is "on a tongue of land where the people are Sunni, but the villages around it are Alawite and Christian. I know it well because my wife comes from a village near there." He said he was very worried that if it turned out that the Sunni villagers, including 34 children, had been murdered by militia men from neighbouring Alawite villages then "I do not know what will happen".

Damascus is deeply affected by the crisis, though this is not always visible. The banks have been cut off from the rest of the world. "All the banks in Lebanon are terrified of doing business with Syria," said one wealthy businesswoman. "My bank manager in Beirut did not want to take a deposit I made even though the cheque was drawn on a British bank." Many in Damascus know first-hand about the physical destruction wrought by the fighting in the centre of the country. There are some 400,000 Syrians displaced by the turmoil, mostly from Homs, who have taken refuge in the capital. Often they move into apartments previously occupied by Iraqi refugees who have returned home, some claiming that for them, Baghdad is now safer than Damascus.

THE WEST IS HORRIFIED BY CHILDREN'S SLAUGHTER NOW. SOON WE'LL FORGET
By Robert Fisk
29 May 2012

Bashar al-Assad will get away with it. He got away with Deraa. He got away with Homs. And he'll get away with Houla. So will the armed opposition to the regime, along with al-Qa'ida and any other outfits joining in Syria's tragedy. Yes, this may be the critical moment, the "tipping point" of horror, when Baathist collapse becomes inevitable rather than probable.

And dear Mr Hague may be "absolutely" appalled. The UN, too. We all are.

But the Middle East is littered with a hundred Houlas, their dead children piled among the statistics, with knives and ropes as well as guns among the murder weapons. And what if Assad's soldiers let their Alawite militia do their dirty work? Didn't the Algerian FLN regime use "home guard" units to murder its opponents in the 1990s? Didn't Gaddafi have his loyalist militias last year, and Mubarak his jailbird drugged-up ex-cops, the baltagi, to bash opponents of his regime? Didn't Israel use its Lebanese Phalangist proxies to intimidate and kill its opponents in Lebanon? Wasn't this, too, "rule by murder"? And come to think of it, wasn't it Bashar al-Assad's uncle Rifaat's Special Forces who massacred the insurgents of Hama in 1982 - speak this not too loudly, for Rifaat lives now between Paris and London - and so who thinks Bashar can't get away with Houla? The Algerian parallel is a frightening one. The FLN's corrupt leadership wanted a "democracy", even held elections. But once it was clear that the Islamist opposition - the luckless Islamic Salvation Front - would win, the government declared war on the "terrorists" trying to destroy Algeria. Villages were besieged, towns were shelled - all in the name of fighting "terror" - until the opposition took to slaughtering civilians around

Blida, thousands of them, babies with their throats cut, women raped. And then it turned out the Algerian army was also involved in massacres. For Houla, read Bentalha, a place we have all forgotten; as we will forget Houla.

And we Westerners, we huffed and puffed, and called upon both sides in Algeria to exercise "restraint", but wanted stability in France's former colony - and let's not forget that Syria is a former French "mandate" territory - and were very worried about al-Qa'ida-style insurgents taking over Algeria and, in the end, the US supported the Algerian military just as the Russians are supporting Syria's military today. And the FLN got away with it, after 200,000 dead - compared to the mere 10,000 killed so far in Syria's war.

And it's worth remembering that, faced with their 1990s insurrection, the Algerians cast around desperately for countries from which they could take advice. They chose Hafez al-Assad's Syria and sent a military delegation to Damascus to learn how the regime destroyed Hama in 1982. Now the Americans - who six months ago were characteristically casting Bashar as a "dead man walking" - prefer a Yemen-type ending to the Syrian war, as if Yemen's crisis wasn't bloody enough. But replacing Assad with a thug from the same patch (the Sanaa "solution") is not what the Syrians will settle for.

Yes, it's a civil war. And yes, Houla may be the turning point. And yes, now the UN are witnesses. But the Baath party has roots that go deeper than blood - ask any Lebanese - and we in the West will soon forget Houla when another YouTube image of death flicks on to our screens from the Syrian countryside. Or from Yemen. Or from the next revolution.

HAGUE SENT PACKING BY RUSSIA AS ANNAN PEACE PLAN CRUMBLES
By Shaun Walker and Patrick Cockburn
29 May 2012

Kofi Annan arrived in Damascus in a desperate bid to rescue his peace plan and prevent Syria from sinking deeper into civil war, but hopes of a united international front were dashed when Russia refused to condemn Bashar al-Assad's regime for the Houla massacre.

Mr Annan held talks with the Syrian President while the British Foreign Secretary, William Hague, sat through a tense press conference in Moscow in which his Russian counterpart, Sergei Lavrov, insisted all sides shared the blame for the recent atrocities.

Russia's backing of a UN Security Council statement condemning the deaths on Friday of more than 100 civilians in Houla had raised hopes that Moscow may finally relax its opposition to putting real pressure on Mr Assad's regime. Mr Lavrov conceded that government forces bore the main responsibility for the massacre, but insisted the presence of knife and bullet wounds on some corpses meant the opposition was also involved. Mr Lavrov also suggested recent bombings in Syria bore "all the hallmarks of al-Qa'ida". He said: "We are dealing with a situation in which both sides evidently had a hand in the deaths of innocent people." Mr Lavrov also repeatedly accused other nations of egging the rebels on and pushing them to break the ceasefire and provoke a response from Mr Assad's forces, in the hope of forcing international intervention. He said: "We should be attempting to implement the peace plan and not trying to change the regime. It's time to choose between pursuing geopolitical goals and saving lives."

The contrast to the language coming out of the US was stark, with Pentagon chief General Martin Dempsey saying there "is always a military option" in dealing with such regimes, adding that "it may come to a point with Syria because of the atrocities".

However, Gen Dempsey, the chairman of the Joint Chiefs of Staff, added that "diplomatic pressure should always precede any discussions about military options".

As Mr Annan arrived in Syria there were reports of escalating fighting in the central city of Hama, where the opposition says Syrian army artillery barrages have killed 41 people.

"I am personally shocked and horrified by the tragic incident in Houla two days ago," Mr Annan said, before entering talks with Mr Assad and other officials.

The UN's peace envoy said that all sides of the conflict had to end the bloodshed, insisting that "this message of peace is not only for the government, but for everyone with a gun".

The Syrian government continues to blame the Houla massacre on "terrorists" and Sunni fundamentalists, but has not spelt out in convincing detail how it believes the killings occurred.

Anti-government opposition sources in Damascus said they have been told by survivors of Houla that, after fighting between the Free Syrian Army and regular government forces last Friday, Alawite militiamen began the massacre, saying they were acting in retaliation for the killing of a government informant in their village a month ago, but this could not be independently confirmed.

The mood in Damascus is becoming increasingly tense as people absorb the shock of the atrocity at Houla. There is the sound of sporadic shooting in some parts of the capital and the explosion of a bomb near a school in one suburb sent parents racing to pick up their children. Government control is tight and there are many more checkpoints at night.

Mr Annan's original plan envisioned a ceasefire beginning on 12 April, but it is now being broken on a daily basis, according to the UN monitoring team. Few Syrians expect Mr Assad or the leadership of the regime he represents to consider giving up or even sharing power unless they face the prospect of losing their last allies. They also look for support to Iran, allied with Syria for 30 years, and, to a lesser extent, Iraq.

Mr Annan faces a difficult task to get either the Syrian government or the rebels to implement his six-point peace plan signed seven week ago.

A national dialogue now looks unlikely because of the hatred and distrust between the two sides.

And the government does not feel strong enough to allow the release of detainees or a withdrawal of heavy weapons from cities as it promised.

Summer 2012

Inconvenient Truth

WESTERN AGREEMENT 'COULD LEAVE SYRIA IN ASSAD'S HANDS FOR TWO MORE YEARS'
By Robert Fisk
20 June 2012

President Bashar al-Assad of Syria may last longer than his opponents believe - and with the tacit acceptance of Western leaders anxious to secure new oil routes to Europe via Syria before the fall of the regime. According to a source closely involved in the possible transition from Ba'ath party power, the Americans, Russians and Europeans are also putting together a deal that would permit Assad to remain leader for at least another two years in return for political concessions to Iran and Saudi Arabia in both Lebanon and Iraq.

For its part, Russia would be assured of its continued military base at Tartous in Syria and a relationship with whatever government in Damascus eventually emerges with the support of Iran and Saudi Arabia. Russia's recent concession - that Assad may not be essential in a future Syrian power structure - is part of an understanding in the West which may accept Assad's presidency in return for an agreement that stops a further slide into civil war.

Information from Syria suggests that Assad's army is now "taking a beating" from armed rebels, who include Islamist as well as nationalist forces; at least 6,000 soldiers are believed to have been killed in action since the rebellion against Assad began 17 months ago. There are unconfirmed reports that during any one week up to a thousand Syrian fighters are being trained by mercenaries in Jordan at a base used by Western authorities for personnel seeking "anti-terrorist" security exercises.

The US-Russian negotiations - easy to deny, and somewhat cynically hidden behind the mutual accusations of Hillary Clinton and her

Russian opposite number, Sergei Lavrov - would mean the superpowers would acknowledge Iran's influence over Iraq and its relationship with its Hezbollah allies in Lebanon, while Saudi Arabia - and Qatar - would be encouraged to guarantee Sunni Muslim rights in Lebanon and in Iraq. Baghdad's emergence as a centre of Shia power has caused much anguish in Saudi Arabia whose support for the Sunni minority in Iraq has led to political division.

But the real object of talks between the world powers revolves around the West's determination to secure oil and gas from the Gulf states without relying upon supplies from Moscow. "Russia can turn off the spigot to Europe whenever it wants - and this gives it tremendous political power," the source says. "We are talking about two fundamental oil routes to the West - one from Qatar and Saudi Arabia via Jordan and Syria and the Mediterranean to Europe, another from Iran via Shia southern Iraq and Syria to the Mediterranean and Europe. This is what matters. This is why they will be prepared to let Assad last another two years. They would be perfectly content with that. And Russia will have a place in the new Syria."

Diplomats who are still discussing these plans should, of course, be treated with some scepticism. It is one thing to hear political leaders excoriating the Syrian regime for its abuse of human rights and massacres - another to realise that Western diplomats are prepared to put this to one side for the "bigger picture" which, as usual in the Middle East, means oil and gas. They are prepared to tolerate Assad's presence until the end of the crisis, rather than insisting his departure is the start of the end. The Americans apparently say the same. Now Russia believes that stability is more important than Assad himself.

It is clear that Assad should have gone ahead with extensive reforms when his father Hafez died in 2000. At that stage, say Syrian officials, Syria's economy was in a better state than Greece is today. And the saner voices influencing Assad's leadership were slowly deprived of their power. An official close to the president called him during the height of last year's fighting to say that "Homs is burning". Assad's reaction was to refuse all personal conversation with the official in future, insisting on only text messages. "Assad no longer has power over all that happens in Syria," the informant says. "Not because he doesn't want to - there's just too much going on across the country."

What Assad is still hoping for, according to Arab military veterans, is an Algerian solution. After the cancellation of democratic elections in Algeria, its army and generals fought a merciless war against rebels and Islamist guerrillas across the country throughout the 1990s, using torture and massacre to retain government power but leaving an estimated 200,000 dead.

Amid this crisis, the Algerian military sent a delegation to Damascus to learn from Hafez al-Assad's Syrian army how it destroyed the Islamist rebellion in Hama - at a cost of up to 20,000 dead - in 1982. The Algerian civil war - remarkably similar to that now afflicting Assad's regime - displayed many of the characteristics of the current tragedy in Syria: babies with their throats cut, families slaughtered by mysterious semi-military "armed groups", whole towns shelled by government forces.

And, more interesting to Assad's men, the West continued to support the Algerian regime with weapons and political encouragement during the 1990s while huffing and puffing about human rights. Algeria's oil and gas reserves proved more important than civilian deaths - just as the Damascus regime now hopes to rely upon the West's desire for via-Syria oil and gas to tolerate further killings. Syrians say Jamil Hassan, the head of Air Force intelligence in Syria is now the "killer" leader for the regime - not so much Bashar's brother Maher whose 4th Division is perhaps being given too much credit for suppressing the revolt. It has certainly failed to crush it.

The West, meanwhile has to deal with Syria's contact man, Mohamed Nassif, perhaps Assad's closest political adviser. The question remains as to whether Assad - however much he fails to control military events on the ground - really grasps the epic political importance of what is going on in his country. Prior to the rebellion, European and Turkish leaders were astonished to hear from him that Sunni forces in the northern Lebanese city of Tripoli were trying "to create a Salafist state" that would threaten Syria.

How this extraordinary assertion - based, presumably on the tittle-tattle of an intelligence agent - could have formulated itself in Assad's mind, remained a mystery.

SYRIAN WAR OF LIES AND HYPOCRISY
By Robert Fisk
29 July 2012

Has there ever been a Middle Eastern war of such hypocrisy? A war of such cowardice and such mean morality, of such false rhetoric and such public humiliation? I'm not talking about the physical victims of the Syrian tragedy. I'm referring to the utter lies and mendacity of our masters and our own public opinion - eastern as well as western - in response to the slaughter, a vicious pantomime more worthy of Swiftian satire than Tolstoy or Shakespeare.

While Qatar and Saudi Arabia arm and fund the rebels of Syria to overthrow Bashar al-Assad's Alawite/Shia-Baathist dictatorship, Washington mutters not a word of criticism against them. President Barack Obama and his Secretary of State, Hillary Clinton, say they want a democracy in Syria. But Qatar is an autocracy and Saudi Arabia is among the most pernicious of caliphate-kingly-dictatorships in the Arab world. Rulers of both states inherit power from their families - just as Bashar has done - and Saudi Arabia is an ally of the Salafist-Wahabi rebels in Syria, just as it was the most fervent supporter of the medieval Taliban during Afghanistan's dark ages.

Indeed, 15 of the 19 hijacker-mass murderers of 11 September, 2001, came from Saudi Arabia - after which, of course, we bombed Afghanistan. The Saudis are repressing their own Shia minority just as they now wish to destroy the Alawite-Shia minority of Syria. And we believe Saudi Arabia wants to set up a democracy in Syria?

Then we have the Shia Hezbollah party/militia in Lebanon, right hand of Shia Iran and supporter of Bashar al-Assad's regime. For 30 years, Hezbollah has defended the oppressed Shias of southern Lebanon against Israeli aggression. They have presented themselves as the defenders of Palestinian rights in the West Bank and Gaza. But faced with the slow collapse of their ruthless ally in Syria, they have lost their tongue. Not a word have they uttered - nor their princely Sayed Hassan Nasrallah - about the rape and mass murder of Syrian civilians by Bashar's soldiers and "Shabiha" militia.

Then we have the heroes of America - La Clinton, the Defence Secretary Leon Panetta, and Obama himself. Clinton issues a "stern warning" to Assad.

Panetta - the same man who repeated to the last US forces in Iraq that old lie about Saddam's connection to 9/11 - announces that things are "spiralling out of control" in Syria. They have been doing that for at least six months.

Has he just realised? And then Obama told us last week that "given the regime's stockpile of nuclear weapons, we will continue to make it clear to Assad ... that the world is watching". Now, was it not a County Cork newspaper called the Skibbereen Eagle, fearful of Russia's designs on China, which declared that it was "keeping an eye ... on the Tsar of Russia"? Now it is Obama's turn to emphasise how little clout he has in the mighty conflicts of the world. How Bashar must be shaking in his boots.

But what US administration would really want to see Bashar's atrocious archives of torture opened to our gaze? Why, only a few years ago, the Bush administration was sending Muslims to Damascus for Bashar's torturers to tear their fingernails out for information, imprisoned at the US government's request in the very hell-hole which Syrian rebels blew to bits last week.

Western embassies dutifully supplied the prisoners' tormentors with questions for the victims. Bashar, you see, was our baby.

Then there's that neighbouring country which owes us so much gratitude: Iraq. Last week, it suffered in one day 29 bombing attacks in 19 cities, killing 111 civilian and wounding another 235. The same day, Syria's bloodbath consumed about the same number of innocents. But Iraq was "down the page" from Syria, buried "below the fold", as we journalists say; because, of course, we gave freedom to Iraq, Jeffersonian democracy, etc, etc, didn't we? So this slaughter to the east of Syria didn't have quite the same impact, did it? Nothing we did in 2003 led to Iraq's suffering today. Right?

And talking of journalism, who in BBC World News decided that even the preparations for the Olympics should take precedence all last week over Syrian outrages? British newspapers and the BBC in Britain will naturally lead with the Olympics as a local story. But in a lamentable decision, the BBC - broadcasting "world" news to the world - also decided that the passage of the Olympic flame was more important than dying Syrian children, even when it has its own courageous reporter sending his despatches directly from Aleppo.

Then, of course, there's us, our dear liberal selves who are so quick to fill the streets of London in protest at the Israeli slaughter of

Palestinians. Rightly so, of course. When our political leaders are happy to condemn Arabs for their savagery but too timid to utter a word of the mildest criticism when the Israeli army commits crimes against humanity - or watches its allies do it in Lebanon - ordinary people have to remind the world that they are not as timid as the politicians. But when the scorecard of death in Syria reaches 15,000 or 19,000 - perhaps 14 times as many fatalities as in Israel's savage 2008-2009 onslaught on Gaza - scarcely a single protester, save for Syrian expatriates abroad, walks the streets to condemn these crimes against humanity. Israel's crimes have not been on this scale since 1948. Rightly or wrongly, the message that goes out is simple: we demand justice and the right to life for Arabs if they are butchered by the West and its Israeli allies; but not when they are being butchered by their fellow Arabs.

And all the while, we forget the "big" truth. That this is an attempt to crush the Syrian dictatorship not because of our love for Syrians or our hatred of our former friend Bashar al-Assad, or because of our outrage at Russia, whose place in the pantheon of hypocrites is clear when we watch its reaction to all the little Stalingrads across Syria. No, this is all about Iran and our desire to crush the Islamic Republic and its infernal nuclear plans - if they exist - and has nothing to do with human rights or the right to life or the death of Syrian babies. Quelle horreur!

SYRIA'S ANCIENT TREASURES PULVERISED
By Robert Fisk
5 August 2012

The priceless treasures of Syria's history - of Crusader castles, ancient mosques and churches, Roman mosaics, the renowned "Dead Cities" of the north and museums stuffed with antiquities - have fallen prey to looters and destruction by armed rebels and government militias as fighting envelops the country. While the monuments and museums of the two great cities of Damascus and Aleppo have so far largely been spared, reports from across Syria tell of irreparable damage to heritage sites that have no equal in the Middle East. Even the magnificent castle of Krak des Chevaliers - described by Lawrence of Arabia as "perhaps the best preserved and most wholly admirable castle in the world" and which Saladin could not capture - has been shelled by the Syrian army, damaging the Crusader chapel inside.

The destruction of Iraq's heritage in the anarchic aftermath of the Anglo- American invasion of 2003 - the looting of the national museum, the burning of the Koranic library and the wiping out of ancient Sumerian cities - may now be repeated in Syria. Reports from Syrian archeologists and from Western specialists in bronze age and Roman cities tell of an Assyrian temple destroyed at Tell Sheikh Hamad, massive destruction to the wall and towers of the citadel of al-Madiq castle - one of the most forward Crusader fortresses in the Levant which originally fell to Bohemond of Antioch in 1106 - and looting of the magnificent Roman mosaics of Apamea, where thieves have used bulldozers to rip up Roman floors and transport them from the site. Incredibly, they have managed to take two giant capitols from atop the colonnade of the "decumanus", the main east-west Roman road in the city.

In many cases, armed rebels have sought sanctuary behind the thick walls of ancient castles only to find that the Syrian military have not hesitated to blast away at these historical buildings to destroy their enemies. Pitched battles have been fought between rebels and Syrian troops amid the "Dead Cities", the hundreds of long-abandoned Graeco-Roman towns that litter the countryside outside Aleppo, which once formed the heart of ancient Syria.

Syrian troops have occupied the Castle of Ibn Maan above the Roman city of Palmyra and parked tanks and armoured vehicles in the Valley of the Tombs to the west of the old city. The government army are reported to have dug a deep defensive trench within the Roman ruins.

"The situation of Syria's heritage today is catastrophic," according to Joanne Farchakh, a Lebanese archaeologist who also investigated the destruction and plundering of Iraq's historical treasures after 2003, and helped the Baghdad museum to reclaim some of its stolen artifacts. "One of the problems is that for 10 years before the war, the Syrian regime established 25 cultural museums all over the country to encourage tourism and to keep valuable objects on these sites - many placed stone monuments in outside gardens, partly to prove that the regime was strong enough to protect them. Now the

Homs museum has been looted - by rebels and by government militias, who knows? - and antique dealers are telling me that the markets of Jordan and Turkey are flooded with artifacts from Syria."

There is, of course, a moral question about our concern for the destruction of the treasures of history. Common humanity suggests that the death of a single Syrian child amid the 19,000 fatalities of Syria's tragedy must surely carry more weight than the plundering and erasure of three thousand years of civilisation. True. But the pulverisation and theft of whole cities of history deprives future generations - in their millions - of their birthright and of the seeds of their own lives. Syria has always been known as "the Land of Civilisations" - Damascus and Aleppo are among the world's oldest inhabited cities and Syria is the birthplace of agrarian society - and the terrible conflict now overwhelming the country will deprive us and our descendants of this narrative for ever.

To their enormous credit, Syrian archaeologists have themselves anonymously catalogued the destruction of their native country's historical sites. They include government shelling of villages that exist within ancient cities; rebels have apparently been sheltered, for example, in the small civilian township built inside the wonderful ruins of Bosra which contains one of the best-preserved Roman theatres in the world - which did not prevent several buildings from being destroyed. Similar bombardments have smashed the fabric of Byzantine-era buildings in al-Bara, Deir Sunbel and Ain Larose in northern Syria.

In the monastery of Sednaya, apparently founded by the Emperor Justinian - the people of the village still speak Aramaic, the language of Jesus - shellfire has damaged the oldest section of the building, which dates back to 574. The Umayyad Mosque in Deraa, one of the oldest Islamic-era structures in Syria, built at the request of the Caliph Omar Ibn al-Khattab, has also been damaged. Dr Bassam Jamous, the government-appointed director general of antiquities in Syria, says that "terrorists" - ironically, the Western world's own nomenclature for state enemies - have targeted historic buildings in Damascus, Aleppo, Bosra, Palmyra and the Citadel of Salah al-Din (Saladin), a crusader fortress seized by the Kurdish warrior hero in 1188, the year after he recaptured Jerusalem for the Muslims from Balian of Ibelin.

Several months ago the Syrian authorities reported the theft of the golden statue of an 8th century BC Aramaic god - still unfound, although it was reported to Interpol - and admitted thefts at government museums at Deir ez-Zor, Raqqa, Maarat al-Numan and Qalaat Jaabar. Hiba Sakhel, the Syrian director of museums, has confirmed that items from the Aleppo museum have been transferred to the vaults of the central bank in Damascus for safekeeping.

"Syrian Archeological Heritage in Danger", a group of Syrian specialists who list the destruction and looting of the country's treasures on their own website, has revealed that Syria's Prime Minister, Adel Safar, wrote to fellow ministers on 11 July last year warning that "the country is threatened by armed criminal groups with hi-tech tools and specialised in the theft of manuscripts and antiquities, as well as the pillaging of museums". The archaeologists find this note "very odd" because it appears to warn of looting which had not yet occurred - and thus suggests that officials in the regime might be preparing the way for their own private theft and re-sale of the country's heritage, something which did indeed occur under President Assad's father Hafez al-Assad.

So the looting and destruction lies at the door of all sides in the Syrian conflict, along with the thieves who move in on all historic sites when the security of the state evaporates. In truth, Syria has always suffered - and the regime always tolerated - a limited amount of theft from historical sites, to boost the economy in the poor areas in the north of the country and to enrich the regime's own mafiosi. But what is happening now is on an epic and terrifying scale. "As for the old churches, old houses, old streets of Homs, you can forget it - they don't exist any more," archaeologist Joanne Farchakh says. A specialist in heritage in times of war in Lebanon, Iraq and northern Cyprus as well as Syria, she gloomily reports new information from the second millennium BC sites in which looters have dug huge holes, metres wide, to unearth the treasures of pre-history.

Much of this destruction is taking place not only in the world of ancient Rome, the Crusaders and the Muslim conquest and revival, but in the land of the original "terrorists", the Assassins whose murderous attacks on all authority a thousand years ago were led by "the Old Man of the Mountains". He once besieged Al-Madiq castle - whose bombardment by the Syrian army is now available on videotape.

UN LEAVES SYRIA TO ITS BLOODY FATE
By Robert Fisk
19 August 2012

The UN's commander in Damascus bid a miserable goodbye to his mission yesterday, unconvincingly claiming that the UN would not abandon Syria, but in fact turning the country into a free-fire zone the moment his last 100 soldiers begin their retreat tomorrow. Whenever the UN withdraws its personnel from the Middle East, calamity always follows in its wake - the departure of UN weapons inspectors from Iraq in 2003 presaged the Anglo- American invasion - and, privately, the UN fears the way is now open for the West and Gulf Arabs to pour heavy weapons into Syria to assist the rebellion against the Assad regime.

As General Babacar Gaye was standing in the lobby of the luxury Damas Rose Hotel, absurdly wishing Muslims a happy Eid holiday following the fasting month of Ramadan, and insisting that "the UN will not leave Syria", his own officers were packing their bags and queuing to pay their last hotel bills on the other side of the atrium. "They couldn't even wait until Lakhdar Brahimi got here to take over as UN envoy," one of Gaye's officials grumbled. The general declined to tell journalists whether more Syrian lives might have been saved if the UN stayed on.

Outside, in the bright, hot Damascus afternoon, the often empty streets and shuttered shops spoke of lassitude rather than collapse. Bashar al-Assad's regime does not appear to be on the verge of departure - as American and French diplomats fondly believe - but the signs of dislocation are everywhere. Soldiers are billeted in the old Ottoman Haj station in central Damascus - from which no trains have left for Syrian cities in months - but the daily Syrian government-controlled press (there is no other) carries front-page stories from the war front each day. The capture of "Free Syrian Army" weapons, the assassination of civilians in and around Damascus - always attributed to "terrorists", of course - and fighting speeches by government acolytes make no secret of the nation's peril.

Perhaps for this reason, Syrians in Damascus speak with increasing freedom about the chances of the regime's survival, openly debating Bashar's victory or defeat in cafés and restaurants. All know that just a few miles outside the capital, a dark zone begins, a land -

thousands of square kilometres of it – in which terrible deeds are taking place hourly. The main highways north have been cut and phone lines to Aleppo have largely collapsed; most travellers choose to fly to the city from Damascus, even though the road from Aleppo airport to the city centre is itself dangerous. Syrian Arab Airlines' main ticket office in Damascus was packed with passengers yesterday, all seeking flights out of the country or pleading for overbooked seats for relatives on planes from Aleppo.

And yet. The regime, whose history and roots go deep into the land of Syria - however brutal and corrupting its opponents believe those roots to be - seems to have more life in it than the Clintons and the Panettas and the Laurent Fabiuses of this world might believe. When French foreign minister Fabius - after listening to refugees' stories of atrocities in Syria - announces that Bashar al-Assad "doesn't deserve to be on this earth", his words appear infantile rather than threatening; indeed they sound like the kind of nonsense often spouted by Arab dictators. Damascenes are looking to their families rather than revenge; one middle-class man I have known for years told me yesterday how his wife worked for a government office but he had "moved her to home" so that she would be safe. The information ministry have produced a DVD packed with tapes of "terrorist" bomb explosions across the country - while admitting that the disk doesn't yet take in last week's truck bombing near the UN's hotel.

General Gaye's last goodbye was as bleak as it was short. After UN troops had arrived on 21 April to monitor the withdrawal of heavy weapons and a ceasefire, violence declined, he said, but "by the middle of June, it was clear that the parties were no longer committed to the ceasefire". UN observers then tried "to facilitate pauses in the fighting" to assist humanitarian work. "I call upon all parties to stop the violence which is causing such suffering to the Syrian people," General Gaye proclaimed, adding that humanitarian law must be respected.

But, needless to say, humanitarian law is not - and will not - be respected, and from tomorrow there will be no-one left to "facilitate pauses in the fighting". When I asked the good general how he personally felt about the failure of his mission, he replied that he was comforted by the fact that "the UN will stay in Syria". But this was preposterous. Save for a tiny UN office - with perhaps 10 staff - which has still not been approved, there is no UN observer mission left here, save for the post-1967 war UNTSO (UN Truce Supervision Organization) force which is fully engaged on keeping the Syrian-Israeli peace on the Golan Heights. The UN soldiers who have bravely sat through the shellfire of Aleppo and Homs will be there no longer.

Should the UN's Syrian mission have been led by a diplomat rather than a soldier - no-one here appears to understand why the Norwegian General Mood, General Gaye's predecessor, left his post - and should it have spent more time talking to opposition forces outside Syria, were questions still being debated within the UN yesterday. And why end the mission now? Because there were some in UN headquarters in New York who knew from the start that the assignment was not intended to succeed? Or because the Western nations and Gulf sponsors do not want UN observers snooping into the amount of new and more lethal weaponry which they may be planning to send to the "Free Syrian Army" and its more bearded allies in those parts of Syria in which Bashar's writ no longer runs?

Autumn 2012

Divided State

ANOTHER WEEK IN THE VIOLENT, MURDEROUS AND DIVIDED WORLD OF SYRIA
By Robert Fisk
1 September 2012

A weed is a long time in violence. It seems only yesterday - five days ago, in fact - that armed men shot Sheikh Abu Haitham al-Bortawi outside the el- Noor mosque in the Rukenadin suburb of Damascus. Went to the scene.

Middle class area. Tree shaded, clean street. Ten in the morning. Turns out he was the cleric who knelt right next to Bashar al-Assad for the Eid prayers at the end of Ramadan. A dagger to the heart of the body politick.

I meet an old friend the next day at a café in Mezzeh, and he's crying. His dentist lived in Zabadani, in the hills near the Lebanese border, in Free Syria Army country. His son was warned the family home was unsafe because of incoming fire. From the army? No one's sure. But a shell hit the house and the dentist has just arrived at the French Hospital. Dead, his grieving family still at the morgue.

Then there's the two Christian guys outside town. One runs a DVD store, the other a pharmacy. Murdered. Next day, their funeral cortege is car-bombed. Twelve dead, at least 40 wounded. Turns out they had brothers in the Syrian army, apparently conscripts. Hardly a sin. But the opposition says the two men were "connected to the military".

A Syrian journalist calls me. Six Armenians have been "slaughtered with knives" in their homes. I race to the Armenian church and there is brown- robed Bishop Armesh Nalbandian next to the ancient chapel of Saint Sarkis - he has around 6,500 parishioners in Damascus

- and only a few metres from the memorial to the 1915 Armenian genocide. Many of those one and a half million victims of Ottoman Turkish slaughter were put to death in the deserts north of Damascus, now the scene of another Calvary.

But the "six-dead" story is untrue, Armesh says. Good news. But no. Three Damascus Armenians have just been murdered, apparently shot. Thirty- nine-year-old Bedros Matosian died along with his younger brother Kevork and the son of one of them - the bishop isn't sure which - called Levon, who was only 22. Armed men. No identity. But the Matosians had Alawite and Sunni neighbours who were also massacred, because, so the local story goes, they refused to join the Free Syria Army.

The story depends on where you go in this divided capital. Yesterday, I take another prowl, through the Damascus suburbs; Malayha, Harasta, Zamalka, Bab Shawkeh. Thirty government checkpoints, maybe 40, but in Harasta, the Syrian Arab Republic has no sway. There are dozens of painted green, white and black FSA flags on the walls. "The free people of Harasta are denied their liberty," a slogan informs us. "Assad should go." There's a mosque so packed that the crowds have spilled on to the boiling roadway; a guy in a pick-up tells us it's safe to head for the motorway. An opposition man. A Syrian soldier in sunglasses waves us back to the autostrade of the Syrian Arab Republic.

We drive through the Assad Suburb, government housing, though some home-owners have rented to people from Zabadani - maybe a little security problem? - and just past the Tishreen military hospital (former student, one Bashar al-Assad), there's an explosion and a car with headlights zipping the street dust under its shrieking tyres and a pulverised dead dog lying inside a garage.

Up to the Kassioun mountain overlooking Damascus for lunch at Al Montagna - the only guests, save for three tired Syrian officers - and we look across at the Omayad mosque and there's a roar from the government guns on the other side of the jebel and a rumble of sound relayed mountain-to- mountain on the other side of the city. Fifteen seconds later, there's a pop far away on the edge of the Palestinian camp at Yarmouk and a smudge of grey smoke. Then another report and another rumble and another pop a bit to the right, four miles away through the heat haze. Palestinians. I close my notebook for the week.

SYRIA'S ROAD FROM JIHAD TO PRISON
By Robert Fisk
2 September 2012

They came into the room one by one, heads bowed, wrists crossed in front of them as if they were used to wearing handcuffs. In one of Syria's most feared military prisons, they told their extraordinary story of helping the armed opponents of Bashar al-Assad's regime. One was French-Algerian, a small, stooped man in his forties with a long beard; another Turkish, with what looked like a black eye, who spoke of his training at a Taliban camp on the Afghan-Pakistan border. A Syrian prisoner described helping two suicide bombers set off a bloody explosion in central Damascus, while a mufti spoke of his vain efforts to unite the warring factions against the Syrian government.

Given the unprecedented nature of our access to the high-security Syrian prison, our meetings with the four men - their jailers had other inmates for us to interview - were a chilling, sobering experience. Two gave unmistakable hints of brutal treatment after their first arrest. It took 10 minutes to persuade the prison's military governor - a grey-haired, middle- aged general in military fatigues - and his shirt-sleeved intelligence officer to leave the room during our conversations. Incredibly, they abandoned their office so that we could speak alone to their captives. We refused later requests by the Syrian authorities for access to our tapes of the interviews.

Two of the men spoke of their recruitment by Islamist preachers, another of how Arab satellite channels had persuaded him to travel to Syria to make jihad. These were stories that the Syrian authorities obviously wanted us to hear, but the prisoners - who must have given their interrogators the same accounts - were clearly anxious to talk to us, if only to meet Westerners and alert us to their presence after months in captivity. The French-Algerian wolfed down a box of chicken and chips we gave him. One of the Syrians admitted he was kept in constant solitary confinement. We promised all four that we would give their names and details to the International Red Cross.

Mohamed Amin Ali al-Abdullah was a 26-year-old fourth-year medical student from the northern Syrian city of Deir el-Zour. The son of a "simple" farming family in Latakia, he sat in the governor's brown leather chair in a neat striped blue shirt and trousers - given to him, he said, by the authorities - and told us he had encountered "psychological problems" in his second year. He twice broke down in tears while he spoke. He said he had followed medical advice as a student but also accepted psychological help from a "sheikh" who suggested he read specific texts from the Koran.

"This was a kind of entrance to my personality and from time to time the second man gave me disks about the Salafist cause, mostly of speeches by Saudi sheikhs such as Ibn Baz and Ibn Ottaimin. Later, he gave me videos that rejected all other sects in Islam, attacking the Sufis, attacking the Shia." The "sheikh" was imprisoned for a year but later joined Mohamed as a roommate in Damascus. "Then he used to show me videos of operations by jihadi people against NATO and the Americans in Afghanistan."

When the uprising began in Syria last year, Mohamed said, he was advised by the "sheikh" and two other men to participate in anti-regime demonstrations. "When Friday prayers were over, one of us would stand in the middle, among the crowd, to shout about injustice and the bad situation; the other four would go to the corners and shout 'Allahu Akbar' [God is great] to encourage the crowd to do the same."

Around this time, Mohamed said, he was introduced to a Salafist called "Al- Hajer" who asked him to help in his movement's "medical and logistic support - to hide men wanted by the authorities and to find safe houses". Al- Hajer began frequenting Mohamed's home, "and he offered me a kind of allegiance, where you shake hands with this man and tell him that you acknowledge him as a leader whom you will obey, and will follow jihad and will not question him". Al-Hajer brought strangers to Mohamed's home.

"They took me into their circle. I left my mind 'outside' at this period and then I recognised that this group was al-Qa'ida. On 10 April this year, one of these people asked me to go with him in a car. I went to a place where I saw cylinders 2.5m high, with cases to fill them up with explosives. There were about 10 people there. I don't know why they asked me there - maybe to drag me into involvement. There was a Palestinian and a Jordanian who were to be suicide bombers and three Iraqi citizens. We left in a car in front of the two bombers. I don't know where they were going to bomb, but 15 minutes after I arrived back home, I heard the explosion and two minutes later there was a much stronger explosion. The catastrophe came for me when I watched the television and saw the bomb had gone off in a crowded street in the Bazzaz district; there were houses crushed in the bombings and all the inhabitants [targeted] were middle class and poor people. I was so sorry."

Later, one of the Salafists asked Mohamed to visit his mother in hospital - because he was a doctor and the Salafist would be recognised - but the Syrian Mukhabarat intelligence service was waiting for him. "I said very frankly to them: 'I am happy to be arrested - better than to get involved in such a group or have a role in wasting more blood.' I don't know how I got involved with these people. I put myself in a kind of 'recycle bin'. Now I want to write a book and tell people what happened to me so that they should not do as I did. But I have not been given pencil and paper."

Mohamed saw his father, a schoolteacher, his mother and a sister two months ago. Was he mistreated, we asked him. "Just one day," he said. "It was not torture." We asked why there were two dark marks on one of his wrists. "I slipped in the toilet," he said.

Jamel Amer al-Khodoud, an Algerian whose wife and children live in Marseille and who served in the French army in the 1st Transport Regiment, was a more subdued man, his 48 years and his rather pathetic tale of a search for jihad - encouraged by al-Jazeera's coverage of Muslim suffering in Syria, he said - leaving him a somewhat disillusioned man. Born in Blida, he had emigrated to France, but though a fluent French speaker, he found only a life of odd jobs and unemployment, until, "after a long hesitation, I decided to go to Turkey and help the Syrian refugees".

He was, he said, a "moderate Salafist", but in the Turkish refugee camps had met a Libyan sheikh, many Tunisians and a Yemeni imam "who gave me lessons in jihad". He crossed the Syrian border with a shotgun, and with other men had attacked military checkpoints and slept rough in abandoned houses and a mosque in the mountains above Latakia. Trained on French weapons, he had never before fired a Kalashnikov - he was allowed to fire three bullets at a stone for target practice, he said - but after several miserable weeks of discovering that a jihad in Syria was not for him, he resolved to walk back to Turkey and return to France. "What I saw on television I didn't see in Syria."

Captured by suspicious villagers, he was taken to a city (probably Aleppo) and then by helicopter to Damascus. Why didn't he choose

Palestine rather than Syria for his jihad, we asked. "A Palestinian friend told me his people needed money more than men," he replied. "Besides, that is a difficult border to cross." When I asked him if he had been treated badly in captivity, he replied: "Thank God, I am well." To the same question, he repeated the same answer.

A Syrian imam - of the Khadija al-Khobra mosque in Damascus - with a lean, dark face, told us of his meetings this year with four Syrian "militant groups" in the city which had different nationalist and religious aims, of how he tried to unite them, but discovered that they were thieves, killers and rapists rather than jihadis. Or so Sheikh Ahmed Ghalibo said. Sprinkling the names of these men throughout his conversation, the sheikh said he had been appalled at how the groups had liquidated all who disagreed with them, merely on suspicion, "cutting the bodies up, decapitating them and throwing them in sewage". He said he had witnessed seven such murders; indeed, the disposal of corpses in sewage has been a common occurrence in Damascus.

Knowing that he was a mufti at the al-Khobra mosque and apparently aware that he had met the four extremist leaders, the Syrian security police arrested Ahmed Ghalibo on 15 April this year. He told us he had made a full confession because "these militants are not a 'Free Army'", insisted he had received "very good treatment" from his interrogators, condemned the Emir of Qatar for stirring revolution in Syria, and said he believed he would be released "because I have repented".

Cuma Öztürk comes from the south-eastern Turkish city of Gaziantep, and crossed into Syria after months of training, he said, in a Taliban camp on the Afghan-Pakistan border. He could not speak Pashtu - or Arabic - but had left behind his pregnant wife Mayuda and their three-year old daughter in Gaziantep to travel to Damascus. He spoke only vaguely of jihad but said he had been asked to set up a "smuggling" trail from Turkey to the Syrian capital which would also involve moving men across the border. He was arrested when he visited Aleppo for his mother-in-law's funeral. "I regret all that happened to me," he said mournfully; he was receiving good treatment "now". He asked us to let the Turkish authorities know of his presence in the prison.

When our four and a half hours of interviews were over, we appealed to the Syrian prison governor to give his inmates greater access to their families, a request which his tired smile suggested might be outside his remit. We also asked for a pen and paper for Mohamed al-Abdullah and we spoke - however fruitlessly - of the need for international law to be applied to those in the prison. The inmates shook hands with the governor in friendly fashion, although I noticed that little love seemed lost between them and the shirt- sleeved intelligence man. Each prisoner returned to his cell as he had arrived at the governor's office - with his head bowed and his eyes on the floor.

'THE FINAL STRAW': TURKEY AUTHORISES ATTACK ON SYRIA
By Kim Sengupta and Justin Vela
5 October 2012

Turkey's parliament yesterday authorised the country's military to carry out cross-border operations after clashes drew Syria's neighbour deeper into its 18-month civil war.

NATO and the UN Security Council also held emergency meetings after a Syrian mortar strike on Wednesday killed five members of a family in the Turkish town of Akcakale, provoking retaliation from Ankara. The Turkish armed forces have been shelling Syrian positions since late on Wednesday, killing several soldiers.

Turkish officials have warned that further retaliation may take place and have been moving reinforcements and ammunition supplies up to frontier bases. "This last incident is pretty much the final straw," said Bulent Arinc, Turkey's Deputy Prime Minister. "There has been an attack on our land and our citizens lost their lives, which surely has adequate response in international law."

A Syrian apology did come later in the day, following pressure from Russia. Besir Atalay, a Turkish minister, announced: "Syria accepts that it did it and apologises. They said nothing like this will happen again. That's good. The UN mediated and spoke to Syria."

Although the apology will go some way towards defusing tensions, the Turkish government stressed there will be no immediate change to its military posture. Speaking at a press conference in Akcakale yesterday, the Prime Minister, Recep Tayyip Erdogan, said he has no intention of starting a war.

"We want peace and security and nothing else. We could never be interested in something like starting a war," he said.

But he added: "The Turkish Republic is a state capable of defending its citizens and borders. Nobody should try and test our determination on this subject."

In Damascus, the Information Minister, Omran Zoabi, insisted that Syria respected the sovereignty of other states and said an investigation was underway. But he appeared to hold Turkey at least partly responsible, due to its support for the rebellion against President Bashar al-Assad.

"The Syrian-Turkish border is a long one and is being used for smuggling weapons and terrorists," said Mr Zoabi. "Neighbouring countries should act wisely and rationally and responsibly, especially in cases of the presence of armed terrorist groups who have their different agendas that are not targeting the Syrian national security but the regional security."

Akcakale was hit by four shells on Wednesday. One of the shells hit a grain mill. The others landed on a residential street just a few hundred feet from the border. Three of those who died in the blast were children who had come to the gate of their house after the first two blasts, eyewitnesses said. Two women were also killed.

Residents in Akcakale said they had been increasingly concerned that such an incident was looming. "For the last 10 days our houses have been shaking from the shelling," said Abdul Halil, 70, a farmer. Mr Halil said that many in the town were leaving. He estimated that 70 per cent of the residents had already moved away. "We do not want war, but if they attack again we want the government to attack back," he said.

There had earlier been unusual public rebuke from Russia - which has so far been a staunch supporter of Syria - with the "advice" that it needed to acknowledge that the deaths were a "tragic accident" and ensure they were not repeated. "We think it is of fundamental importance for Damascus to state that officially," said Foreign Minister, Sergei Lavrov.

After meeting to discuss the border clashes yesterday evening, the UN Security Council condemned "in the strongest terms" Syria's shelling.

"This incident highlighted the grave impact the crisis in Syria has on the security of its neighbours and on regional peace and stability," a statement said. The statement came after the council managed to bridge differences between the US and its Western allies who were demanding a strong text and Syria's most important ally, Russia, which tried to weaken the text.

NATO ambassadors also met yesterday and issued a statement saying the alliance "continues to stand by" Turkey, and demanding "the immediate cessation of such aggressive acts against an ally".

Turkey could theoretically invoke Article 5, under which an armed attack on any NATO member is considered an attack on all. However, Article 5 does not automatically result in collective military action.

The British Foreign Secretary, William Hague, said Turkey's actions were "understandable, an outrageous act has taken place, Turkish citizens have been killed inside Turkey by forces from another country". The US Secretary of State, Hillary Clinton said she too was "outraged" by the mortar attack.

HOW REBELS WERE SOLD EXPLODING RIFLES - BY A BRITON NAMED 'EMILE'
By Kim Sengupta
27 October 2012

To the Syrian rebels, the offer was enticing: Kalashnikov AK-47 rifles and ammunition at below-market price, with supplies plentiful. The dealers were convincing: two of them had European passports, one a British passport, and they claimed to have been involved in supplying arms during the Bosnia war.

Three meetings took place in Istanbul between representatives of the rebels and the dealers, including the Briton, calling himself Emile, to organise shipments. An initial payment of around $40,000 was made.

The delivery was on time, as had been a previous shipment. But it soon became apparent that something was wrong.

Rifles exploded during a firefight. There was a second such "accident", and a third, leading to injuries. An examination of the remaining consignments revealed that propellants inside some of the cartridges had been replaced with ground explosives with three or four times design-pressure, with the aim of bursting them in the breach.

With Syria's civil war getting increasingly vicious and dirty, the opposition has come across "abandoned" government arms that were proved to have been doctored.

But the presence of the arms traffickers, including the Briton, has led to claims that the Syrian regime is using foreign agents to undermine the opposition.

Abdurrahman Abu-Nasr, a rebel representative who attended one of the meetings with the dealers in Istanbul three weeks ago, recalled "Emile" as a man in his late 40s who was of Arab - part-Syrian - origin. "He spoke fluent English, he told us that he had lived in England. Another man had a Belgian passport, but I think his family were from somewhere like Morocco. They were giving good prices, only around $ 2.50 per round [The average price had gone up to $5 at times].

"The man with the British passport told us he had supplied the Mujahedin in Bosnia, he knew a lot about defence equipment. My friend and I asked whether they were acting on behalf of their governments. They did not admit they were, but did not deny it totally either. It was clever, it left us wondering."

There is no evidence to suggest that the man calling himself "Emile" has any connection with the British intelligence agencies.

The UK government is supplying "non-lethal" aid to the Syrian opposition, including satellite communications equipment, and thus, say security sources, it would not have been possible for regime agents to have infiltrated such a chain.

Speaking about arms supplies, the Foreign Secretary, William Hague, said recently: "I don't rule out any option in the future because we don't know how the situation will develop." He denied that supplies are being "outsourced" through Qatar or Saudi Arabia.

The rebels who met "Emile" and his colleagues are investigating the role of a conduit who had acted as a referee.

Sabotaging ammunition is not new to counter-insurgency warfare. The British engineered the supply of doctored bullets in the Second Matabele War in the 1890s and the Waziristan campaign in the 1930s. The Americans used the tactic in Vietnam, and both they and the Russians have carried out such operations in Afghanistan.

'WE LEFT HOMS BECAUSE THEY WERE TRYING TO KILL US. THEY WANTED TO KILL US BECAUSE WE ARE CHRISTIANS'
By Kim Sengupta
2 November 2012

The red Mitsubishi Lancer GT with "go faster" stripes was a source of great pride to Hamlig Bedrosian. It was the only one of its kind in the city, pointed out on the streets as he roared along, an object of admiration and envy among his friends in Aleppo.

The car may have been the reason why the 23-year-old student was ambushed and taken hostage, along with a female friend, as they were travelling to a shopping complex. The revolutionary fighters with Kalashnikovs who led them away subjected Mr Bedrosian - blindfolded and tied up - to savage beatings and threats of execution before the pair was finally freed in exchange for a ransom.

Or there may have been a different reason for the attack: they were targeted by the Sunni Muslim rebels because they were Christians. Mr Bedrosian did not wait long to find out, leaving - along with his brother - for Lebanon.

Others from the Syrian Armenian community followed, abandoning their homes.

The Haddad family had no doubts about why they had to escape from Homs. "We left because they were trying to kill us," said 18-year-old Noura Haddad. She is now staying with relations in the town of Zahle in the Bekaa Valley. "They wanted to kill us because we were Christians. They were calling us Kaffirs, even little children saying these things. Those who were our neighbours turned against us.

"At the end, when we ran away, we went through balconies. We did not even dare go out on the street in front of our house. I've kept in touch with the few Christian friends left back home, but I cannot speak to my Muslim friends any more. I feel very sorry about that."

Mr Bedrosian and Ms Haddad are among thousands who have left Syria as the 20 month-long civil war gets increasingly vicious and increasingly sectarian. The prospect of reconciliation between the Alawites, from which the ruling elite are drawn, and the overwhelmingly Sunni opposition, gets more remote by the day after each round of strife. But now it is the Christians, who have largely sought to remain neutral, who are on the receiving end of abuse and attacks. For many, the choice now is between leaving the country or risking an uncertain and hazardous future.

Some in the Church are adamant about who is to blame - not just those carrying out the persecution, but those who are encouraging it to happen. For Archbishop Issam John Darwish of Furrzol, Zahle and the Bekaa, the responsibility for the attacks lay with "an influx of jihadists in the rebels in the last six, seven months". There is for him, as in so many such situations in the Middle East, the spectre of a "hidden hand". "I think the situation is being manipulated by the USA and maybe Israel - they want this to happen," he insisted.

The Archbishop and others like him feel there is a lack of understanding in Europe about what Christians in the area are going through. Speaking at his diocese, he continued: "I have raised this with officials in the West, they must bring peace. The jihadis will not stop here, the war will spread to Europe. What will England be like in ten or 15 years?"

Fear continues to grow. The recent bombing in Beirut was probably the work of the Syrian regime aiming to kill Brigadier General Wissam al- Hassan, the head of Lebanon's domestic intelligence. A blast in Damascus the following day killing 13 people was targeted at a police station. But both took place in Christian areas of the respective cities and this has added to the trepidation in the community in both Syria and Lebanon, as has the recent inroads made into Christian parts of Aleppo by rebel fighters.

There are now busy campaigns to publicise the plight of the Christians, with a nun from the Homs area being one of its most prominent faces. Mother Agnes-Mariam de la Croix's Greek-Melkite monastery of St James the Mutilated was blown up a few months ago. The culprits, she says, are Islamists, who tried to blame the regime for the destruction.

Mother Agnes-Mariam, who is of Palestinian and Lebanese descent, is on an international tour and is due to visit Britain. She believes that opposition fighters have driven out 80,000 Christians from the Homs region alone and that she escaped after being warned that she was the target of abduction. "Aggressive, armed gangs that wished to paralyse community life, abducting people, beheading, bringing terror even to schools," she said, maintaining that many of them are affiliated to "al-Qa'ida and with Muslim Brotherhood backgrounds".

Only one in 20 are Syrians, the rest come from a wide array of states, from Britain to Pakistan, Chechnya to North Africa, she says. Many are veterans of Iraq and Afghanistan, and now "their cause is being recycled to kill Syrians".

Mother Agnes-Mariam has witnessed the plight of the Syrians first hand, but some of her assertions are open to dispute. In five trips into Syria with rebels, I did not once find large numbers of foreign fighters, although the numbers of domestic jihadist groups had undoubtedly grown and is a source of concern among the more secular revolutionaries. Some groups have banned the chant "Christians to Beirut, Alawites to their graves", which started early in the uprising.

Mother Agnes-Mariam also claimed that the Houla massacre, in which more than 100 civilians died, more than half of them children, was a rebel hoax. A UN commission of inquiry has concluded that regime forces were responsible for the killings. Unsurprisingly, she has critics among her co- religionists. A group opposed to the Assad regime, Syrian Christians for Democracy, charged: "Mother Agnes and those helping her are harming the Syrian people by disseminating negative pro-Assad propaganda and tearing at Syria's social and religious fabrics. The Christians in Syria do not need rumours and propagation of inaccurate information."

The organisation pointed out that many Christians had played a part in the protest movement against Syrian President Bashar al-Assad and his regime and some had paid with their lives as a result.

But there are also those like Mr Bedrosian, who had supported reform, but then found themselves being victimised by the rebels. As a student at Aleppo University in a country without a free media he had, at first, accepted the regime's propaganda that the protesters were terrorists.

"But then I saw the reports being put out by the opposition, saw what Assad's people were doing, the brutal things and began to support the protests," he said. "My friend and I were taken to a villa in the outskirts of Aleppo after we were captured [in the Anadan district]. I was being beaten with rifle butts, punched and kicked. None of the men holding us were foreigners, they were all Syrians and it was one of them who was really violent. They accused me of fighting for the regime, but I told them I was a Syrian Armenian - we didn't want to fight either side. I also told them that I had taken part in marches at university. But they said I would be killed unless money was paid for the girl and myself."

The kidnappers called Mr Bedrosdian's parents and got through to his mother's mobile phone - which had as a ringtone a song in praise of Bashar al-Assad: the regime receives, in general, more support in the older generation. That got him another beating, but the ransom was delivered by his father, bargained down to $12,000, and the couple were freed. The kidnappers kept the car. The first thing Mr Bedrosian did on returning home was to change his mother's ringtone.

Two months ago, Aleppo's 14th century covered market was burnt down. The regime and the rebels blamed each other while the Souk al-Medina, one of the finest examples of its kind in the Middle East, lay in ruins. Jiraryr Terzian, a jewellery trader, was one of dozens who lost their store that day. He is now in Beirut with his Syrian Armenian family; their locked-up home is in one of the Christian neighbourhoods overrun last week by revolutionary fighters. "The business was started by my grandfather 60 years ago and I hoped my children would take it over after me" he said.

"The history of my family is in Aleppo and we did not like leaving. I think both sides are at fault in what is happening. Our country is being destroyed. The fact is we can only go back if Assad wins. I don't like saying this, we don't want the regime to stay as it is, but we will be safer under them."

Another Christian refugee, who wants to be known as Boutros, says he knows what happens when the revolutionaries take over. At his home town, Qusayr, the rebels were, he acknowledges, local Sunnis, not foreigners. "But they told us we must fight with them against the government. When we refused they began to threaten and insult us. They started killing Christians. Mathew Kasouha was the first they killed. He was a good man."

Local Christians took up arms after a while, said Boutros, and in March there was a "showdown". More Christians were killed and he fled to Lebanon. Two months ago at Al-Bab, a satellite town of Aleppo, I was discussing what lay in store for Syria when the bloodletting ends with a group of young activists, all Muslims but committed to democracy with the Alawites and Christians playing their parts. But they were also aware of just how difficult that was going to be to achieve. One of them, Bari, who was later shot but survived in Aleppo, said: "It is not just the fighting and the destruction, but the division between different groups that is such a big problem. We're convinced it is the regime that's responsible for creating this, but the damage has been done. I don't know if people from different communities will ever trust each other again."

Winter 2013

Horror Upon Horror

SYRIA: THE DESCENT INTO HOLY WAR
By Patrick Cockburn
16 December 2012

It is one of the most horrifying videos of the war in Syria. It shows two men being beheaded by Syrian rebels, one of them by a child. He hacks with a machete at the neck of a middle-aged man who has been forced to lie in the street with his head on a concrete block. At the end of the film, a soldier, apparently from the Free Syrian Army, holds up the severed heads by their hair in triumph.

The film is being widely watched on YouTube by Syrians, reinforcing their fears that Syria is imitating Iraq's descent into murderous warfare in the years after the US invasion in 2003. It fosters a belief among Syria's non- Sunni Muslim minorities, and Sunnis associated with the government as soldiers or civil servants, that there will be no safe future for them in Syria if the rebels win. In one version of the video, several of which are circulating, the men who are beheaded are identified as officers belonging to the 2.5 million-strong Alawite community. This is the Shia sect to which President Bashar al-Assad and core members of his regime belong. The beheadings, so proudly filmed by the perpetrators, may well convince them that they have no alternative but to fight to the end.

The video underlines a startling contradiction in the policy of the US and its allies. In the past week, 130 countries have recognised the National Coalition of Syrian Revolutionary and Opposition Forces as the legitimate representatives of the Syrian people. But, at the same time, the US has denounced the al-Nusra Front, the most effective fighting force of the rebels, as being terrorists and an al-Qa'ida affiliate. Paradoxically, the US makes almost exactly same allegations of terrorism against al-Nusra as does the Syrian government. Even more bizarrely, though so many states now recognise the National Coalition as the legitimate representative of the Syrian people, it is unclear if the rebels inside Syria do so. Angry crowds in rebel-held areas of northern Syria on Friday chanted "we are all al-Nusra" as they demonstrated against the US decision.

Videos posted on YouTube play such a central role in the propaganda war in Syria that questions always have to be asked about their authenticity and origin. In the case of the beheading video, the details look all too convincing.

Nadim Houry, the deputy director for Human Rights Watch in the Middle East and North Africa, has watched the video many times to identify the circumstances, perpetrators and location where the killings took place. He has no doubts about its overall authenticity, but says that mention of one district suggests it might be in Deir ez-Zhor (in eastern Syria). But people in the area immediately north of Homs are adamant the beheadings took place there. The victims have not been identified. The first time a version of the film was shown was on pro-government Sama TV on 26 November, but it has been widely viewed on YouTube in Syria only over the past week.

The film begins by showing two middle-aged men handcuffed together sitting on a settee in a house, surrounded by their captors who sometimes slap and beat them. They are taken outside into the street. A man in a black shirt is manhandled and kicked into lying down with his head on a concrete block. A boy, who looks to be about 11 or 12 years old, cuts at his neck with a machete, but does not quite sever it. Later a man finishes the job and cuts the head off. The second man in a blue shirt is also forced to lie with his head on a block and is beheaded. The heads are brandished in front of the camera and later laid on top of the bodies. The boy smiles as he poses with a rifle beside a headless corpse.

The execution video is very similar to those once made by al-Qa'ida in Iraq to demonstrate their mercilessness towards their enemies. This is scarcely surprising since many of the most experienced al-Nusra fighters boast that they have until recently been fighting the predominantly Shia government of Iraq as part of the local franchise of al-Qa'ida franchise. Their agenda is wholly sectarian, and they have shown greater enthusiasm for slaughtering Shias, often with bombs detonated in the middle of crowds in markets or outside mosques, than for fighting Americans.

The Syrian uprising, which began in March 2011, was not always so bloodthirsty or so dominated by the Sunnis who make up 70 per cent of the 23 million-strong Syrian population. At first, demonstrations were peaceful and the central demands of the protesters were for democratic rule and human rights as opposed to a violent, arbitrary and autocratic government. There are Syrians who claim that the people against the regime remains to this day the central feature of the uprising, but there is compelling evidence that the movement has slid towards sectarian Islamic fundamentalism intent on waging holy war.

The execution video is the most graphic illustration of deepening religious bigotry on the part of the rebels, but it is not the only one. Another recent video shows Free Syrian Army fighters burning and desecrating a Shia husseiniyah (a religious meeting house similar to a mosque) in Idlib in northern Syria. They chant prayers of victory as they set fire to the building, set fire to flags used in Shia religious processions and stamp on religious pictures. If the FSA were to repeat this assault on a revered Shia shrine such as the Sayyida Zeinab mosque in Damascus, to which Iranian and Iraqi pilgrims have flooded in the past and which is now almost encircled by rebels, then there could be an explosion of religious hatred and strife between Sunni and Shia across the Middle East. Iraqi observers warn that it was the destruction of the Shia shrine in Samarra, north of Baghdad, by an al-Qa'ida bomb in 2006 that detonated a sectarian war in which tens of thousands died.

The analogy with Iraq is troubling for the US and British governments. They and their allies are eager for Syria to avoid repeating the disastrous mistakes they made during the Iraqi occupation. Ideally, they would like to remove the regime, getting rid of Bashar al-Assad and the present leadership, but not dissolving the government machinery or introducing revolutionary change as they did in Baghdad by transferring power from the Sunnis to the Shia and the Kurds. This provoked a furious counter-reaction from Baathists and Sunnis who found themselves marginalised and economically impoverished.

Washington wants Assad out, but is having difficulty riding the Sunni revolutionary tiger. The Western powers have long hoped for a split in the Syrian elite, but so far there is little sign of this happening. "If you take defections as a measure of political cohesion, then there haven't been any serious ones," said a diplomat in Damascus.

Syria today resembles Iraq nine years ago in another disturbing respect. I have now been in Damascus for 10 days, and every day I am struck by the fact that the situation in areas of Syria I have visited is wholly different from the picture given to the world both by foreign leaders and by the foreign media. The last time I felt like this was in Baghdad in late 2003, when every Iraqi knew the US-led occupation was proving a disaster just as George W Bush, Tony Blair and much of the foreign media were painting a picture of progress towards stability and democracy under the wise tutelage of Washington and its carefully chosen Iraqi acolytes.

The picture of Syria most common believed abroad is of the rebels closing in on the capital as the Assad government faces defeat in weeks or, at most, a few months. The Secretary General of NATO, Anders Fogh Rasmussen, said last week that the regime is "approaching collapse". The foreign media consensus is that the rebels are making sweeping gains on all fronts and the end may be nigh. But when one reaches Damascus, it is to discover that the best informed Syrians and foreign diplomats say, on the contrary, that the most recent rebel attacks in the capital had been thrown back by a government counteroffensive. They say that the rebel territorial advances, which fuelled speculation abroad that the Syrian government might implode, are partly explained by a new Syrian army strategy to pull back from indefensible outposts and bases and concentrate troops in cities and towns.

At times, Damascus resounds with the boom of artillery fire and the occasional car bomb, but it is not besieged. I drove 160 kilometres north to Homs, Syria's third largest city with a population of 2.3 million, without difficulty. Homs, once the heart of the uprising, is in the hands of the government, aside from the Old City, which is held by the FSA. Strongholds of the FSA in Damascus have been battered by shellfire and most of their inhabitants have fled to other parts of the capital. The director of the 1,000- bed Tishreen military hospital covering much of southern Syria told me that he received 15 to 20 soldiers wounded every day, of whom about 20 per cent died. This casualty rate indicates sniping, assassinations and small-scale ambushes, but not a fight to the finish.

This does not mean that the government is in a happy position. It has been unable to recapture southern Aleppo or the Old City in Homs.

It does not have the troops to garrison permanently parts of Damascus it has retaken. Its overall diplomatic and military position is slowly eroding and the odds against it are lengthening, but it is a long way from total defeat, unless there is direct military intervention by foreign powers, as in Libya or Iraq, and this does not seem likely.

This misperception of the reality on the ground in Syria is fuelled in part by propaganda, but more especially by inaccurate and misleading reporting by the media where bias towards the rebels and against the government is unsurpassed since the height of the Cold War. Exaggerated notions are given of rebel strength and popularity. The Syrian government is partially responsible for this. By excluding all but a few foreign journalists, the regime has created a vacuum of information that is naturally filled by its enemies. In the event, a basically false and propagandistic account of events in Syria has been created by a foreign media credulous in using pro-opposition sources as if they were objective reporting.

The execution video is a case in point. I have not met a Syrian in Damascus who has not seen it. It is having great influence on how Syrians judge their future, but the mainstream media outside Syria has scarcely mentioned it. Some may be repulsed by its casual savagery, but more probably it is not shown because it contradicts so much of what foreign leaders and reporters claim is happening here.

PERSECUTION OF THE CHRISTIANS
By Patrick Cockburn
18 December 2012

Two masked men armed with Kalashnikov assault rifles tried to kidnap a businessman called George Alumeh in the ancient Christian town of Maloula, north-west of Damascus, last week. It was not the first kidnap attempt on richer members of the Christian community here and Mr Alumeh was prepared. He fought back, first drawing a pistol, hurling his car keys away so his car could not be stolen, and then trying to escape. He got away, but was hit by a burst of gunfire from the kidnappers which has sent him to hospital with stomach, leg and hand wounds.

Father Mata Hadad, the priest of the Convent of St Tikla built into the mountain wall that towers over Maloula, tells the story to illustrate how life has become more dangerous for Christians, particularly for those thought to have money. The 10 per cent of the Syrian population who are Christians are debating with trepidation the likely outcome of the Syrian crisis and its effect on them.

The omens are not good. Every country in the Middle East seems to be becoming more Islamic and more sectarian. Syrian Christians have seen since 2003 how an outcome of the invasion of Iraq was the destruction of Christian communities in Iraq that had survived for almost 2,000 years. If the opposition National Coalition, recognised by 130 countries as the legitimate government of Syria, does ultimately take power then its most effective fighting force will be Jadhat al-Nusra, with an ideology similar to al-Qa'ida. It is prospects like this that fill Syrian Christians with alarm.

Maloula is a good place to talk about these fears. It is an hour's drive from Damascus, some 20 miles from Lebanon, and occupies a spectacular site in a cleft in the mountains. Its rocky defiles have always been a place of refuge. It was here that St Tikla, fleeing imperial soldiery, took refuge in a cave high up in the cliffs.

Maloula's isolation helped preserve its Christianity and also gave it the distinction of being the only place where Western Aramaic, the language of Jesus, is still spoken by Christians.

There is a mood of uncertainty about the future. So far there have been four kidnappings that the Syrian army post just beyond the entrance to the town has not been able to do much to prevent. Religious tourism has disappeared. "I used to sell guide books and souvenirs," says Samir Shakti, gesturing towards his small shop, "but now I sell fruit and vegetables".

Another sign of edginess is the bursts of anger against foreigners, in the present case myself, as a symbol of European powers accused of arming Islamic fundamentalists. Even the Mother Superior of the Convent, Pelagia Sayaf, demanded to know why the Europeans were aiding "people who kill with the knife". She said many people were leaving the town (though this was denied by some others in Maloula).

Mother Superior Pelagia looked strained. She has been at her post for 23 years, ruling over 14 nuns and 33 orphans from Christian families all over the Middle East. The orphans wear a red uniform and tartan caps, giving them a surprisingly Scottish appearance. "It is going to be a sad Christmas in Maloula," the Mother Superior said. "Sanctions are punishing the people, not the government."

Christians may feel more frightened than other Syrians, but everybody feels vulnerable. There was no fighting on the road from Damascus to Maloula, but there are many wrecked buildings from battles in the past couple of months. Once the main road to Homs was crowded with car showrooms, but these are now closed and their plate glass windows are protected from blast damage by hurriedly built walls of concrete blocks.

Better-off Christians are able to escape abroad, but for those with little money this is a difficult option. One Armenian, who did not want his name published, said "we can go to Lebanon, but it is expensive to stay there, jobs are difficult to get and Lebanese don't like Syrians much because our army was there for so long". He himself was seeking Armenian citizenship.

As with others in Damascus the degree of danger felt depends on precise location. Many Christians live in Jaramana district that is now dangerous from snipers and bombers. The Christian parts of the Old City are safer, but there are electricity cuts and a shortage of diesel. So far the sufferings of the Christians of Syria are no worse than those of the Muslims, but they feel that whatever the outcome of the civil war, their future will most likely be worse than their past.

SYRIAN REGIME CAPTURES AL-QA'IDA CHIEF'S BROTHER ON 'AID MISSION'
By Kim Sengupta
5 January 2013

The brother of the head of al-Qa'ida is reported to have been captured by regime forces in Syria. Mohamed al-Zawahiri is said to have been seized in Deraa in the south-west where he was meeting opposition activists.

Rebel fighters insisted Mohamed al-Zawahiri was engaged on a humanitarian mission and had not been involved in violent acts. They also claimed that he had, in fact, proposed a local truce to enable aid to get through.

However the Syrian regime is likely to try to capitalise on Mr Zawahiri's presence in the country - if indeed they have him under arrest - as proof of their repeated charge that the revolution has been taken over by "terrorists".

Ayman al-Zawahiri, who took over as al-Qa'ida leader following the killing of Osama bin Laden, has declared that it is the duty of Muslims to take part in a jihad against the "pernicious, cancerous regime" of Bashar al-Assad and warned the opposition against depending on the West for help.

Jabhat al-Nusra, an Islamist rebel group with links to al-Qai'da, has become increasingly powerful in the conflict, overshadowing the more moderate fighters, and its leader, Abu Muhammad al-Julani, is said to be in personal contact with Ayman al-Zawahiri.

There is also evidence of groups of foreign volunteers, albeit not in large numbers, joining the uprising. Mohamed al-Zawahiri has, however, denied in the past that he wanted to get involved in the Syrian struggle. Speaking in Cairo recently, he stated that he had no plans to join the rebellion. Mr Zawahiri spent 14 years in an Egyptian prison on charges of being involved in the assassination of President Anwar Sadat in 1981 and taking part in terrorist acts. But he has protested his innocence and insisted that he now devotes his time to attempt reconciliation between jihadists and mainstream Islam.

Mohamed al-Zawahari is a former military commander of the Islamic Jihad movement, but has, he has stressed, turned away from violence. He claims to have been a conduit for talks between hardline Salafist groups in the Sinai and the Egypt's Muslim Brotherhood government. Last year Mr Zawahiri offered to help in negotiations between the US and Islamists and maintained that his attempts at reconciliation had made him a target for hardline Islamists who have accused him of betraying the cause. There is no evidence that his offer was taken seriously by the US administration.

The reports of his presence in Syria have come from rebel factions but remain unconfirmed.

Deraa, near the Jordanian border, has, however, become a stronghold for Jabhat al-Nusra where its "emir", the organisation has announced, is Abu Julaybib, a brother-in-law of the former leader of al-Qa'ida in Iraq who was killed in an American air strike in 2006.

Jabhat al-Nusra denied reports on Al Jazeera that Abu Julaybib and Mr Julani, who has been described as an emissary of the al-Qa'ida leader Ayman al- Zawhari, were recently killed in fighting in Deràa.

SYRIA'S CARNAGE IS NOT IN DISPUTE. BUT THE NUMBERS ARE IMPOSSIBLE TO QUANTIFY
By Robert Fisk
7 January 2013

Notice how Syria's civil war casualty figures shot up by 15,000 overnight last week? The world's press had happily settled into the "Syrian Observatory for Human Rights" statistic of 45,000 dead in almost three years.

But then at New Year's the UN's Human Rights Commission tells the world that the real figure is close to 60,000. Come again? Did 15,000 Syrians climb into a mass grave on 1 January, 2013?

First, however, a health warning. No-one disputes the carnage in Syria. But figuring out just how many souls die in a civil war - and whose "side" they were on when they expired - is a mighty dangerous game.

News desks beware, for history suggests that the "bad guy" must always be held responsible for the greatest number of deaths - at least in the Middle East - and that civilians who become "fighters" end up in civilian death lists, while men and women killed by the "good guys" don't get on lists at all. It's not just a question of lies, damned lies and statistics; in a war, each side produces its own rules for the dead. And none of them tell the truth, the whole truth and nothing but the truth.

For example, how many Syrian soldiers, pro-government militiamen, pro- government supporters and civilian sympathisers are counted among the statistics. SANA, the Syrian government news agency, once spoke of 2,000 dead among Assad's military. Assad's own officers suggested to me in Damascus last year that this figure had reached at least 6,000. I suspect it may be nearer to 10,000 pro-Assad soldiers who have now been killed. So does this mean that at least one sixth of the UN figures actually comprise the army which is accused by the West of committing atrocities? And if this is true, how many more "pro-Assad" civilians should be added to the list?

Hundreds of recent victims of the Syrian war have been Christians - who could scarcely rank among the insurgents. Does this account for one figure, which puts pro-government dead as more than 13,000?

One reason, of course, why the pro-opposition "Syrian Observatory" suspects the UN figure is inflated is that the ladies and gentlemen of the Human Rights Commission want to heap more coals of derision upon the slumbering - and certainly impotent - UN Security Council. The UN, after all, is not a committee of wise men, but a monumental political beast, not unlike a giant donkey. Give it the carrot of a bigger mass grave and it might plod a little faster.

So how many rebels have been killed in Syria? We are told that almost 5,500 military defectors are among the dead. So are 372 Palestinians, killed in inter-Palestinian fighting around the largest refugee camp in Damascus.

It's sobering to remember how we have wrestled with the same kind of statistics in the past. In "our" Iraq war from 2003-2009 - note how we assume the conflict ended when "we" abandoned the country, although another 4,500 Iraqis were killed in 2012 alone - every blue-eyed Western casualty was meticulously listed. But the Western occupation authorities went along with General Tommy Franks' obscene invention about the Iraqi dead, that "we don't do body counts". The Pentagon was later revealed to have kept a list of civilian dead up to 2005 - the total was 25,902 - but these figures were slyly contrived. They listed only civilians killed by insurgents: unarmed Iraqis killed by Western military forces found no place in the Pentagon's figures.

But you can go further back. Armenians claim - with good reason - that a million and a half of their people were victims of the 1915 Turkish genocide. But the Turks still peddle the myth that these figures were falsified, and that Armenians died in the "chaos" of internal conflict during the First World War.

And what about the Second World War? Did 40 million die, as we used to believe, or was it 70 million (more likely if you include the Sino-Japanese war)? Against this hecatomb, a 15,000 discrepancy in the killing fields of Syria is hardly surprising.

NEW FEARS ON SYRIA'S CHEMICAL WEAPONS
By Kim Sengupta
9 January 2013

The prospect of Syria's chemical arsenal falling into the hands of Islamists who are fighting in the country's bloody civil war is a matter of mounting concern for the West.

General Sir David Richards, the head of the British military, has raised his worries in Whitehall in recent weeks and European and American officials have held a series of meetings with governments in the region about the issue.

Although the American and British governments still think a beleaguered regime on its last legs may use weapons of mass destruction, they also fear there is a danger of jihadist fighters gaining possession of stockpiles. The Obama administration has proscribed the Al-Nusra Brigade, one of the strongest of the rebel groups and one which declares itself affiliated to al- Qa'ida, as a terrorist organisation.

The possibility that President Bashar al-Assad may unleash chemical weapons was one of the key reasons given for the deployment this week of NATO Patriot missiles to the Turkish border. At the end of last year Barack Obama warned that the use of chemical weapons would mean the Assad regime had crossed a "red line" and must bear the consequences. The regime appeared to have stopped in its tracks in preparing such attacks and the US Defence Secretary, Leon Panetta, stated subsequently that the threat has been reduced.

An SAS team is believed to have observed an exercise carried out by US and Jordanian special forces in preparation for any operation which may have to be undertaken to secure the stockpiles. Defence sources in London stated there are no plans at present to deploy British personnel for such a mission.

There is bound to be public scepticism towards claims about the Syrian regime and weapons of mass destruction after the exposure of similar false reports about Saddam Hussein's arsenal used by the Bush and Blair administrations to justify invading Iraq.

Western officials insist, however, that there is ample evidence that the Damascus regime has the means to carry out chemical warfare and also evidence, of a more limited nature, that it has a biological warfare programme. One cause of apprehension is that the regime's command and control of WMD has been severely damaged by casualties and defections.

A series of meetings have taken place involving military personnel from the US, France, countries in the region and Israel, whose Prime Minister, Benjamin Netanyahu, according to media reports in Jerusalem, met King Abdullah II of Jordan in Amman to discuss the matter. One aspect of Israeli concern is that Hezbollah, some of whose fighters have been fighting for the Assad regime, may be able to smuggle chemical weapons into Lebanon.

The vulnerability of the chemical stock is believed to have been discussed between American and Russian officials on a number of occasions. The Russian Foreign Minister, Sergey Lavrov, subsequently stated that the chemical stock was being kept in two centres and it would be "suicidal" for the Assad regime, which his government has supported throughout the uprising, to use them.

General Adnan Sillu, the recently defected former head of Syria's chemical weapons programme, has claimed that the regime has already used sarin gas in an attack last month on the Al-Bayyadh district of Homs.

The opposition Free Syrian Army maintains that the regime has used chemical weapons on 18 separate occasions. Western officials maintain, however, that photographs and testimonies they have received do not back up the charge.

An independent chemical and biological analyst, Dr Sally Leivesley, said: "If there really was an attack involving sarin, then one would expect a significant number of fatalities. From what one hears about the symptoms it's possible that a harassing agent rather than a nerve agent was used."

Dr Leivesley, who trained as a scientific adviser with the Home Office, said: "Reports of Syria's bio-warfare programme go back to the mid-90s and there was a report to the US Congress in 2004 and NATO reports. The material on all this is interesting because it was put together a long time before current events and thus one can't say that it has been put together to fit a particular agenda."

Problems with biological agents, Dr Leivesley held, may start by accident rather than the design of either the regime or rebels. "Pathogens such as anthrax, plague, tularemia, botulinum, smallpox, aflatoxin, cholera and ricin can become exposed by people stumbling across them in insecure bases."

Spring 2013

Barbaric Beyond Belief

WEST HAS NEVER UNDERSTOOD SYRIA - JUST TAKE A LOOK AT THE HISTORY BOOKS
By Robert Fisk
4 March 2013

In Syria these days, we are resorting to our racist little maps. The Alawite mountains and the town of Qardaha, home of the Assad family - colour it dark red. Will this be the last redoubt of the 12 per cent Alawite minority, to which the President, below, belongs, when the rebels "liberate" Damascus? We always like these divisive charts in the Middle East. Remember how Iraq was always Shias at the bottom, Sunnis in the middle, Kurds at the top? We used to do this with Lebanon: Shias at the bottom (as usual), Shias in the east, Sunnis in Sidon and Tripoli, Christians east and north of Beirut. Never once has a Western newspaper shown a map of Bradford with Muslim and non-Muslim areas marked off, or a map of Washington divided into black and white people. No, that would suggest that our Western civilisation could be divvied up between tribes or races. Only the Arab world merits our ethnic distinctions.

The problem, of course, is that Syria - as secular and assimilated as any Arab nation before its current tragedy - doesn't lend itself to this neat distribution of religious minorities. Aleppo was always a home to Christians, Sunnis and Alawites. The Alawites were "citified" many years ago - hence their presence in Damascus - and many of them came not from the mountains but from Alexandretta, which is now in the Turkish province of Hatay. Yet even if we know where they live, there has been precious little research into this community - save, perhaps, in France.

For now Sabrina Mervin, the French author and researcher, has put together a remarkable document in which she traces the history of a people who used to call themselves "Nusayris" - after the founder of their faith, Muhammad Ibn Nusayr - and whose religion was founded "in the bosom of Shiism" in the 9th and 10th centuries. Mervin's work, published now in that splendid French institution Le Monde Diplomatique, should be essential reading for every Syria "expert", for it suggests that the Alawites are victims of a long history of religious dissidents, persecution and repression.

As long ago as 1903, the Belgian-born Jesuit and Orientalist, Henri Lammens, was identifying the Alawites as former Christians - until he met a Sheikh who insisted he belonged to Shia Islam. Lammens, a typical imperialist, suggested that the Alawites - who appeared to believe in the transmigration of souls and a trinity (the Prophet Muhammad, his cousin and son-in-law Ali, and Salman, a companion) - might become Christians "which would allow France to interfere in your favour". Indeed, France did indeed show favour to the Alawites in later years.

The Ottomans had tried to integrate the Alawites who, according to Ms Mervin, were exploited by Sunni landowners and often illiterate. By 1910, their religious dignitaries were opening relations with the Shias of southern Lebanon and Iraq, calling themselves "Alawites" after Ali and distancing themselves from Nusayr. The French mandate authorities in Syria went along with this, not least because they wished to divide them from the Sunnis. Popular myth would have it that the Alawites collaborated with the French while the Sunnis fought for independence. In fact, one prominent Alawite, Saleh al-Ali, fought the French army in the mountains between December of 1918 and 1921 - and was subsequently recognised as a national hero by the first independent Syrian government in 1946. Another prominent Alawite, a would-be shepherd-saint called Sulieman al-Mourchid, met a less happy end, hanged in 1946 for treason.

The Alawites were themselves divided over French rule, some favouring the short-lived Alawite state created by Paris, others the Syrian nationalism espoused by the Sunnis. The latter stood behind Sulieman al-Ahmed, claiming adherence to Islam and in 1936 publishing a text stating that they were Muslim Arabs; and successfully seeking a "fatwa" from the grand Mufti of Jerusalem, Haj Amin al-Husseini, which included the Alawites in the "umma". And yes, this was the same Haj-Amin who would meet Hitler - though this had nothing to do with the Alawites.

Supported by Iraqi Shias, the Alawites founded their own religious institutions, constructed mosques and published works on their faith, receiving the acknowledgement of the Mufti of Syria in 1952.

This rapprochement with the Shias continued under the first Alawite president - Hafez, father of Bashar - and in 1973, Imam Moussa Sadr, the most politicised of Shia leaders in Lebanon (later believed to have been killed on the orders of a certain Muammar Gaddafi), declared that the Alawites were indeed Muslims; Shia religious schools were then opened at Sayeda Zeinab in the suburbs of Damascus - thus the story of the "shia-isation" of Syria. And henceforth Alawites ascended in the Syrian military and in the Baath party, albeit that most Syrian generals were Sunni.

Yet within the Alawite community, not everyone found favour. Tribal organisations and religious influence, according to Ms Mervin, declined under the Assads. So too did the great traditional families. Poverty still undermines the Alawite hinterland north of Damascus. Even to speak of the Alawites in sectarian terms has been, of course, forbidden.

Cruellest of all was the habit adopted by Syrians of referring to the Alawites with the code word "Germans" - in Arabic, "alawiyyin" (Alawites) and "almaniyyin" (Germans) are similar. What's in a name? But please, no more maps.

CONFLICT IN SYRIA CREATES NEW WAVE OF BRITISH JIHADISTS
By Kim Sengupta
14 March 2013

The bloody uprising against Bashar al-Assad is creating a new wave of jihadists in Britain, with Syria now the main destination for militant Muslims wishing to fight abroad, The Independent has learnt.

Syria has replaced Pakistan and Somalia as the preferred front line where Islamist volunteers can experience immediate combat with relatively little official scrutiny, security agencies said.

The worrying development has been taking place as extremist groups, some with links to al-Qa'ida, have become the dominant force in the uprising against the Damascus regime.

More than 100 British Muslims are believed to have gone to fight in Syria with the numbers continuing to rise. The situation presents a unique problem for Western security and intelligence services. In Syria, unlike Pakistan and Somalia, they have to keep track of jihadists who are being backed by Britain and its allies.

The Syrian rebels are drawing recruits from a variety of national backgrounds in the UK. Only a handful of those who have returned from the fighting there have been arrested and all for a specific offence: their alleged role in the kidnapping of a British freelance photographer, John Cantlie, in Idlib province last summer. Others who have been taking part in the armed struggle against the Assad regime are not deemed to be doing anything illegal.

Mr Cantlie, along with a Dutch colleague, Jeroen Oerlemans, are believed to have been abducted by a group called al-Dawa al-Islamiyya, which encouraged British and other Western volunteers to join the struggle against the Assad regime. The hostages were rescued by moderate fighters.

Abo Mohamad al-Shami, the leader of al-Dawa al-Islamiyya, was executed five weeks later, supposedly by the Farouq Brigade, a unit of the Free Syrian Army, which had become alarmed at the activities of the extremists.

But since then the Islamists, and in particular one group, Jabhat al-Nusra - which proclaims links with al-Qa'ida and has been proscribed by the US administration as a terrorist group - have grown in size and influence largely due to supplies of money and arms from backers in Qatar, Saudi Arabia and other states in the Gulf.

It is to counter the growth of the extremists that the British Foreign Secretary William Hague successfully campaigned for a partial easing of European Union sanctions on Syria. The UK will supply armoured cars and body armour to "moderate" rebels.

David Cameron announced earlier this week that if the EU rescinds the easing of the rules, the UK will go ahead with supplying more lethal weapons to the "democratic" opposition.

Security officials point out that the volatility of the strife in Syria, with khatibas (battalions) forming, merging and disbanding, makes it difficult to keep track of whether British jihadists have ended up fighting for so-called moderate groups or extremists.

The Independent has come across revolutionaries who were avowedly "secular" in the past who now declare themselves Islamists. Some do so to get funding from the Gulf states.

The Russian Foreign Minister, Sergei Lavrov, whose government has backed the Assad regime, declared during a visit to London yesterday that any attempt by Britain to arm the rebels would be a violation of international law and strenuously opposed by the Kremlin.

"International law does not permit the supply of arms to non-governmental actors," he said.

Standing beside him at a press conference, Mr Hague and the Defence Secretary Philip Hammond stated that the UK "had not ruled anything out" in arming the rebels. Mr Lavrov warned weapons may fall into the hands of extremists.

"We don't know who is going to receive the arms, how they are going to use them. The most dangerous and effective group fighting the regime is the Jabhat al-Nusra which, we note, the US has declared a terrorist organisation," the Russian Foreign Minister said.

IRAQI AL-QA'IDA DECLARES TAKEOVER OF LEADING SYRIAN REBEL FACTION
By Patrick Cockburn
10 April 2013

Al -Qa'ida in Iraq has said it has united with the most militant and effective Syrian rebel group, the al-Nusra Front, in a move likely to embarrass Western countries supporting Syrian insurgents seeking to overthrow the government of President Bashar al-Assad.

Abu Bakr al-Baghdadi, the leader of al-Qa'ida's umbrella organisation in Iraq, the Islamic State of Iraq, said in a statement posted on Islamic fundamentalist websites yesterday that his group had helped create al- Nusra, had funded it and reinforced it with experienced al-Qa'ida fighters from Iraq. He said: "It's now time to declare in front of the people of the Levant and the world that al-Nusra Front is but an extension of the Islamic State of Iraq and part of it." The US has labelled al-Nusra a "terrorist" group.

Al-Nusra has been at the forefront of the fighting in and around Aleppo and appears to have been behind a series of car bombings in Damascus. Some 15 people were killed by a suicide bomber who blew himself up near the Central Bank in Damascus on Monday. Its use of suicide bombers, foreign volunteers and fundamentalist rhetoric, targeting non-Sunni Syrians as heretics or disbelievers, is similar to the tactics and ideology of al-Qa'ida in Iraq.

Many opposition military and political factions have sought to downplay evidence that the uprising in Syria is dominated by jihadi and salafi movements preaching holy war. Al-Nusra is not the only such organisation and it was Ahrar al-Sham, another well-organised Islamic fundamentalist group, which led the assault on Raqqa, the first provincial capital to fall to the opposition earlier this year. Al-Nusra also played an important role in the fighting while the Western-backed Free Syrian Army was largely absent. Religious courts have been set up in Raqqa, and al-Nusra has sought to ban the sale of cigarettes as un-Islamic.

Mr Al-Baghdadi said in a 21-minute audio talk that the new united group operating in both Iraq and Syria would in future be called The Islamic State of Iraq and Sham, Sham being the name for Syria and the surrounding area.

He said that al-Qa'ida in Iraq had been devoting half its budget to supporting al-Nusra, of which the overall leader will apparently be Mr Al-Baghdadi himself.

The Sunni majority areas of Iraq in Western Anbar and Nineveh provinces share a common border with eastern Syria which is increasingly falling under rebel control. The degree of co-ordination was underscored early last month when 48 Syrian soldiers who had fled into Iraq were ambushed and killed at Akashat as they were being returned to Syria. An Iraqi intelligence officer was quoted as saying that al-Qa'ida in Iraq and al-Nusra have three joint training camps in the border area where they share training, logistics, intelligence and weapons.

The US, Britain and France, along with Turkey, Saudi Arabia and Qatar, have promoted and financed other factions of the opposition. But, while supposedly more moderate, these have often been denounced by Syrians in areas they control as being little more than bandits and incapable of maintaining civil government.

A BARBARIC WAR THROWS UP A HORROR STORY THAT MAKES VILLAINS OF ALL
By Robert Fisk
15 April 2013

Horror of horrors. A young Syrian, clean-shaven, perhaps in his early twenties, in a windcheater and with a Kalashnikov rifle slung over his left shoulder, holds the head of a decapitated man. The head appears to have been hacked from his unseen corpse with a knife. Just last week, we are told. It has short hair, a thin moustache, eyes mercifully closed. And - here we need an infinitely more terrible word than horror - the young man is holding the head over a smouldering barbecue.

The boy is described as a member of the Free Syria Army (FSA), the ragtag militia of government army deserters who now fight against the Assad regime. The head, so a website caption would have us believe, is that of a Syrian air force officer who survived the crash of a helicopter in Idlib province after the machine was shot down by a ground-to-air missile.

Propaganda? Most certainly. Truth? Perhaps. But the internet has so skewed the Syrian war that propaganda has become truth and truth, propaganda - even myth. Everyone believes what they want to believe. And this awful image is not just a challenge to humanity. It is also, in its most obvious form, a challenge to journalism.

Here I am in Damascus when a website - most assuredly sympathetic to the regime - produces "evidence" of a war crime and lists the names and ranks of the other seven air force "martyrs" who last week apparently endured the terror and pain of decapitation with the man in the picture.

I first heard of this gruesome picture in conversation with a friend yesterday morning. By midday, I saw it running from printing machines in the Ministry of Information in the Mezze suburb of the city, not for distribution to the press but for the files of the staff. Several could not bring themselves to look at the photograph, one woman leaving the room in order to avoid vomiting. This was not play-acting for my benefit.

By chance, I was about to meet briefly with the information minister himself, Omran Zoubi. "I can't confirm this," he said to me. "I need to ask first." By last night, he had made no further comment. It would have been easy for Mr Zoubi to have said that he believed every word. But he had clearly never heard of this before.

So let us begin with the air force dead. For the record, they are listed as General Souhel Akram, parachute Major Youssef Ma'alla, Air Force Captain Hussam Asaad (who had allegedly survived an earlier massacre of air force personnel), Air Force Captain Ayham Al-Hussain, First Lieutenant Mohamed Ali Al-Dikar, First Lieutenant Maias Ramadan, and Sergeants Sarot Ghanija and Mohamed Diben.

Most assuredly, the Syrian air force can confirm - indeed, must confirm - if these are real names. And the details on the website - which appears to have come from Lebanon and is highly sectarian (in this case, anti-Sunni Muslim) in tone - are quite straightforward: the air force men were flying on a helicopter from Latakia airport on the Mediterranean coast, carrying food and humanitarian aid to villages and army units around Maaret al-Noman when they were shot down over Idlib province. All survived. They were then beheaded.

The website implies that the executioners were Sunnis and that the victims were Shias - or from that intriguing offshoot of Shiism, the Alawites, to which President Bashar Assad belongs. But there is no evidence to what religion the dead men - if they are dead - belonged. And there is another weird side to all this. The killers were described as "Free Syria Army gangs", yet most of the atrocities - and decapitations - carried out by the armed opposition to the regime have been the responsibility of extreme Islamist groups. Why would the largely secular - a painfully inaccurate word in any Syrian context - FSA commit such a war crime?

If it was committed. Pictures and video from the Iraq war show that Islamist groups were prepared - and happy - to carry out such executions. Yet the Syrian regime has itself indulged in barbarity. And if even part of yesterday's horror story is true, was the military helicopter taking only "humanitarian" supplies across Idlib? And did this horror of horrors actually happen? Did these men even exist?

Alas, in war, photoshop technology and the internet have made villains of us all.

HISTORY LESSONS THE WEST REFUSES TO LEARN
By Patrick Cockburn
12 May 2013

In the aftermath of the First World War, Britain and France famously created the modern Middle East by carving up what had been the Ottoman Empire. The borders of new states such as Iraq and Syria were determined in keeping with British and French needs and interests. The wishes of local inhabitants were largely ignored.

Now, for the first time in over 90 years, the whole postwar settlement in the region is coming unstuck. External frontiers are no longer the impassable barriers they were until recently, while internal dividing lines are becoming as complicated to cross as international frontiers.

In Syria, the government no longer controls many crossing points into Turkey and Iraq. Syrian rebels advance and retreat without hindrance across their country's international borders, while Shia and Sunni fighters from Lebanon increasingly fight on opposing sides in Syria. The Israelis bomb Syria at will. Of course, the movements of guerrilla bands in the midst of a civil war do not necessarily mean that the state is finally disintegrating. But the permeability of its borders suggests that whoever comes out as the winner of the Syrian civil war will rule a weak state scarcely capable of defending itself.

The same process is at work in Iraq. The so-called trigger line dividing Kurdish-controlled territory in the north from the rest of Iraq is more and more like a frontier defended on both sides by armed force. Baghdad infuriated the Kurds last year by setting up the Dijla (Tigris) Operations Command, which threatened to enforce central military control over areas disputed between Kurds and Arabs.

Dividing lines got more complicated in Iraq after the Hawaijah massacre on 23 April left at least 44 Sunni Arab protesters dead. This came after four months of massive but peaceful Sunni protests against discrimination and persecution. The result of this ever-deeper rift between the Sunni and the Shia-dominated government in Baghdad is that Iraqi troops in Sunni- majority areas behave like an occupation army. At night, they abandon isolated outposts so they can concentrate forces in defensible positions. Iraqi government control in the northern half of the country is becoming ever more tenuous.

Does it really matter to the rest of the world who fights whom in the impoverished country towns of the Syrian interior or in the plains and mountains of Kurdistan? The lesson of the last few thousand years is that it matters a great deal. The region between Syria's Mediterranean coast and the western frontier of Iran has traditionally been a zone where empires collide. Maps of the area are littered with the names of battlefields where Romans fought against Parthians, Ottomans against Safavids, and British against Turks.

It is interesting but chilling to see the carelessness with which the British and French divided up this area under the Sykes-Picot Agreement of 1916. The British were to control the provinces of Baghdad and Basra and have influence further north. The French were to hold south-east Turkey and northern Syria and the province of Mosul, believed to contain oil. It turned out, however, that British generosity over Mosul was due to Britain having promised eastern Turkey to Tsarist Russia and thinking it would be useful to have a French cordon sanitaire between themselves and the Russian army.

Sykes-Picot reflected wartime priorities and was never implemented as such. The British promise to give Mosul to France became void with the Bolshevik revolution in 1917 and the Bolsheviks' unsporting publication of Russia's secret agreements with its former French and British allies. But in negotiations in 1918-19 leading up to the Treaty of Versailles, only the most perfunctory attention was given to the long-term effect of the distribution of the spoils.

Discussing Mesopotamia and Palestine with David Lloyd George, Georges Clemenceau, the French Prime Minister, who was not very interested in the Middle East, said: "Tell me what you want." Lloyd George: "I want Mosul." Clemenceau: "You shall have it. Anything else?" Lloyd George: "Yes, I want Jerusalem too." Clemenceau agreed with alacrity to this as well, though he warned there might be trouble over Mosul, which even then was suspected to contain oil.

Those negotiations have a fascination because so many of the issues supposedly settled then are still in dispute. Worse, agreements reached then laid the basis for so many future disputes and wars that still continue, or are yet to come. Arguments made at that time are still being made.

Not surprisingly, the leaders of the 30 million Kurds are the most jubilant at the discrediting of agreements of which they, along with the Palestinians, were to be the greatest victims. After being divided between Iraq, Turkey, Iran and Syria, they sense their moment has finally come. In Iraq, they enjoy autonomy close to independence, and in Syria they have seized control of their own towns and villages. In Turkey, as the PKK Turkish Kurd guerrillas begin to trek back to the Qandil mountains in northern Iraq under a peace deal, the Kurds have shown that, in 30 years of war, the Turkish state has failed to crush them.

But as the 20th century settlement of the Middle East collapses, the outcome is unlikely to be peace and prosperity. It is easy to see what is wrong with the governments in present-day Iraq and Syria, but not what would replace them. Look at the almost unanimous applause among foreign politicians and media at the fall of Colonel Gaddafi in 2011, then look at Libya now, its government permanently besieged or on the run from militia gunmen.

If President Bashar al-Assad did fall in Syria, who would replace him? Does anybody really think that peace would automatically follow? Is it not far more likely that there would be continued and even intensified war, as happened in Iraq after the fall of Saddam Hussein in 2003? The Syrian rebels and their supporters downplay the similarities between the crises in Iraq and Syria, but they have ominous similarities. Saddam may have been unpopular in Iraq, but those who supported him or worked for him could not be excluded from power and turned into second-class citizens without a fight.

US, British and French recipes for Syria's future seem as fraught with potential for disaster as their plans in 1916 or 2003. In saying that Assad can play no role in a future Syrian government, the US Secretary of State, John Kerry, speaks of the leader of a government that has still only lost one provincial capital to the rebels. Such terms can only be imposed on the defeated or those near defeat. This will only happen in Syria if Western powers intervene militarily on behalf of the insurgents, as they did in Libya, but the long-term results might be equally dismal.

THE DAY I MET THE CANNIBAL COMMANDER'S BRIGADE
By Kim Sengupta
16 May 2013

Even by the standards of a particularly murderous war, a fighter eating the freshly cut out lungs of a dead enemy soldier reached a new depth of savagery; the images on the internet were, to the outside world, gruesome evidence of a depraved and babaric conflict.

Yet Abu Sakkar, the man who has introduced cannibalism into the Syrian civil war, was, until quite recently, seen as someone in the mainstream of the revolutionaries trying to overthrow Basher al-Assad; something of a hero even for his part in the defence of Baba Amr when the district in Homs came under onslaught from regime forces.

Indeed his khatiba, or brigade, Omar al-Farouq, had won praise for taking a stand against the Islamist extremists in rebel ranks who are becoming more of a worry to Western governments than the Damascus regime. They had arrested and executed a commander, Mohammed al-Absi, leader of a group of foreign jihadists, who was suspected over the kidnapping of a British photographer and was affiliated to Jabhat al-Nusra, an organization since prescribed as a terrorist organisation by the Obama administration.

I had spent some time with members of al-Farouq in Syria. What was clear was that they were not among the more wild eyed, prepared to pledge allegiance to al-Qa'ida, as al-Nusra has done. On a number of occasions they talked earnestly at length about the problems the country will face post- Assad and how difficult it would be to repair the fractures between warring communities. What was also clear was that they, like most other khatibas on the ground, have little regard for the Free Syrian Army, the supposed umbrella group for rebels. Khalid al-Hamad (Abu Sakkar is his nom de guerre) was not always a bloodthirsty man of violence. People in Baba Amr remember him taking part in marches in the very early days of protests which declaimed sectarianism among the opposition and urged the need for a united front to achieve the reforms being denied by the regime.

The question remains what turned al-Hammad, below, into the man seen in a video mutilating a corpse?

Haitham Mohammed Nassr, a former al-Farouq fighter, currently in Turkey, acknowledged the video footage was extremely damaging to the opposition, but insisted it should be put in the context of crimes committed by the Shabiha, the pro-regime militia.

There have been reports that members of Abu Sakkar's own family were raped by regime forces. "I do not know any family who has not suffered," Mr Nassr said. "He [Abu Sakkar] should not have done what he did, doing that was haram [wrong in religion] and unwise. But it was a message to the Shabiha. They film young men and women being tortured to try and frighten people and this was meant as a warning to them."

He went on: "Everyone has been changed by this war; when all you are seeing are fires, bombs, bodies it is very difficult to remain normal. We all want Basher to go, the longer this goes on the more violent people become, it will be difficult to have a normal society after all this, whatever happens."

Summer 2013

The Media is Getting It Wrong

WAR WITHOUT END IN A LAND AWASH WITH ARMS
By Kim Sengupta
1 June 2013

The failure of the European Union to renew the arms embargo on Syria was hardly unexpected. David Cameron and William Hague indicated two months ago that Britain would demand that the terms were relaxed so that the option would be there to send weapons to the rebels. This, it was acknowledged, was unlikely to succeed because of strong opposition from some other member states, and thus the sanctions regime would cease to exist.

Britain and France, which also supported the call on the embargo, have been locked into a position and timeline from which it has become impossible to retreat without losing political credibility. The chain of unintended consequences of this may be that the Cameron Government will actually succeed in uniting all interested parties - in irritation against itself.

Since the uprising began in Syria two years ago, moderate opposition fighters - of which there were many - had begged for arms. Britain and France could and should have given them this help, but did not. In that time, the Islamists, receiving weapons and money from Gulf states, have grown enormously in power. Jabhat al-Nusra was a small, unimpressive group, big on jihadist talk, short on action, when I first met them in Aleppo last summer. Now they are the largest and most effective of the rebel khatibas, or battalions, in the process becoming described by the US as a terrorist organisation. The moderates are seen as counterweights to the terrorists, but they have dwindled in numbers.

Having failed to seize the momentum in helping its natural allies, Britain and France have now announced that they will (probably) arm the rebels. The timing is unfortunate. Despite bitter accusations and recriminations from the protagonists, there is still hope that the planned conference in Geneva next month can begin the process of ending the savage strife which has claimed about 80,000 lives so far.

It is true that the Syrian National Council, the opposition's dysfunctional umbrella group, says it may not attend. But it has become well known for making contradictory statements and, if push comes to shove and the Americans and the Arab League tell it to turn up, it will. The SNC is also aware that there are other opposition organisations that would be only too willing to take their place. John Kerry and Sergei Lavrov have been working hard at this, and although the White House says it broadly supports ending the sanctions by Brussels, there is annoyance in the State Department at yet another unwelcome problem in the run-up to Geneva.

The Russians are protesting about the end of the embargo, pointing out that David Cameron had publicly said he was heartened after his recent meeting with Vladimir Putin that both of them wanted an unfragmented Syria to achieve peace. A day after the EU meeting, deputy foreign minister Sergei Ryabkov warned that the Kremlin would now go ahead with the supply of the S-300 missiles to the Assad regime. The contract for the system had long been signed, but has not so far been delivered, at the request of the US, European states and Israel. This, in turn, has boosted Assad's confidence and will make it that much harder to impose any kind of a "no-fly zone" in the future.

Israel says the S-300 falling into the hands of Hezbollah across the border in Lebanon would be a game-changer; defence minister Moshe Yaalon threatened more air strikes on Syria if the missiles arrive. At the same time, Tel Aviv does not want the rebels to be armed with weapons which could be turned against the Jewish state. Tel Aviv's position remains ambivalent at best. Efraim Halevy, a former head of Mossad, says Assad remains "Israel's man in Damascus". A column in Haaretz said "Israel can stand to gain from war" and its current stalemate.

What about the rebels themselves? The news from Brussels was followed within hours by the SNC asking the EU to send "specialised weaponry". Abu Qasem, a commander I spent time with in Idlib province, said in an excited phone call from Turkey, where he had gone to obtain ammunition, that the khatibas were expecting, above all, Manpads (shoulder-launched surface-to- air missiles). Having seen cold-blooded killings meted out from the air by Assad's warplanes, I can understand the desire to strike back. But it seems highly unlikely that Britain and France will supply such weapons. There is deep apprehension that they may end up with Islamists. The Americans are still trying to secure Manpads looted from Gaddafi's arsenal in Libya. I saw some in Mali being used by al-Qa'ida to try to shoot down French helicopters.

The British and French are likely to supply, through a third party, small arms and ammunition. Qasem and his comrades will probably be very disappointed and then resentful towards the West as their high expectations are dashed. Other questions remain. How are AK-47s going to swing the balance against the regime, or, indeed, the heavily armed Islamists? What are the chances that al-Nusra would not get hold of them anyway? This particular reasoning has become a bit of a cliché, but is of concern, nevertheless. We have seen Islamists help themselves, from depots, to food donated from abroad: why shouldn't they be able to do so with arms? Also, driven by necessity, some remaining moderate groups are having to work alongside jihadists; it is easy for weapons to change hands in battlefield conditions.

William Hague wants to help people suffering at the hands of a vicious regime. He does not desire the arms option as an imperialist conspiracy, as some of his more swivel-eyed critics charge. The aim is not to prolong the war, he says, but to pressure the regime to the negotiating table. But it also means Assad's allies abroad will use this as an excuse to add more to his arsenal and the risk that the move may jeopardise the first real chance of negotiations to end the bloodshed - the Geneva conference.

BRITISH JIHADI ONE OF THREE WESTERNERS KILLED IN BATTLE WITH SYRIAN REGIME
By Kim Sengupta
1 June 2013

A young British man has been killed along with an American woman and another Western national during a gun battle in Syria, the main destination for young Muslims from this country wishing to take part in jihad abroad.

The Assad regime claimed that 22-year-old Ali Almanasfi, from London, Nicole Lynn Mansfield, 33, from Michigan in the United States, and their companion - who is believed to be a Canadian - were killed fighting for Jabhat al-Nusra, an Islamist group which had pledged allegiance to al-Qa'ida.

Graphic photographs of bodies, in Idlib province, alongside the passports and driving licences of Mr Almanasfi and Ms Mansfield, along with a bullet- marked car and the black flag of al-Nusra, were shown on state-run television in Damascus.

It has, however, been the policy of the regime to describe all opposition groups as Islamist extremists and tie them to al-Nusra, which has been prescribed as a terrorist organisation by the Obama administration.

Last night as police visited Mr Almanasfi's home in Acton, west London, a family member said that he had been in Syria for four months and out of contact for a few weeks. He added: "We are sitting tight to hear, but it looks like it could be him." Kusai Noah, the brother of Mr Alamasfi's wife, Bushra, said that a missing person's report was made with the police after Ali first went missing several months ago.

More than 100 British Muslims have taken part in the bloody uprising against Bashar al-Assad. Not all have been fighters; Issa Abdur Rahman, a 26-year-old graduate of London University's Imperial College who died last Wednesday, was treating injured people at a clinic when the building was shelled by regime troops.

Abu Hajer, a commander with the Suqur Al-Sham brigade, said yesterday that Mr Almanasfi and Ms Mansfield were with his fighters when they were killed in an engagement with the Shabiha, a militia from the Alawite community from President Assad and the ruling elite are drawn.

He said: "We had engaged in several shoot-outs with Shabiha forces, we launched an attack against a government checkpoint and managed to kill several Shabiha. Another group of rebels came from Al-Akrad mountains to join us. They wanted to avoid the centre of Idlib and took a back route through the suburbs. They didn't know there was a Syrian army checkpoint there; the army shot up the car and the British guy was killed."

The complex and changeable nature of rebel organisations can, at times, make it difficult to demarcate different between different groups. Suqour al- Sham has been described as Islamist, but not necessarily extremist. Its leader, Ahmed Abu Issa, has stated in a sermon that Muslims are losing their honour because they are abandoning jihad. But he has also maintained that his vision after the downfall of Assad would be of Syria as a moderate Islamist state.

Mohammed Ali Razaq, a rebel fighter from the Binesh area, said last night: "We have had quite a few brothers who have joined us from other countries because they want to get rid of the cruel Assad. I have seen some of them become influenced by jihadists and they change. They also know that jihadists like Al-Nusra are the most effective groups so they are attracted."

Ms Mansfield, who was raised a Baptist, converted to Islam five years ago. Her aunt, Monica Mansfield Speelman, said the FBI had informed the family of the death. "I am just devastated, evidently she was fighting with opposition forces."

On Facebook, Ms Mansfield's daughter, Triona Lynn, posted a memorial message saying: "I will never forget everything you taught me. I wish I could honour in some other way but I have no control what happens to you now. I will try to not give up on life even though I really want to. I just want to see your face, hear your voice, and touch your skin again. But I'll stay strong.

And you will never be forgotten."

The Britons fighting in Syria are drawn from a variety of national backgrounds. Only a handful of those who have returned from the fighting there have been arrested and all for a specific offence: their alleged role in the kidnapping of a British freelance photographer, John Cantlie, in Idlib province last summer. Others who have been taking part in the armed struggle against the Assad regime are not deemed to be doing anything illegal.

Unlike Pakistan or Somalia, the rebels in Syria are being backed by the British government which is sending aid including communications equipment and body armour to them and has declared that military supplies may follow in the future.

FOREIGN MEDIA PORTRAYALS OF THE CONFLICT IN SYRIA ARE DANGEROUSLY INACCURATE
By Patrick Cockburn
30 June 2013

Every time I come to Syria I am struck by how different the situation is on the ground from the way it is pictured in the outside world. The foreign media reporting of the Syrian conflict is surely as inaccurate and misleading as anything we have seen since the start of the First World War. I can't think of any other war or crisis I have covered in which propagandistic, biased or second-hand sources have been so readily accepted by journalists as providers of objective facts.

A result of these distortions is that politicians and casual newspaper or television viewers alike have never had a clear idea over the last two years of what is happening inside Syria. Worse, long-term plans are based on these misconceptions. A report on Syria published last week by the Brussels-based International Crisis Group says that "once confident of swift victory, the opposition's foreign allies shifted to a paradigm dangerously divorced from reality".

Slogans replace policies: the rebels are pictured as white hats and the government supporters as black hats; given more weapons, the opposition can supposedly win a decisive victory; put under enough military pressure, President Bashar al-Assad will agree to negotiations for which a pre- condition is capitulation by his side in the conflict. One of the many drawbacks of the demonising rhetoric indulged in by the incoming US National Security Adviser Susan Rice, and William Hague, is that it rules out serious negotiations and compromise with the powers-that-be in Damascus. And since Assad controls most of Syria, Rice and Hague have devised a recipe for endless war while pretending humanitarian concern for the Syrian people.

It is difficult to prove the truth or falsehood of any generalisation about Syria. But, going by my experience this month travelling in central Syria between Damascus, Homs and the Mediterranean coast, it is possible to show how far media reports differ markedly what is really happening. Only by understanding and dealing with the actual balance of forces on the ground can any progress be made towards a cessation of violence.

On Tuesday I travelled to Tal Kalakh, a town of 55,000 people just north of the border with Lebanon, which was once an opposition bastion. Three days previously, government troops had taken over the town and 39 Free Syrian Army (FSA) leaders had laid down their weapons. Talking to Syrian army commanders, an FSA defector and local people, it was evident there was no straight switch from war to peace. It was rather that there had been a series of truces and ceasefires arranged by leading citizens of Tal Kalakh over the previous year.

But at the very time I was in the town, Al Jazeera Arabic was reporting fighting there between the Syrian army and the opposition. Smoke was supposedly rising from Tal Kalakh as the rebels fought to defend their stronghold. Fortunately, this appears to have been fantasy and, during the several hours I was in the town, there was no shooting, no sign that fighting had taken place and no smoke.

Of course, all sides in a war pretend that no position is lost without a heroic defence against overwhelming numbers of the enemy. But obscured in the media's accounts of what happened in Tal Kalakh was an important point: the opposition in Syria is fluid in its allegiances. The US, Britain and the so- called 11-member "Friends of Syria", who met in Doha last weekend, are to arm non-Islamic fundamentalist rebels, but there is no great chasm between them and those not linked to al-Qa'ida. One fighter with the al-Qa'ida- affiliated al-Nusra Front was reported to have defected to a more moderate group because he could not do without cigarettes. The fundamentalists pay more and, given the total impoverishment of so many Syrian families, the rebels will always be able to win more recruits. "Money counts for more than ideology," a diplomat in Damascus told me.

While I was in Homs I had an example of why the rebel version of events is so frequently accepted by the foreign media in preference to that of the Syrian government. It may be biased towards the rebels, but often there is no government version of events, leaving a vacuum to be filled by the rebels. For instance, I had asked to go to a military hospital in the al-Waar district of Homs and was granted permission, but when I got there I was refused entrance. Now, soldiers wounded fighting the rebels are likely to be eloquent and convincing advocates for the government side (I had visited a military hospital in Damascus and spoken to injured soldiers there). But the government's obsessive secrecy means that the opposition will always run rings around it when it comes to making a convincing case.

Back in the Christian quarter of the Old City of Damascus, where I am staying, there was an explosion near my hotel on Thursday. I went to the scene and what occurred next shows that there can be no replacement for unbiased eyewitness reporting. State television was claiming that it was a suicide bomb, possibly directed at the Greek Orthodox Church or a Shia hospital that is even closer. Four people had been killed.

I could see a small indentation in the pavement which looked to me very much like the impact of a mortar bomb. There was little blood in the immediate vicinity, though there was about 10 yards away. While I was looking around, a second mortar bomb came down on top of a house, killing a woman.

The pro-opposition Syrian Observatory for Human Rights, so often used as a source by foreign journalists, later said that its own investigations showed the explosion to have been from a bomb left in the street. In fact, for once, it was possible to know definitively what had happened, because the Shia hospital has CCTV that showed the mortar bomb in the air just before it landed - outlined for a split-second against the white shirt of a passer-by who was killed by the blast. What had probably happened was part of the usual random shelling by mortars from rebels in the nearby district of Jobar.

In the middle of a ferocious civil war it is self-serving credulity on the part of journalists to assume that either side in the conflict, government or rebel, is not going to concoct or manipulate facts to serve its own interests. Yet much foreign media coverage is based on just such an assumption.

The plan of the CIA and the Friends of Syria to somehow seek an end to the war by increasing the flow of weapons is equally absurd. War will only produce more war. John Milton's sonnet, written during the English civil war in 1648 in praise of the Parliamentary General Sir Thomas Fairfax, who had just stormed Colchester, shows a much deeper understanding of what civil wars are really like than anything said by David Cameron or William Hague. He wrote:

For what can war but endless war still breed? Till truth and right from violence be freed,

And public faith clear'd from the shameful brand Of public fraud. In vain doth valour bleed

While avarice and rapine sharethe land.

VIOLENCE IS ONE THING, BUT WHAT CAUSES REAL TERROR IS THE THREAT OF KIDNAPPING
By Patrick Cockburn
11 August 2013

Numbers of dead and wounded and signs of physical destruction are usually taken as a measure of the violence and breakdown of order in any civil war. But, in practice, kidnapping can carry a greater charge of fear for a community. People are more terrified by an ever-present risk that they, their children or other relatives may be kidnapped than they are by a more momentary fear of being hit by a shell, a bomb or a bullet.

Kidnappings in Syria contribute far more to the atmosphere of insecurity and instability than is generally appreciated by non-Syrians. They are crimes that take place in the shadows, as both perpetrators and victims have an interest in keeping them secret.

Over the past year, they have become big business and everybody is vulnerable, particularly families with money since most abductions are carried out by criminal gangs working for profit. This is not the only motive - many kidnappings are tit-for-tat actions between hostile communities, either as a form of vengeance or to enable an exchange of hostages for a person held by the other side. Along the Syrian Lebanese border, Shia and Alawites have been seized to get a relative freed from a Syrian government prison. The distinction between commercial and political kidnappings is not definitive, as gangsters pretend to act on behalf of their community or in opposition to the government.

Sometimes the identity and motive of the kidnappers is frighteningly obscure, and it never becomes clear if people are being held for ransom or are already dead. What happened, for instance, to two eminent Christian clerics from Aleppo, the Greek Orthodox Bishop Boulos Yazigi and his Syriac Orthodox counterpart Yohanna Ibrahim, who went on a mission of mercy on 22 April this year into rebel-controlled territory to try to free two kidnapped priests? They were themselves abducted by a jihadi gang, which was reportedly led by Chechens, and nothing has been heard from them since, leading to fears they were murdered.

You do not have to go far in Syria or among well-off Syrians abroad to find stories of relatives kidnapped and bought back or still being held prisoner. Earlier this summer in Damascus, the Syrian deputy foreign minister, Faisal Mekdad, who comes from near Daraa in the south, told me that his 84-year- old father had been kidnapped in May and held for 14 days. His nephew had similarly been abducted and mistreated. Two senior Syrian army officers asked me not to mention their names for fear that family members might be kidnapped or killed. The situation in Syria is now getting as bad as Iraq after 2003, when I did not know a single well-off Iraqi family that had not had a close relative grabbed by gunmen and held for ransom.

Kidnappings take place largely though not exclusively in rebel areas and they are on the increase. Peter Bouckaert, the Geneva-based emergencies director of Human Rights Watch, confirms this in an interview with the website Syria Deeply: "The kidnappings have been going on for about a year," he said. "It's really intensified. It started mostly when fighting broke out in Aleppo, and has developed and grown since then into a broader trend across many parts of Syria, and is also spilling into neighbouring countries."

Kidnap gangs are becoming better organised and have good intelligence about when and where their victims will be easy to snatch. Mr Bouckaert cites the recent case of a prominent member of the Armenian community in Aleppo, who was travelling to Beirut by bus when it was stopped by gunmen who asked for him by name and took him away, knowing that the Armenian community in Damascus would pay to get him back. Again, there is an ominous parallel with Iraq, where gangs would pay informants a cut of the ransom for identifying a vulnerable and lucrative target. To this day, people selling houses in Baghdad do so without publicity because neither the seller nor the buyer wants it known that a large sum of money is about to change hands. Wealthy doctors used to be favourite targets, as kidnappers could gain easy access to them by pretending to be in need of medical attention.

Kidnappings spur flight and demoralise those who stay behind. They also have a long-term political impact. They have done much to discredit the Syrian opposition because it is in rebel-held areas that most people are seized and held (though there are stories of people being taken in government-controlled areas, too). US Senator John McCain, a militant advocate of Western help for the rebels who slipped into Syria to be photographed with rebel leaders, was embarrassed when one of them was alleged to be the kidnapper of 11 Lebanese Shia pilgrims. Two Turkish pilots were abducted from a bus outside Beirut airport last week to put pressure on Turkey to use its influence to get the pilgrims released.

The criminalisation of the opposition in Syria is following the same pattern as in Chechnya after 1999 and in Iraq after 2003. In all three cases, heroic militiamen who may have begun as defenders of their community became indistinguishable from bandits. Their former supporters came to feel that, as cruel and violent as the authorities might be, the alternative was even worse. In Chechnya, I remember going see President Aslan Maskhadov in the Chechen capital, Grozny, at the start of the Second Chechen War and noticing that his presidential guard was more worried that I and the party of foreign journalists I was with would be kidnapped than they were by possible attacks by Russian aircraft.

Many journalists who used regularly to visit rebel-held zones in Syria are expressing reluctance to continue doing so. Earlier this year, one internationally known television crew were seized by kidnappers who said they would hold them for three months and ask for $1m in ransom. In the event, they escaped after 10 days. Last year, the NBC chief correspondent, Richard Engel, and his crew were held for five days and were lucky to get free when their abductors unexpectedly ran into a checkpoint operated by another opposition group - there are 1,200 in Syria - and were shot.

Reporters Without Borders says it is "aware of a total of 15 cases of foreign journalists disappearing or being abducted in Syria".

Syrian rebels are thus losing the great advantage they had of giving greater access to reporters while the government handed out few visas. The international media may have been credulous in lapping up opposition propaganda, but the government had only itself for blame for creating a vacuum of information that was filled by its enemies.

Even rebel strongholds are no longer safe for visting foreign journalists. Two weeks ago, a Polish journalist called Marcin Suder was kidnapped from an opposition media centre by a gang of gunmen in the rebel-held town of Saraqeb in the north-western Idlib province. An opposition militant who tried to stop the kidnappers was beaten to the ground with rifle butts.

The Syrian opposition is discrediting itself in the same way as insurgents in Chechnya and Iraq. Kidnappings and the inability to provide even basic security alienate people at home and abroad. The methods of a police state begin to appear acceptable if they mean that your children can go to school in safety.

SYRIA CONFLICT: THE DARKEST DAY YET?
By Kim Sengupta
22 August 2013

The victims were laid out in a hospital, on beds and on the tiled floor, their eyes lifeless and staring. Many of them were very young children, even babies. Others were in convulsion, mouths foaming, as medics frantically tried to save them, using hand-pump respirators.

These were the scenes from videos showing, it was claimed by the Syrian opposition, the devastating aftermath of a massacre of more than 1,300 people by Bashar al-Assad's forces using chemical weapons in Ghouta, east of Damascus.

The regime has denied the allegations, accusing "terrorists and their supporters" in the international media of disseminating false propaganda.Such recriminations have become standard in the vicious civil war. But, for the first time since reports of the use of weapons of mass destruction began to circulate, there is now a United Nations inspection team not only inside the country, but in the vicinity of the affected area. It arrived in the Syrian capital on Sunday after months of negotiations with the regime to investigate three occasions where chemical agents have, allegedly, been used in the past.

One of these was at the village of Khan al-Assal near Aleppo where the two sides in the conflict accused each other of carrying out the attack resulting in 26 deaths; the location of the other two sites has not been confirmed.

A number of Western states asked the UN team to investigate the latest deaths, which prompted an emergency meeting of the UN Security Council in New York last night.

The British Foreign Secretary, William Hague, said that if the claims were verified they would "mark a shocking escalation in the use of chemical weapons". "I hope this will wake up some who have supported the Assad regime to realise its murderous and barbaric nature," he added later. Russia had backed up the Assad regime's denials, by saying the attack looked like a rebel "provocation" to discredit him.

The French President François Hollande declared it was imperative that the team be allowed "to shed full light" on what had taken place and the German Foreign Minister Guido Westerwelle demanded that the inspectors be given immediate access.

The head of the 20-strong team of inspectors, Ake Sellstrom, a scientist from Sweden, said in Damascus: "It sounds like something that should be looked into. It will depend on whether any UN member state goes to the Secretary General and says we should look at this event. We are in place to do so."

What happened was recent enough for the inspectors to be able to form a view on what had happened, according to specialists on chemical warfare. Such a development may have a major impact on the course of the conflict.

Evidence that the regime has indeed used WMDs, with such a massive number of fatalities, would greatly strengthen the hands of those pressing for large-scale supplies of advanced weapons to the rebels.

Evidence that the footage was fabricated would further dent the already fragile credibility of the disjointed opposition and weaken the position of their Western sponsors.

Ghazwan Bwidany, a doctor treating the casualties, held that the symptoms indicated the use of sarin gas. "It may be sarin, most probably it is sarin" he said. "We don't have the capacity to treat all this number of people. We're putting them in mosques, in schools. We are lacking medical supplies now, especially atropine, which is the antidote for chemical weapons."

Bayan Baker, a nurse at the Douma Emergency Collection facility, initially put the death toll at 213. "Many of those affected are women and children. They arrived with their pupils dilated, cold limbs and foam in their mouths. The doctors say these are typical symptoms of nerve gas victims."

Local co-ordination committees of activists in the area said the numbers killed had risen to 1,360, while George Sabra, the deputy chief of the Syrian National Coalition, the main umbrella group of the opposition, announced a figure of 1,300. He said: "This is the coup de grâce which kills all hopes for a political solution in Syria. This is not the first time they have used chemical weapons, but it constitutes a significant turning point; this time it was for annihilation rather than terror."

However, there are questions as to why the regime would want to have recourse to WMDs at a time when it was making gains using conventional arms and with the knowledge that UN inspectors were present in the country. "If you look at the way they have sought legitimacy through having the UN team there, in a carefully orchestrated fashion, with the help of the Russians and the Iranians, the use of chemical weapons does not make sense," said a European diplomat.

Robert Emerson, a security analyst, added: "Assad has not been doing too badly in the publicity stakes with the excesses of Islamists among the rebels like the cannibal commander, et cetera. Deploying WMDs at this stage would be a hell of an own goal."

Jean Pascal Zanders, a senior research fellow at the EU Institute for Security Studies in Paris, was also puzzled as to why the regime would carry out such an attack with UN experts there. But he continued: "It is clear that something terrible has happened. The scenes could not have been stage-managed. None of the victims appeared to have external wounds from blast, shrapnel or bullets. The footage seems to offer more convincing evidence of poisoning through asphyxiation - witness the pinkish-bluish hue on the faces of some of the fatalities. Further elements that seem to confirm exposure to toxicants are the unfocused and rolling eyes, severe breathing difficulties and possible signs of urination or defecation on trousers."

Autumn 2013

Hopes For A Hollywood Ending

ONCE WASHINGTON MADE THE MIDDLE EAST TREMBLE - NOW NO ONE THERE TAKES IT SERIOUSLY
By Robert Fisk
2 September 2013

Watershed. It's the only word for it. Once Lebanon and Syria and Egypt trembled when Washington spoke. Now they laugh. It's not just a question of what happened to the statesmen of the past. No one believed that Cameron was Churchill or that the silly man in the White House was Roosevelt - although Putin might make a rather good Stalin. It's more a question of credibility; no one in the Middle East takes America seriously anymore. And you only had to watch Obama on Saturday to see why.

For there he was, prattling on in the most racist way about "ancient sectarian differences" in the Middle East. Since when was the president of the United States an expert on these supposed "sectarian differences"?

Constantly we are shown maps of the Arab world with Shias and Sunnis and Christians colour-coded onto the nations which we generously bequeathed to the region after the First World War. But when is an American paper going to carry a colour-coded map of Washington or Chicago with black and white areas delineated by streets?

But what was amazing was the sheer audacity of our leaders in thinking that they could yet again bamboozle their electorates with their lies and trumperies and tomfooleries.

This doesn't mean that the Syrian regime did not use gas "on its own people" - a phrase we used to use about Saddam when we wanted a war in Iraq - but it does mean that our present leaders are now paying the price for the dishonesty of Bush and Blair.

Obama, who is becoming more and more preacher-like, wants to be the Punisher-in-Chief of the Western World, the Avenger-in-Chief. There is something oddly Roman about him. And the Romans were good at two things. They believed in law and they believed in crucifixion. The US consititution - American "values" and the cruise missile have a faintly similar focus. The lesser races must be civilized and they must be punished, even if the itsy-bitsy tiny missile launches look more like perniciousness than war.

Everyone outside the Roman Empire was called a barbarian. Everyone outside Obama's empire is called a terrorist.

And as usual, the Big Picture has a habit of taking away some of the little details we should know about.

Take Afghanistan, for example. I had an interesting phone call from Kabul three days ago. And it seems that the Americans are preventing President Karzai purchasing new Russian Mi helicopters - because Moscow sells the same helicopters to Syria. Well, how about that. The US, it seems, is now trying to damage Russian trade relations with Afghanistan - why the Afghans would want to do business with the country that enslaved them for eight years is another matter - because of Damascus.

Now another little piece of news. Just over a week ago, two massive car bombs blew up outside two Salafist mosques in the north Lebanese city of Tripoli. They killed 47 people and wounded another 500. Now it has emerged that five people have been charged by the Lebanese security services over these bombings and one of them is said to be a captain in the Syrian government intelligence service.

His charge is "in absentia", as they say, and we all like to think that men and women are innocent until proved guilty. But two sheikhs have also been charged, one of them apparently the head of a pro-Damascus Islamist organization. The other sheikh is also said to be close to Syrian intelligence. Typically, Obama is so keen on bombarding Syria for gassing that he has missed out on this nugget of information which has angered and infuriated millions of Lebanese.

But I guess this is what happens when you take your eye off the ball.

It reminds me of a book that was published by Yale University Press in 2005. It was called The New Lion of Damascus by David Lesch, a professor at Trinity University in Texas. Those were the days when

Bashar al-Assad was still being held up as the bright new broom in Syria.

"Bashar," Lesch concluded, "is, indeed, the hope - and the promise of a better future."

Then last year - by which time the West had abandoned its dreams of Bashar - the good professor came up with another book, again published by Yale. This time it was called Syria: The Fall of the House of Assad, and Lesch concluded: "He (Bashar) was short-sighted and became deluded. He failed miserably."

VIOLENCE BURSTS IN TO SHATTER CHRISTIANS' MOUNTAIN REFUGE
By Patrick Cockburn
8 September 2013

At the end of last year I visited the ancient Christian town of Maloula in a deep gorge in the mountains 20 miles north-west of Damascus. It has been a place of refuge for 2,000 years, its cliffs riddled with caves and its buildings clinging to towering walls of rock. It is one of the few towns in Syria where Christians are a majority and the only place where Western Aramaic, the language of Jesus, is still spoken.

People in Maloula were nervous when I was there, wondering just how long they would remain immune or at least largely unaffected by the violence that had engulfed the rest of Syria. Already, they were feeling its impact, mostly in the shape of criminal attacks on well-off Christians.

Maloula's uncertain immunity from the civil war in Syria lasted for another nine months. But, at 5.40am last Wednesday, a suicide bomber in a vehicle packed with explosives blew himself up at the checkpoint, killing some eight soldiers. Then, 20 pick-up trucks with machine guns mounted in the back stormed into the town, firing into the air. They took over an ugly white- washed hotel on top of a cliff as their command post and told people to stay in their houses. There was no resistance and fighting only started when the Syrian army arrived later in the day, government aircraft bombed and the rebels finally retreated. Heavy fighting around Maloula was reported yesterday.

What happened during the capture of Maloula is revealed in convincing detail by Matthew Barber in the online newsletter Syria

Comment. He has rapidly combined film and statements by the insurgents with phone interviews with local people. The result is that, unlike most episodes in the Syrian war, it is possible to follow events with a fair degree of accuracy.

Going by their own declarations, the rebel units were mostly from jihadi groups led by the al-Qa'ida-linked Jabhat al-Nusra and including the Ahrar al-Sham, the Baba Amr brigade and the Free Syrian Army (FSA) commando unit. Local people say they were aided by Sunni Muslim refugees from the militant town of Douma on the outskirts of Damascus.

This is not a story of sectarian bloodbath, but the Christians in Maloula must have worried that it could turn into one. One rebel group called the operation a case of "an eye for an eye" in retaliation for the poison gas attack on rebel-held Ghouta on 21 August. There are postings with quotes from the Koran saying "Allah give us patience and victory over the infidel". Pictures taken by the insurgents show the bodies of Syrian army soldiers killed by the suicide bomber. The insurgent fighters finally retreated, but not before they had demonstrated that they considered Maloula a stronghold of government supporters. As with other such clashes, the government sent aircraft to bomb rebel positions, a tactic that has done so much to turn millions of Syrians into refugees inside and outside the country.

The occupation of Maloula illuminates other developments in Syria that differ markedly from what is being reported by the media or said by the Obama administration in an attempt to win Congressional assent for air strikes. On 5 September, the very day the al-Nusra stormed Maloula, the US Secretary of State, John Kerry, told a Congressional hearing about the rebels: "I just don't agree that a majority are al-Qa'ida and the bad guys. That's not true. There are about 70,000 to 100,000 oppositionists... Maybe 15 per cent to 25 per cent might be in one group or another who are what we would deem to be bad guys." Rebel commanders have been happily assuring American newspaper columnists that the supposedly moderate FSA is dominant around Damascus, unlike northern and eastern Syria.

The attack on Maloula is evidence of another aspect of the war: after its successes in the early summer in the battle for Qusayr, government forces have not been as successful on the battlefront as many expected. They have made some advances in Homs but still do not hold the whole city. If they did use poison gas against rebel-held suburbs in Damascus it may have been frustration at the army's inability to capture them by other means and its lack of manpower to sustain the casualties inevitable in street fighting.

Maloula is not far from the main Damascus-Homs road, emphasising that this crucial highway could be cut by the insurgents if they are prepared to take the losses.

Maloula used to be one of the safer places in Syria for Christians, who once made up 10 per cent of the population. Many have already fled from Aleppo and northern Syria. Their priests and bishops have been kidnapped and murdered. In their part of the Old City of Damascus they are under mortar fire from rebel districts leaving no doubt that they are being punished as government supporters. Those with money have mostly left the country. Even a previously secure place in the mountains such as Maloula, where persecuted Christians once sought refuge, is safe no longer.

Suppose US missile strikes take place, will they tip the military balance decisively towards the insurgents? It looks unlikely, though elimination of the Syrian air force would enable the rebels to gain ground. The stalemate will continue. Syria has a failed government and a failed opposition. Both still think they can win if they get enough outside support but have few ideas other than to fight on. The only good news here is that government and rebels have become so much the dependent proxies of foreign powers that the US and Russia could force them to negotiate at least a ceasefire. But this may come too late for Maloula.

CUT! OBAMA'S HOPES FOR A HOLLYWOOD ENDING IN SYRIA WERE ALWAYS GOING TO END IN TRAGEDY
By Robert Fisk
16 September 2013

What on earth was going on in Washington and Geneva last week? I'm not trying to cheapen the unspeakable tragedy of Syria, nor the apparent common sense that suddenly gripped world leaders on Saturday when the US and Russia agreed a framework for the destruction of Syria's chemical weapons, but the Obama administration is still getting weirder and weirder. First - and let's remember the narrative of events - Obama last year was really, terribly, awfully worried that Syria's chemical weapons would "fall into the wrong hands". In other words, he was frightened they would fall into the hands of al-Qa'ida or the al-Nusra front. Seemingly they were still, at that moment, in the "right hands" - those of the regime of President Bashar al-Assad of Syria. But now Obama and the US Secretary of State, John Kerry, have decided that they are in the wrong hands after all, since they are now accusing the "right hands" of firing sarin gas shells at civilians. And that crosses the infamous "red line".

I am overlooking, for the moment, the almost magical moment when Kerry told the world that America's strike would be "unbelievably small", followed by Obama telling us all that he doesn't do "pin pricks". What does all this twaddle mean?

And then - wait for it - as the Russian President, Vladimir Putin, suggested an international collection of all the rusty old chemical shells in Syria, Pentagon "sources" said it would need up to 75,000 armed troops to protect the chemical inspectors. Seventy-five thousand! If that isn't boots on the ground, I don't know what is.

And all this amid yet more nonsense in America last week about Hitler and the Second World War. Maybe the Americans should offer 250,000 men and see if Putin won't pitch in with another quarter of a million and the two great statesman can recreate the Grand Alliance of Yalta - Cameron, I'm afraid, doesn't get to play Churchill this time round - and do a re-run of the Second World War in Syria with live bullets: D-Day, Arnhem - no, on reflection perhaps not Arnhem - Stalingrad, the Battle of the Kursk Salient, the whole shebang. Believe me, the convoys would stretch for miles.

Of course, Putin and Lavrov kept clear of references to the Second World War. Russia suffered too grievously from the real Hitler for that. I've said this before, but I really do suspect that leaders who have no experience of war - I am excepting McCain and the indefatigable UN envoy Lakhdar Brahimi here - actually thought they were making a Hollywood movie.

Kerry's preposterous "unbelievably small" strike is obviously a low budget film for recession-hit America. Obama promises widescreen drama. Think Steven Spielberg. And then the Russians, who can spot a dead cat when they see one, zap the whole project.

None of the above should cheapen the unspeakable tragedy of Syria. The world, I suspect, is not totally convinced that the regime was responsible for using chemical weapons in Ghouta on 21 August - though I bet the Russians know who did. Now we've got rebels chopping off prisoners' heads, I'm not sure what scruples they'd have about using sarin. But it was interesting to see the Syrian government agreeing to put their chemical weapons in international hands - I couldn't help noticing that they didn't demand the same of the insurgents...

But without dismissing the Geneva shenanigans out of hand, let's have a closer look at the Kerry-Lavrov timetable. The Syrians have to come up with a list of their nasties within a week. Inspectors are to be on the ground by mid-November. Then every chemical weapon has got to be destroyed (or "secured") by the middle of next year. And this amid a civil war! Peace in our time. O brave new world.

Of course, while the inspectors are battering their way through the front lines - if Assad hasn't got all his weapons in Tartous, Banias and Lattakia on the Mediterranean coast, which I suspect - the Syrians continue to kill each other, the Syrian government goes on trying to break the rebels and the Islamist insurgents go on attacking Christian towns and chopping off the heads of captives. Put bluntly, they can use rifles, shells, knives and swords to slaughter each other - but absolutely no sarin. There is something deeply offensive and deeply cynical about all this. Russia re-enters the Middle East, Obama is off the hook after playing World War 2 - and the Syrians go on dying.

I do hope that all this will work, that we will have a "Geneva 2" conference at last, and that America and Russia will no longer spat over the Syrian bloodbath. But I am not at all sure the rebels will go along with this, because Assad is clearly not leaving power. Not now, anyway. And the Saudis? And the Qataris? And any other Gulf Sunnis who've been funding and arming the rebels? And the whole timetable seems so hopelessly optimistic that I wonder what Kerry and Lavrov put in their coffee in Geneva before addressing the press. For there are fearful pitfalls along the way.

However, there is another story going on here, and that's Iran. For now, the leader of Iran appears to be a wise and sane man, Putin can surely resurrect his own ideas on Iranian nuclear material, and the Iranian-Syrian alliance could be hooked up together to end the whole miserable failure of politics and perhaps even the war in Syria. Then Obama can claim a world-shaking political victory (brought about only by his threat to use force, of course) and Kerry can go back to making peace between Palestinians and Israelis.

And now that the Egyptian army is helping the Israeli army enforce the siege of Gaza again, Obama could find a few old Dakotas and run a postwar Berlin- style airlift to drop food and fuel to the Palestinians below. Ah, just another movie.

A sinister warning for the Druze militia leader as his mother dies.

A week ago, one of Lebanon's great ladies died. At 85 years old, Princess May Shakib Arslan was the widow of humanist, philosopher and politician Kamal Jumblatt, who was murdered in 1977 - so the family are convinced - by Syrian assassins. Ms Arslan was also the mother of Walid Jumblatt, the present Druze leader, head of the ruthless Druze militia in the Lebanese civil war and perhaps the bravest current critic of the Syrian regime. Thousands trooped to her funeral in Mukhtara, hundreds queued to offer their condolences.

But one sinister, indeed venomous letter arrived at the Jumblatt home from a certain General Jamil Sayyed, the former - and very pro-Syrian - director of Lebanon's General Security. General Sayyed is a man you listen to. Here is part of what he wrote: "I hope in these sad circumstances and in view of the genuine tears you have shed over your late mother, that you yourself remember... the thousands of mothers, widows and orphans that you made cry through the killings you perpetrated in your wars... I implore the mercy of God for [Princess May Shakib Arslan's] soul and his forgiveness for all sins that she accidentally or deliberately committed. It is not her fault that she made you as you are. It's not too late for Jumblatt to ask forgiveness or change who he is."

Is it a warning?

AS THE WEST LOOKS AWAY, THE ISLAMISTS CLAIM SYRIA'S REBELLION FOR THEMSELVES
By Kim Sengupta
26 November 2013

One of the last scenes we saw heading out of Syria was a convoy near Aleppo, a long, snaking line coming from the east in a swirl of dust.

The passengers on the flat-bed trucks and cars, riding pillion on motor bikes, waved their Kalashnikovs and rocket-propelled grenade launcher. They flew the black flag of al-Qa'ida.

These were the fighters of a group named ISIS, the Islamic State of Iraq and Syria, returning after it had become quite clear that despite all the threats, Barack Obama was not going to take military action over the crossing of his "red line" on chemical weapons by Bashar al-Assad's forces.

ISIS and Jabhat al-Nusra, the other main Islamist organisation among the rebels, had convinced themselves that the US would take the opportunity of air strikes on the regime to target them as well. Elaborate security precautions had been taken, moving men, weapons and Western hostages away from their bases, in some instances all the way to Anbar province in Iraq.

That was two months ago. Since then, Syria's chemical stock, at least the portion of it that was in regime hands, is in the process of being destroyed. But no one knows when the supposed next stage in the process, the Geneva II talks aimed towards a negotiated settlement, will ever actually take place despite yet another date being set for January.

Meanwhile the killings have continued; hundreds of civilians and also of fighters on both sides. The rebels, however, are not just getting killed by regime forces, but also by ISIS and Jabhat al-Nusra. This reached the ghoulish depths of farce when they executed a fellow Islamist, a member of the Ansar al-Sham "by mistake".

Mohammed Fares was captured and had the misfortune to think that his captors were the Shabiha, the militia of the Alawite community from which President Assad and the ruling elite are drawn. In a desperate hope of ingratiating himself, he took the names of the Shia imams, Ali and Hussein; the enraged Sunnis of ISIS promptly beheaded him.

Other killings have not been through mistakes. Two of those I met in Syria in September, members of the relatively moderate Farouq Brigade, have died fighting against ISIS. Kamal Hammami, a senior officer in the Free Syria Army (FSA), which is supposedly in charge of the opposition militias, had gone to try and prevent a sectarian massacre by besieging rebels and was shot dead, also by members of ISIS.

Last week, one of the highest profile of the rebel commanders was eliminated - this time not killed by fellow rebels but the regime in an air strike. But the life and death of Abdulkader al-Saleh, who most of us knew as Hajji Marea, was intrinsically linked to the deep divisions in the opposition. We had first met him last year as a co-leader of the Tawhid, one of the largest brigades taking part in the battle for Aleppo. His fame grew rapidly and we would often see the tall and rangy figure, a former honey merchant, at the front lines of fighting in the city.

I travelled with him on a number of occasions when he would maintain that, with international help for the revolution, President Assad could be toppled within weeks.

But as the power of the Islamist groups grew, the power of Tawhid declined. Many of its members were killed or driven out by ISIS. Hajji Marea did not confront the Islamists, insisting that doing so would have just led to more bloodshed, and he believed that he could achieve more through mediation.

Not everyone supported his stance. One of them, Abu Haitham, who left Syria disillusioned and is now staying across the border in Turkey, reflected: "I felt sorry, of course, on a personal level for Hajji Marea's death, but at the end many of us felt that he gave up what we as a khatiba (battalion) stood for, he gave in to the Salafis. Who knows who gave his location to regime so they could kill him?"

But others also bear much responsibility. George Sabra, until recently the acting president of the Syrian National Coalition, the opposition government in exile which replaced the dysfunctional National Council, gave a fulsome public eulogy for the dead commander.

But the disunity of the opposition politicians has ensured they lack authority in the rebel-held parts of the country, allowing the extremists to hold sway.

And what of the Western states which encouraged Syrians to rise up and then did little while the Gulf states armed al-Nusra and ISIS?

In an interview with my colleague from The Daily Telegraph Richard Spencer, Hajji Marea had been scathingly dismissive of the type of aid that was being given to the rebels by Britain. "Mr Hague after all this bombing of the city said he would send us 'communications devices'. It's like coming to a man who is dying and offering him sunglasses."

There is a price to pay for this. Syria has now superseded Pakistan as the first choice of Muslims from the UK seeking terrorist training. They post messages on social networks inviting other to join the "five-star jihad".

The head of MI5, Andrew Parker, has echoed his predecessor in pointing out the risk that this development poses to Britain.

The moderate fighters in Syria, meanwhile, feel that they have been abandoned by the West where public opinion increasingly sees all the rebels as extremists.

The West has ensured that Bashar al-Assad has got the enemy he wanted.

Winter 2014

Destroying The Past Too

THE ROAD FROM IRAQ TO DAMASCUS
By Patrick Cockburn
5 December 2013

In Damascus, Shia men from Iraq fight to the death to defend the Shia shrine of Sayyida Zaynab, the daughter of Ali and Fatimah and the grand- daughter of the Prophet Mohamed. They battle with less enthusiasm, however, for the Baathist government of President Bashar al-Assad, which reminds them of the regime of Saddam Hussein.

Sattar Khalaf, an Iraqi wounded in Damascus, says: "Fighting in Syria is to defend the shrines of the Prophet's family and not the regime of Bashar al- Assad and the Baath Party."

This is not always a distinction easily made. Shia leaders say that at any one time there are between 3,800 and 4,700 Iraqi fighters in Syria, but new volunteers have not been registered for the last five months. The 20 million Shia Mulims in Iraq feel threatened by the Sunni-dominated opposition in Syria's bid to overthrow the regime there, and its repercussions in Iraq. The Islamic State of Iraq and the Levant (Isil), the al-Qa'ida umbrella organisation which has been fighting against Syrian regime forces, draws no distinction between its attacks on the Syrian army and non-Sunni Syrians. In Iraq, Shia and Kurdish civilians are its main target.

But the Shia political and religious leadership in Iraq is reluctant to be drawn into the war next door despite Iranian promptings. Grand Ayatollah Ali al-Sistani and the Shia religious establishment have refused to issue a fatwa calling for Iraqi Shia to go to fight in Syria, though they have not condemned those who do volunteer. In contrast to the Iranian religious authorities in Qom, the message from their Iraqi counterparts in Najaf is more emphatic that Muslims should not fight Muslims.

Iraqi fighters cross into Syria by land, though the road via the Sunni Anbar province is so dangerous that they fly instead by plane to Damascus from Baghdad or Najaf. Flights have been easier since the Syrian army cleared the area around the international airport. Sattar Khalaf, a 43-year-old from Baghdad who was part of 200-strong detachment travelling on five buses, says, "When we got into Syrian territory we were escorted by Syrian troops along the long road that was under the control of the army."

He joined a group whose overall leader was an Iranian colonel. "The day I entered the shrine of Sayyida Zaynab I joined a group of a dozen fighters and our job was to plant bombs on road sides surrounding the area where the shrine is." Other fighters with him were told to make hit-and-run attacks using rocket-propelled grenade launchers or to take part in street fighting.

He says, "In April I was hit in my shoulder while fighting near the airport and was taken back to Baghdad. Once I recover from my wound I will continue jihad in defending the shrine of Sayyida Zaynab." He reckons between 12 and 20 Iraqi volunteers are being killed in Syria every month.

The Iraqi volunteers fighting in Syria are not as significant militarily as the experienced and battle-hardened Hezbollah units from Lebanon. They have played an important role as assault troops in capturing the strategic town of Qusayr near Homs, and in aiding the Syrian army in its advance into rebel- held parts of south Damascus.

Overall, foreign volunteers are less numerous among the pro-Assad forces than they are among the rebels. But the Iraqis' presence underlines the degree to which Syria has become the main battle ground in the conflict between Shia and Sunni that is raging across the Muslim world. Last week, a jihadist group in Derna in Libya released a video of the shooting of an Iraqi Shia professor, Khalaf Hassan al-Sa'idi, shot in revenge for Sunni insurgents being executed by the Shia-led government in Baghdad.

Iran has been keen to encourage Iraqi Shia to fight in Syria and many of those who have done so come from Iranian-influenced groups such as Asa'ib Ahl al-Haq with between 2,000 and 3,000 fighters in Iraq in addition to some 800 combat-experienced troops from Hezbollah in Iraq (different from the Lebanese group of the same name). The motives of the men who volunteer for service are a mixture of ideology and poverty. "Ordinary fighters were offered a $700

(£427) a month salary, ex-fighters were paid according to their rank," says Sattar Khalaf. "The non-commissioned officers with battle experience were offered $850 monthly and former officers' salaries depended on their rank, starting from $1,500 per month."

These are tempting sums in a society like Iraq where so many are jobless. Ghafil Khayoun Khadim is a 38-year-old unemployed construction worker with a wife and two children who lives in a tough Shia neighbourhood in east Baghdad. His story is worth recounting at length because it explains why so many men with little desire to fight anybody join militias not only in Iraq but in Syria, Lebanon and Libya.

Ghafil says he had no work in July and "I found myself penniless, my kids hungry and my wife in need of money, so I came around to the idea of fighting in Syria." Another motive was that he is self-consciously Shia and "it is my duty to defend the shrine of the Sayyida Zaynab." He received $500 up front and some military training.

Ghafil says he learned early on that there were two types of fighter: the ideologues who belonged to political parties and were well-trained, and the less political recruits who are taught "to disassemble and reassemble weapons."

His group was flown to Damascus airport from where he was driven to the Sayyida Zaynab district. Next morning they were split up into units of 12, with his units consisting of seven Iraqis, two Iranians, a Lebanese leader, a Syrian captain and a civilian Syrian fighter.

What happened next was unexpected. Ghafil, who seems a little naive, said Iraqi militiamen at the shrine were praying for six martyrs killed in the fighting who had not died near the shrine itself. He says, "I showed astonishment, saying our mission is to defend Sayyida Zaynab shrine, not the Syrian regime and its army, but nobody listened to me." A Syrian army vehicle took Ghafil's unit to a position an hour's drive away to the airport road where they took up positions: "They told us that the enemy might attack us at any time and we should shoot at anybody."

Ghafil refused to fire his gun, saying he would only fight for the shrine and, if this did not happen, then he demanded to be taken back to Iraq, which was what ultimately happened. He says his friends and relatives in Baghdad are unsympathetic and believe he should have stayed and fought.

But he is adamant he did the right thing saying, "The reason I came back to my country is that I volunteered to fight in defence of

Sayyida Zaynab shrine and not in defence of the Baathist regime in Syria."

WEST SUSPENDS AID FOR ISLAMIST REBELS IN SYRIA
By Patrick Cockburn
12 December 2013

Britain and America decided to suspend deliveries of non-lethal aid to Islamist rebels operating in northern Syria yesterday after fighters from the Islamic Front drove the Western-backed Free Syrian Army (FSA) out of bases and warehouses containing American-supplied equipment in the north-western Syrian province of Idlib.

The significance of the British and US action is that it underlines their disillusionment with the Syrian rebels opposed to President Bashar al- Assad, whom they once lauded as the future rulers of Syria. Washington and London have been trying to target aid to groups opposed to the Islamic State of Iraq and the Levant (ISIL), the umbrella group for al-Qa'ida in Iraq and Syria, and the al-Nusra Front, another extreme jihadi Sunni military organisation.

In this case Britain and the US are moving against the Islamic Front, an alliance of leading rebel groups including Ahrar al-Sham, Liwa al-Tawhid, Liwa al-Haq, Ansar al-Sham and the Kurdish Islamic Front, all with good relations with the al-Nusra Front.

Saudi Arabia has started to take a stronger leadership role in funding Syrian rebels since last summer, replacing Qatar which previously cooperated with Turkey in supporting the insurgency in Syria. Saudi willingness to spend seemingly limitless funds and the creation of the Islamic Front has inevitably weakened the Free Syrian Army's Supreme Military Council and the Western-backed National Coalition, and is likely to increase fragmentation among rebels inside and outside Syria's borders.

Louay Meqdad, a spokesperson for the FSA, said the move by the US and Britain yesterday was rushed and mistaken. "We hope our friends will rethink and wait for a few days when things will be clearer," he said.

American intelligence officials estimate that there are around 1,200 rebel military units operating in Syria, ranging from groups based on extended families to those able to field several thousand fighters.

THE SYRIAN REBELS HAVE TAKEN ICONOCLASM TO NEW DEPTHS, WITH THEIR DESTRUCTION OF SHRINES, STATUES AND EVEN A TREE - BUT TO WHAT END?
By Robert Fisk
23 December 2013

Eccentricity marks the path to heaven or hell. Take the Takfiri rebels trying to overthrow Bashar al-Assad's regime in Syria. They have chopped off the heads of their enemies, eaten a few human entrails, massacred Christians and Alawites - the Damascus government, of course, has done its share of civilian bloodletting and war crimes - and even gone to war on the Kurds. But of all the activities of the al-Qa'ida/al-Nusra/Islamic State of Iraq and Greater Syria insurgents in Syria, surely the weirdest has been an iconoclasm worthy of both Henry VIII and the Taliban: the destruction of shrines, tombs and the statues of poets and caliphs.

Take, for example, Abu Tammam Habib ibn Aws who was born near Damascus AD804. He was assistant to a weaver and the son of Christian parents - an obvious provocation to the Nusra lads 2,213 years later - but travelled to Egypt to study poetry. He went to Armenia and Iran, and produced an anthology of other poets' work known as the Hamasah, an anthology of bravery, courage in defeat and revenge.

A work, you might think, that could appeal to the Salafists anxious to rid Syria of its infidel president. But no. In his native town of Jasim in the countryside of Deraa this year, the Islamists destroyed his statue. They simply blew it up with explosives. Was it because he had Christian parents? Unlikely, surely, since some of the current followers of al-Nusra are Muslim converts. Or was it because Abu Tammam brazenly compared the composition of poetry to the sex act? May he be turned to dust!

So let's move on to Abu al-Ala Ahmad ibn Abd Allah al-Ma'arri, who was born almost 170 years after Abu Tammam near Aleppo, the ancient city currently split between rebel and government fighters.

Like Milton, al-Ma'arri was almost blind, but produced a popular collection of poetry called The Tinder Spark and later, in Baghdad - where he was adored by writers but lived in almost hermit-like isolation on a vegetarian diet - wrote Unnecessary Necessity, which complained about the rhyming scheme of poetry. More dodgy, however, al-Ma'arri also described a Dante-like visit to heathen poets in paradise. And a later work was described as a parody of the Koran. He believed, so we are told, in "social justice" - whatever that was in the 9th century - but thought a world without children would spare future generations the pain of life.

Well, you can understand why the al-Nusra boys scratched their heads when they saw al-Ma'arri's turbaned statue. For the poor chap is also credited with telling his readers: "Do not suppose the statements of the prophets to be true... The sacred books are only such a set of idle tales as any age could have..." So off with his head! The al-Nusra guys decapitated the statue in al-Ma'arri's home town of Maarat al-Numan.

Then we come to Harun ar-Rashid himself, the fifth Abbasid caliph of One Thousand and One Nights fame, who ruled Islam's greatest empire, putting down revolts - Assad-style - in Syria, Egypt and Yemen, even bringing Tunisia under his rule. He became an immensely wealthy man whose wife insisted that only gold and silver would hold food on the family table. The palace was packed with singing girls, concubines and servant girls. But... word had it that he maintained a homosexual relationship with Jafar, one of his principal administrators, who was later executed. Luxury, concubines, vice. No chance, then, for Harun's statue in the city of Rakaa - the only town in Syria currently under total Islamist control. His image, in the city's Ar-Rashid Park, no less, was destroyed.

Need one go on? The shrine of the Prophet's companion Hujr ibn Adi has been destroyed in Rif Damascus (the countryside around the capital) and a shrine to a Sufi sheikh in Busaira has been blown up. The Islamists have even announced the cutting down of a 150-year-old tree in the town of Atmeh - next to another shrine which the Salafists had taken over. "Thank God Almighty, the tree... has been removed, after people were worshipping it instead of God," an Islamist informed a French news agency.

But what's new? Didn't the Taliban destroy the Buddhas of Bamiyan, just as the Saudis have reduced every old building in Mecca to rubble and the Islamists hundreds of shrines in Pakistan? Not to mention the destruction in Timbuktu. Think Henry VIII. Think Oliver Cromwell - who would surely have understood the cruelty of the Syrian war. And beware graven images. Pity about the tree.

GRAVEDIGGERS STAY BUSY IN SYRIA AS PEACE TALKS END IN FAILURE
By Patrick Cockburn
1 February 2014

The first session of the Geneva II peace negotiations, which ended yesterday, were more of a failure than they look. It was the sort of international conference of which the sponsors say that useful spadework was done and sceptics respond that the only spades in evidence were those of the grave diggers: some 1,870 Syrians were killed during the week of the peace talks.

For negotiations to have any hope of success they must reflect the balance of power on the ground in Syria. It is all very well for US Secretary of State John Kerry to state that the meeting would be entirely about political transition in Syria during which President Bashar al-Assad should leave power. But why should Mr Assad do anything of the sort when his forces hold 13 out 14 Syrian provincial capitals and are slowly retaking districts in Damascus, Homs and Aleppo captured by rebels in 2012?

If Mr Kerry is sincere in believing that peace can only come if Mr Assad goes, then he is in practice assuming a radical change in the present balance of forces in Syria which could only happen through a long war or full-scale foreign military intervention. The approach of the US and its European allies so far dooms Syrians to devastation and a repeat performance of the Lebanese civil war which lasted 15 years between 1975 and 1990.

It is not that Mr Assad's forces are likely to win a decisive victory. They may be inching their way forward but the rebels still hold great swathes of territory in the north and east of the country. The Syrian Army is short of troops, which must explain why it is blockading rather than recapturing small opposition enclaves in Damascus, Homs and Aleppo. Overall, there is a military stalemate that is unlikely to be broken.

The opposition is in a worse state than ever. It is not only divided but since 3 January is fighting its own civil war within the civil war. The ferocious Islamic State of Iraq and the Levant (ISIS) holds territory to the east and their opponents to the west of Aleppo, while they battle for control of supply lines to Turkey to the north. No outright winner is emerging. The only chance for the opposition to change their military fortunes would be a very long war in which they were fully backed by Saudi Arabia, the Gulf monarchies and Turkey.

These states might calculate that since the majority in Syria is Sunni Arab they will eventually win. But keep in mind that the supposedly "moderate" wing of the Syrian opposition is currently fighting alongside Jabhat al-Nusra, the official Syrian representative of al-Qa'ida. The Alawi, Christians, Druze and Shia - possibly together with the Sunni Kurds - know there is no place for minorities in a Syria run by the present opposition. The Syrian Army may have difficulty getting enough recruits, but in the Christian area where I am staying in Damascus, the young men volunteer to fight Jabhat al-Nusra, attacking their co-religionists in the mountains west of the capital.

So-called confidence-building measures like food being distributed to besieged places like the Old City of Homs and Yarmouk Camp in Damascus are good in themselves. Hungry people get to eat. Sick children live who would have died. But it is doubtful how much confidence is really created between two sides that hate and distrust each other so much. The crimes are not all on one side. The opposition is calling loudly for food and medicine for 2,500 starving people in the Old City of Homs besieged by the government, but it keeps quiet about the rebels' own siege of 45,000 Shia in the towns of Zahraa and Nubl outside Aleppo.

Any attempt at transitional government at this stage in the conflict will not work because power cannot be shared by people who want to kill each other. The only way that power can really be shared at this moment is on a geographical basis whereby each side holds the territory it currently controls under a ceasefire agreement. Given the fragmentation of the rebels this would probably mean a series of local ceasefires in different places.

The days leading up to and during the peace talks were marked by accusations of war crimes against the Syrian government: there were the pictures of tortured and starved prisoners and a report on the demolition of whole neighbourhoods by government forces. But it would be a mistake for foreign observers to imagine that the unpopularity of the Syrian government translates into support for the rebels. As one Syrian in Damascus put it: "These days the people hate them both equally for having ruined our country and are desperate for the war to end."

THE REBEL STRONGHOLD IN THE SKIES
By Patrick Cockburn
4 February 2014

The battle lines of the Syrian civil war are edging closer to Krak des Chevaliers, the most famous Crusader castle ever built. The massive walls and towers of the great fortress on its hilltop glistened white in the sunshine yesterday, as the Syrian Army fought rebels in the valleys below.

The rebels hold the castle and the two nearby villages of al-Zara and al-Hosn while much of the rest of this area, 25 miles west of Homs city and just north of the Lebanese border, is inhabited by Christians who support the government. The 13th century castle was damaged by a Syrian air force attack and mortars last year and the Syrian government says it is eager to prevent further damage.

"We launched an operation to retake this area last week," the governor of Homs, Talal al Barazi, told The Independent. He said that so far the army had taken 50 per cent of al-Zara "and we think the rest of it will be in our hands within a week." Syrian army officers on the spot were more cautious on how long the fighting was going to last, saying it might be a week or two.

The reason why the Syrian army is attacking has less to do with Krak des Chevaliers' strength as a defensive position and more to do with strategic importance of the area in which it stands. This commands the main road between Homs and Tartous on the coast, just as it did in the 13th century when the castle was rebuilt in its present form by the Knights Hospitaller (its original and less romantic name was Crac de l'Ospital).

But Mr Barazi says of more immediate importance is the gas and oil pipelines and electric power lines that run through al-Zara which the rebels can sever at any time. They blew up the Homs-Tartous oil pipeline at al-Zara on 3 January and recently cut the power line leaving Homs city without electricity for 24 hours.

The fighting has led to losses on both sides. Mr Barazi said he had just come back from a hospital in Tal Kalakh, a town just south of Krak, after a day's fighting in which the army "had lost 10 dead and 27 wounded, while we killed 65 terrorists and captured five of them." The battle had eased off yesterday, a day of intense cold for Syria which saw part of the country under snow.

A further reason for the army's push towards Krak and the land around it has to do with the sectarian geography of this part of Syria. The two centres held by the rebels, al Zara-and al-Hosn, the latter just below the castle, are Sunni Muslim and sympathetic to the rebels, but the other villages are Christian and support the Syrian government, often joining the National Defence Force militia.

This part of Syria is much like Lebanon when it comes to sectarian diversity and long-held animosities exacerbated by the civil war.

Syrian army officers said that these worsened recently when two Christians, a man and a women, had a late dinner at a hotel called the Alwadi and were stopped by armed men as they drove home. "As soon as they said they came from a nearby Christian village called Marmarita they were killed," said an officer. In another sectarian killing a Muslim from al-Hosn village was reportedly killed by Christian militiamen.

These stories of sectarian atrocities by all sides may be exaggerated in the telling, but there is no doubt about the extent to which they produce an atmosphere of hatred. An officer in Tal Kalakh produced a picture on his phone of the severed heads of two men being held by what he says were two young rebels inside al-Zara.

The army is getting closer to Krak des Chevalliers but will they try to take it? And, given the way in which the Syrian army relies on its artillery and aerial bombing, might it be destroyed?

Mr Barazi says they are conscious of Krak's historic significance and will do everything to avoid damaging it. But the castle used to hold a garrison of 2,000 men at the height of its power before it was captured by the Mamluk Sultan Baibars in 1271. It could probably give a good account of itself still. On the other hand, the Syrian army strategy has been to blockade places held by the rebels but only to launch ground attacks against those that are strategically important. This is true of the town of al-Zara with its proximity to gas pipelines and electric power lines. Krak might well be spared for the moment but no monument - however famous - is safe in Syria as was shown by the destruction of the medieval market and Ummayad Mosque in Aleppo.

Fighting in Syria has an on-and-off quality because the Syrian army does not have the numbers to sustain heavy losses from ground attacks.

In the battle for Qusayr it was Hezbollah who fought house-to-house and suffered serious casualties. The rebels are fragmented in organisation, lack heavy weapons and are too short of ammunition to launch big offensives. But though the fighting is intermittent, it very seldom stops. On our way back to Homs from Tal Kalakh a tank briefly blocked the road as it took up position and fired a shot from its gun into the al-Wa'ar district of Homs city, whose 400,000 people are Sunni and where government and rebels dispute control.

Army officers based in Tal-Kalakh in charge of the operation were not saying much yesterday. A burly colonel in his command said "the attack is a military secret." But he did explain the reason for launching it was that "this area is strategically important because it is so close to Lebanon."

Last June the government and its Lebanese ally, Hezbollah, had one of its few clear cut victories when they captured the rebel town of al-Qusayr a few miles east of Tal-Kalakh.

THE BATTLE FOR HOMS
By Patrick Cockburn
5 February 2014

The sound of shellfire boomed every few seconds from the besieged Old City. The rebels, surrounded in the densely packed quarter, replied with mortars of their own. Each of them detonated with a sharp crack, shaking the walls of the building I was in, a kilometre from the front line. In between shell bursts the regular chatter of machine guns rang out, lasting for at least six hours before subsiding in the early hours of yesterday morning.

The intensity of the fighting in the battered city of Homs, which began unexpectedly on Monday evening, was greater than anything the people here had experienced in months.

The city is one of the centres of the original uprising and has seen some of the most destructive fighting. Even when there is no fighting the city is tense. The streets clear as soon as darkness falls, unlike Damascus where the shops stay open late and heavy traffic in the government-held centre does not subside until after 8pm.

A few hours before the shooting intensified, I spoke to Captain Mohammed, who said his frontline position in the Bab al-Sebaa district was 30 metres from where the rebels were dug in. "We are completely surrounding them. There is fighting every day but they can't get out." He guessed that the rebels - whom the government side invariably refers to as "terrorists" - numbered over 1,000 fighters.

Contrary to what Captain Mohammed said there are occasional pauses in hostilities. We were standing in a dark, deserted street in the early evening in the Bab al-Sebaa district of Homs, but I did not hear more than a few shots fired in over an hour. But marks of total destruction are everywhere since this is one of Homs's "ghost districts", where the buildings have been torn apart by shell fire and their walls are pock-marked with bullets so that they look as if they had been gnawed by enormous rats. Where buildings survive, their doorways and windows are boarded up and they look abandoned.

Captain Mohammed said he had been fighting in Homs for two-and-a-half years and turned up his right trouser leg to show where he had been wounded by a sniper's bullet. He thought the enemy was penned into the warren of streets that make up the Old City but they had made use of tunnels to get access to the outside world. He said that "some months ago they came through a tunnel that came out behind where our men were positioned and attacked them from behind, but we killed them all." He claimed that for all the international furore about starvation in the Old City "they are not short of food, but weapons and ammunition".

Whatever the Syrian government, under increasing international pressure to allow humanitarian aid into Homs, may want, army commanders on the spot like Captain Mohammed are reluctant to allow their enemies, whom they have been fighting for years, off the hook. Contrary to his belief, aid officials are convinced that people in the Old City are starving.

Sectarianism explains much about the new geography of the city and its hinterland. Homs City and province are much like Lebanon in the number and diversity of their religious sects and ethnic groups including Sunni, Alawi, Christians, Shia, Yazidi, Kurds, Armenians and many other communities. Alawites, the backbone of the National Defence Force militia, are accused of moving into formerly Sunni neighbourhoods. Sunni from the Old City and the "ghost districts" who have not fled to Lebanon or elsewhere in Syria have moved mostly to the al-Wa'ar district of Homs, where 400,000 people have taken refuge. Al-Wa'ar is blockaded and subject to intermittent gunfire. On the main road near Homs oil refinery I saw a tank manoeuvre to position itself facing al-Wa'ar and then fire its cannon towards the modern apartment blocks which are common in the district. I asked the governor's office if I could visit a military hospital on the edge of al-Wa'ar and they said the road was very risky. They added that I could go by myself "but we frankly can't get anybody to go with you there because it is so dangerous."

Sectarian dividing lines and animosities have overlaid the democratic ambitions of those who led the original uprising in 2011. Many of the 1.7 million people in Homs governorate are on the move and fighting for survival. The local head of Unicef, Godfrey Ijumba, says that there are 600,000 internally displaced persons in Homs governorate, adding that "Unicef has distributed winter clothes for half a million of them".

Violence is frequent and the reasons for it not always obvious. I was looking for soldiers wounded in fighting at al-Zaraa, west of Homs, when I came across a wounded man called Ahmed Mohammed in Tal Kalakh hospital. He had been shot through the hand and the upper leg. I asked him who had shot him. Gasping with pain from a leg wound that doctors were examining, he said: "I don't know who shot me. I was milking cows in a field near my village when somebody shot me and killed an old man."

The siege of the Old City of Homs became an international issue at the Geneva II peace conference due to reconvene on 10 February. Ending or at least alleviating the siege has become a test case of whether or not the negotiations could succeed in de-escalating the Syrian conflict. The effort seemed several times to be on the verge of success, but neither government nor opposition wants to hand the other side a real or symbolic victory.

The governor of Homs, Talal al-Barazi, told The Independent that the government will "receive all people from the Old City as refugees who are women, children and old men and they are free to go anywhere." He says the government will give those who stay what they want. The "terrorists" who are Syrians can give up their weapons and also go.

All this sounds good, but the besieged fighters in the Old City do not want to surrender after so long a struggle. The defence of the Old City has become a heroic symbol of their resistance. And those fighters who do want to surrender may well wonder just how far they can trust the Syrian government once they have given up their arms.

There are 30 different armed groups in the Old City, making any agreement with them a problem. But diplomats familiar with the talks say that there are not many jihadis or foreign fighters there, making negotiations at least possible. Mr Ijumba of Unicef in Homs says that "the main stumbling block is that the 30 groups want guarantees that the aid will still be delivered to the Old City once the civilians are evacuated."

Complications are piled on complication. Nobody knows how many civilians and fighters are besieged, so how much food should go in after an evacuation? The government does not want to feed armed opponents. At the same time the Syrian government is feeling the international negative publicity from its strategy of besieging and blockading rebel enclaves across Syria. A less obvious difficulty, say diplomats, is that the rebel negotiators in Geneva have never had much connection with the rebels inside the Old City and the diplomats have to bring the two supposed allies together.

The fighters in the Old City are the defenders of the last bastion of the rebellion in Homs and their determination has a symbolic value for the opposition.

Almost all the rest of the city has fallen or was always controlled by the Syrian army or is, like al-Wa'ar, quite literally under the gun. But, given the level of hatred and fear in Homs, the UN is quite right to believe that a negotiated solution here might open the door for compromise elsewhere in Syria.

Spring 2014

Damascus To Homs

SYRIA'S ROAD TO HELL
By Patrick Cockburn
8 Marach 2014

In every war there is a city, a town, a mountain, a river or a road that all sides see as crucial if they are going to win, or at least avoid defeat. In the Syrian civil war, it is the road linking Damascus to Homs, Syria's third city, 100 miles to the north, which then goes west for 64 miles until it reaches the port city of Tartous on the Mediterranean coast. The route is so important because it connects the parts of Syria held by the government. If it is ever cut off permanently, it will be a crippling blow to the rule of President Bashar al- Assad.

It is a road I have got to know far too well in the past two years. When I think about driving it, I feel a tightening of the muscles in my stomach. There is nothing suicidal about the journey, but the risk is always there, and even after I have discussed the dangers involved with my careful, highly-informed and courageous driver George, a Syrian Christian, I wonder if there is something nasty ahead we don't know about.

We watch for signs that will give us advanced warning of danger, such as a lack of traffic coming towards us on the other side of the road, which could mean vehicles are being stopped by some trouble we cannot yet see. A good flow of traffic probably means that all is well, particularly if there are a lot of buses, since Syrian bus drivers go everywhere and are skilled in assessing risks. Heavy vehicles loaded high with valuable goods are also excellent news, because the driver would not be risking his cargo if he thought it might be stolen or destroyed.

I was last on this road in early February and I knew it had been closed for 17 days a month earlier after rebels captured most of the town of An Nabk, halfway to Homs. But George's mother comes from Nabk and he assured me that government troops were firmly back in control and there was no need to worry. Not everybody was so positive: an experienced foreign journalist advised me to fly to Latakia on the coast in north-west Syria and then drive south to Homs. He said that if I was going to drive to Homs from Damascus, it was worth hiring a second car to drive behind my own to make sure I was not followed. He had got through all right, but the second car had been stolen by armed bandits on the way back to Damascus.

It is the first few miles of the main highway north which make me most nervous. They go past districts such as Qaboun, Harasta, Barzeh and Douma that were or are rebel strongholds, but have been ravaged by artillery fire or systematically bulldozed. Viewed from the car window, I see a landscape of ruins with broken walls and concrete floors sandwiched on top of each other. Most of the time there is nobody to be seen as we speed past mile after mile of ruins, but that does not mean that a sniper is not looking at us through the sights of his rifle. The car showrooms that used to line this road are now burnt out and abandoned. The Mercedes building was a focus for rebel resistance and has taken a terrible battering.

We drive very fast and only stop once at a government checkpoint under a bridge. These are regular troops in uniform and not the National Defence Force (NDF) militia, because the area is still a potential battleground. As in most places in Syria - and this reminds me of Lebanon during the civil war 30 years ago - there is an intricate jigsaw puzzle of zones held by forces loyal to the government and zones controlled by rebels. Even this oversimplifies the situation on the ground, because in places like Barzeh there is a negotiated ceasefire, with rebel Free Syrian Army (FSA) fighters and government soldiers jointly manning checkpoints, while inside Barzeh armed FSA men are still in charge.

The military geography of Syria often follows its sectarian geography. We drive past tall buildings which are undamaged where most of the inhabitants are Alawites, the Shia sect to which President Assad and much of Syria's ruling elite belongs. As we exit the northern outskirts of Damascus, George looks more relaxed and says encouragingly, "That is 80 per cent of the dangerous parts of this journey over". Somehow, I don't feel comforted. A little to my surprise, he is not too worried about the proximity of Ma'loula, a Christian village built in a spectacular ravine in the mountains just off the road to the west that we had visited last summer. These days, all the Christians have fled and it is partly in the hands of Jabhat al-Nusra, the Syrian affiliate of al-Qa'ida, which has gunmen in buildings and caves overlooking the town. I thought it would not take much for these jihadis to push down from the mountain and block the road.

A strange aspect of the war in this part of Syria is how close the combatants are to each other. In a few cases there are negotiated ceasefires, but others seem to be local truces (or a live-and-let-live understanding between the adversaries) that are always fragile and vulnerable to somebody breaking it.

This is particularly true of the part of the road which George and I were about to drive down, because clearly visible on a hill off to the left is the town of Yabroud, which is held by Jabhat al-Nusra, but mysteriously still has a large population of Christians who have not fled. Some deal is evidently in operation, but nobody quite knows what it is. The deal does not apply to strangers, and somebody had fired a shot at us 18 months earlier in just this area, and the bullet had whistled by uncomfortably close to our car. The Syrian Army had been bombarding Yabroud, but this did not necessarily mean it would launch a ground assault. The government is short of combat troops and uses them sparingly, usually to keep open roads vital to itself, or to block routes important to the rebels' supply network.

I had heard a lot in Damascus about the army's coming offensive against Yabroud, but had decided that I would believe it when I saw it. On the other hand, the brief capture of Nabk, a few miles beyond Yabroud, by the opposition in December, might have made the government decide that it was time to secure this important piece of the road, possibly in a combined attack with the Lebanese paramilitary Hezbollah movement, whose forces were just across the border in Lebanon.

Nabk was firmly back in government hands at the time we were there, and the authorities had arranged a victory celebration in the undamaged centre of the town. We turned off the main road to have a look. I am not a great fan of this type of demonstration, with school children playing the main part, because local people are under the gun and do not have any alternative but to take part.

The rally did show, however, that the government was pretty confident that it was in control. I also learnt an interesting fact, which was that the NDF militiamen policing the demonstration had previously been members of the rebel FSA until a couple of months earlier. They had simply switched sides, though nobody knew on what terms.

Unfortunately, nobody should imagine that these deals mitigate the violence of the war anywhere in Syria. In Nabk, there were mutual accusations of atrocities, and just north of the town, at Dayr Atiyah, there was a hospital on a hill where the rebels were said to have killed the doctors. I learnt later that they had also broken into a folk museum and stolen ancient firearms and tried to make them battle-worthy again. Buildings close to the main road were pock-marked with bullet holes and some had been hit by shells, but the damage was not as bad as in Damascus.

Two other points need to be made about this journey. Every six or seven miles, there was a government checkpoint which George and I were likely to get through because we had the right papers and authorisations, but our swift passage was not a complete certainty and a single suspicious soldier might delay us for hours. Secondly, on this road, all the while we were just to the east of the Qalamoun mountain range, which marks the border with Lebanon. It is traditionally a smuggling region and, until last year, nothing much had changed other than the fact that these days, it was men, weapons and ammunition which were being transported. Then in June, the government had won one of its few decisive ground battles of the war, thanks to Hezbollah, whose fighters had stormed al-Qusayr, a rebel-held town on the plain through which the rebels had reinforced and re-supplied their fighters in Homs. I had been in Qusayr just after it had fallen to Hezbollah and it was badly hit, though not wholly destroyed.

I spent the night in Homs and then turned west, taking the road to Tartous, a city where there are many Alawites and which is firmly on the government's side. After success at Qusayr, the government is tightening its grip here.

As we leave Homs, on our right is a big area of tall modern buildings called al-Wa'ar, whose 400,000 inhabitants are Sunni and where Sunnis from the rest of Homs have taken refuge. Wa'ar is blockaded and it is difficult to get in or out, though it is not quite so tightly besieged as the Old City of Homs, which has been at the centre of international attention. Jacoub El Hillo, the head of the UN humanitarian effort, told me later: "I wish that people would understand that there are other sieges in Syria aside from the Old City of Homs."

This is an important strategic area. Homs oil refinery is just to the south of the road and had been hit by mortar fire, though not badly damaged. Later in the day, I saw a Syrian Army tank manoeuvre on the road before firing a shell into Wa'ar. A little further west, the road passes through the Homs Gap, with low mountains on either side of the highway, making this a much- fought-over route down the centuries. Control of the Homs Gap is why the Knights Hospitallers spent so much money in the 13th century building the Krak des Chevaliers, the greatest Crusader castle in the world, with its massive towers and huge concentric masonry walls. I was trying to pick out the fortress on its distant hill when its white stones were suddenly illuminated by a shaft of sunlight - like a castle in a Renaissance painting. I was sorry I could not get closer, but it is held by rebels based in two Sunni villages, al-Zahra and al-Hosn, at its base. The villages have been blockaded for months, but what makes Zahra important are the oil and gas pipes, as well as the electricity lines that go through it - the rebels had been blowing them up.

I visited a hospital in Talkalakh, a town just off the road and close to the Lebanese border, where I hoped to find soldiers wounded in a government attack on Zahra. The doctors denied any wounded were there, but I met a civilian called Ahmad Mohammed, who said he had been shot in the hand and thigh while milking a cow. The old man who was with him had been killed. He appeared to come from an Alawite village and I wondered if he had been shot for sectarian reasons. This part of Syria is very much like Lebanon, with villages with different sectarian allegiances - Sunni, Christian, Alawite - turning into armed camps. A little further west and we were in Tartous, a fine, peaceful city and a government stronghold, but with one wall in the centre covered with pictures of some 2,000 of its young men who have been killed serving in the Syrian Army.

My journey showed that in this part of Syria, the government is expanding its control and the rebels are under pressure. But the expansion is slow and the army is overstretched. The road was more secure than it had been six months earlier, but it was still vulnerable to a sudden attack.

It also reminded me that Syria is more than ever a patchwork of different circumstances, depending on the military situation and which sects predominate. Much of what I had heard in Beirut and Damascus about what was happening turned out to be mistaken, and media reporting has been full of certainties that melted away in the face of reality. In Syria, more than most places, only eyewitness information is worth much and even then it swiftly becomes outdated. That being so, sometime in the course of the year, I am likely to find myself back on the risky but always interesting road from Damascus to Tartous.

SYRIA'S SECULAR UPRISING HAS BEEN HIJACKED BY JIHADISTS
By Patrick Cockburn
20 March 2014

Just after the sarin poison gas attacks on rebel-held districts of Damascus in August last year, I appeared on an American television programme with Razan Zaitouneh, a human rights lawyer and founder of the Violations Documentation Centre, who was speaking via Skype from the opposition stronghold of Douma in East Damascus.

She gave a compelling, passionate, wholly believable account of what had happened. "I have never seen so much death in my whole life," she said, describing people breaking down the doors of houses to find everybody inside dead. Doctors in the few medical centres wept as they vainly tried to treat gas victims with the few medicines they had. Bodies were being tipped, 15 to 20 at a time, into mass graves. She contemptuously dismissed any idea that the rebels might be behind the use of sarin, asking: "Do you think we are crazy people that we would kill our own children?"

Ms Zaitouneh, 36, had been defending political prisoners for a dozen years and was the sort of credible advocate that won the Syrian opposition so much international support in its first years. But on 8 December, gunmen burst into her office in Douma and kidnapped her, along with her husband, Wael Hamada, and two civil rights activists, Samira al-Khalili, a lawyer, and Nazem al-Hamadi, a poet. None of the four has been heard from since. The group suspected of being behind the kidnapping is the Saudi-backed Army of Islam, although it denies being involved. Ms al-Khalili's husband, Yassin al- Hajj Saleh, told the online publication al-Monitor: "Razan and Samira were part of a national inclusive secular movement and this led them to collide with the Islamist factions, who are inclined towards despotism."

The kidnapping and disappearance of Ms Zaitouneh and the others have many parallels elsewhere in Syria, where Islamists have killed civil activists or forced them to flee. Usually, this has happened when the activists have criticised them for killings, torture, imprisonment or other crime. All revolutions have notoriously devoured their earliest and most humane advocates, but few have done so with the speed and ferocity of Syria's.

Instead of modernising Syrian society in a progressive and democratic manner, the Salafi-jihadists want a return to the norms of early Islam and are prepared to fight a holy war to achieve this.

Why has the Syrian uprising, whose early supporters demanded that tyranny should be replaced by a secular, non-sectarian, law-bound and democratic state, so totally failed to achieve these aims? Syria has descended into a nightmarish sectarian civil war as the government bombs its own cities as if they were enemy territory and the armed opposition is dominated by Salafi-jihadist fighters who slaughter Alawites and Christians simply because of their religion. Syrians have to choose between a violent dictatorship in which power is monopolised by the presidency and brutish security services, and an opposition that shoots children in the face for minor blasphemy and sends pictures of decapitated soldiers to their parents.

Syria is now like Lebanon during the 15-year-long civil war between 1975 and 1990. I was recently in Homs, once a city known for its vibrant diversity but now full of "ghost neighbourhoods" where all the buildings are abandoned, smashed by shellfire or bombs. Walls still standing are so full of small holes from machine-gun fire that they look as if giant woodworms have been eating into the concrete.

Syria is a land of checkpoints, blockades and sieges, in conducting which the government seals off, bombards but does not storm rebel-held enclaves unless they control important supply routes. This strategy is working but at a snail's pace, and it will leave much of Syria in ruins.

Aleppo, once the largest city in the country, is mostly depopulated. Government forces are advancing but are overstretched and cannot reconquer northern and eastern Syria unless Turkey shuts its 500-mile-long border. Government success strengthens the jihadists because they have a hard core of fighters who will never surrender. So, as the Syrian army advances behind a barrage of barrel bombs in Aleppo, its troops are mostly fighting the official al-Qa'ida affiliate

Jabhat al-Nusra and the Salafist Ahrar al-Sham, backed by Qatar and Turkey.

The degenerate state of the Syrian revolution stems from the country's deep political, religious and economic divisions before 2011 and the way in which these have since been exploited and exacerbated by foreign intervention.

The first protests happened when they did because of the uprisings in Tunisia, Egypt, Libya, Yemen and Bahrain. They spread so rapidly because of over-reaction by state security forces firing on peaceful demonstrators, thereby enraging whole communities and provoking armed resistance. The government insists that protests were not as peaceful as they looked and from an early stage their forces came under armed attack. There is some truth in this, but if the opposition's aim was to trap the government into a counter-productive punitive response, it succeeded beyond its dreams.

Syria was always a less coherent society than it looked to outside observers, and its divisions were not just along religious lines. In July 2011, the Brussels-based International Crisis Group (ICG) wrote in a report: "The Syrian authorities claim they are fighting a foreign-sponsored, Islamist conspiracy, when for most part they have been waging war against their original social constituency. When it first came to power, the Assad regime embodied the neglected countryside, its peasants and exploited underclass. Today's ruling elite has forgotten its roots."

In the four years of drought before 2011, the United Nations noted that up to three million Syrian farmers had been pushed into "extreme poverty" and fled the countryside to squat in shanty towns on the outskirts of the cities.

Middle-class salaries could not keep up with inflation. Cheap imports, often from Turkey, forced small manufacturers out of business and helped to pauperise the urban working class. The state was in contact with whole areas of life in Syria solely through corrupt and predatory security services. The ICG conceded that there was "an Islamist undercurrent to the uprising" but it was not the main motivation for the peaceful protests that were mutating into military conflict.

Compare this analysis of the situation in the summer of 2011 with that two and a half years later. By late 2013, the war was stalemated and the armed opposition was dominated by the Islamic State in Iraq and the Levant (ISIS), the former official al-Qa'ida affiliate now displaced by Jabhat al-Nusra.

Ideologically, there was not much difference between them and Ahrar al- Sham or the Army of Islam, which also seeks a theocratic Sunni state under Sharia law. Pilloried in the West for their sectarian ferocity, these jihadists were often welcomed by local people for restoring law and order after the looting and banditry of the Western-backed Free Syrian Army (FSA), the loose umbrella group to which at one time 1,200 rebel bands owed nominal allegiance. In Afghanistan in the 1990s the iron rule of the Taliban had at first been welcomed by many for the same reason.

The degree to which the armed opposition at the end of 2013 was under the thumb of foreign backers is well illustrated by the confessions of Saddam al- Jamal, a brigade leader in the Ahfad al-Rasoul Brigade and the former FSA commander in eastern Syria.

A fascinating interview with Jamal, conducted by ISIS and translated by the Brown Moses blog, was recorded after he had defected to ISIS and appears to be reliable, ignoring his self-serving denunciations of the un-Islamic actions of his former FSA associates. He speaks as if it was matter of course that his own group, al-Ahfad, was funded by one or other of the Gulf monarchies: "At the beginning of the Syrian revolution, the file was handled by Qatar. After a while, they switched to Saudi Arabia."

Jamal says meetings of the FSA military council were invariably attended by representatives of the Saudi, UAE, Jordanian and Qatari intelligence services, as well as intelligence officers from the US, Britain and France. At one such meeting, apparently in Ankara, Jamal says the Saudi Deputy Defence Minister, Prince Salman bin Sultan, the brother of Saudi intelligence chief Bandar bin Sultan, addressed them all and asked Syrian leaders of the armed opposition "who have plans to attack Assad positions to present their needs for arms, ammo and money". The impression given is of a movement wholly controlled by Arab and Western intelligence agencies.

The civil war between jihadist groups that started with a co-ordinated attack on ISIS positions on 3 January is damaging the standing of all of them.

Foreign fighters who came to Syria to fight Assad and the Shia find they are being told to kill Sunni jihadists with exactly the same ideological views as themselves.

The Islamic State sent a suicide bomber who killed Abdullah Muhammad al- Muhaysani, the official al-Qa'ida representative in Syria, and also a leader of Ahrar al-Sham (evidence of how al-Qa'ida has links at different levels to jihadi organisations with which it is not formally associated).

Returning jihadists are finding the way home is not easy, since governments in, for example, Saudi Arabia or Tunisia, which may have welcomed their departure as a way of exporting dangerous fanatics, are now appalled by the idea of battle-hardened Salafists coming back. An activist in Raqqa, seeking to speed the departure of Tunisian volunteers, showed them a video of bikini-clad women on Tunisian beaches and suggested that their puritanical presence was needed back home to prevent such loose practices.

It is a measure of Syria's descent into apocalyptic violence that the official representative of al-Qa'ida, Jabhat al-Nusra, should be deemed more moderate than ISIS. The latter may be on the retreat but this could be tactical and it has a vast territory in eastern Syria and western Iraq into to which to retreat and plan a counter-attack. In any case, Jabhat al-Nusra has always sought mediation with ISIS and does not want a fight to the finish. The jihadist civil war has made life easier for the government militarily, since its enemies are busy killing each other, but it does not have the resources to eliminate them.

Crucial to making peace is bringing an end to the proxy war between Saudi Arabia and Iran which is intertwined with the vicious conflict between Shia and Sunni. Russia and the US need to be at one in ending the war, as they briefly seemed to be at the end of last year. Syrians gloomily say the outcome of their civil war is no longer in Syrian hands, but in those of the US, Russia, Saudi Arabia, Iran, Turkey and their various allies.

Peace, if it ever comes, will come in stages and with many false starts such as the failure of the Geneva II peace talks.

FOREIGN JIHADIS IN SYRIA PLEDGE THEIR OWN 9/11
By Patrick Cockburn
4 May 2014

It is only a matter of time before jihadis in al-Qa'ida-type groups that have taken over much of eastern Syria and western Iraq have a violent impact on the world outside these two countries. The road is open wide to new attacks along the lines of 9/11 and 7/7, and it may be too late to close it.

Those who doubt that these are the jihadis' long-term intentions should have a look at a chilling but fascinating video posted recently by the Islamic State of Iraq and the Levant (ISIS), formerly al-Qa'ida in Iraq. It shows a group of foreign fighters burning their passports to emphasise their permanent commitment to jihad. Many of the passports thrown into the flames have grass-green covers and are Saudi; others are dark blue and must be Jordanian. Some of the fighters show their faces while others are masked. As each one destroys his passport, sometimes tearing it in half before throwing it into the fire, he makes a declaration of faith and a promise to fight against the ruler of the country from which he comes.

A Canadian makes a short speech in English before switching to Arabic, saying: "It is a message to Canada, to all American powers. We are coming and we will destroy you." A Jordanian says: "I say to the tyrant of Jordan: we are the descendants of Abu Musab al-Zarqawi [the Jordanian founder of al-Qa'ida in Iraq killed by US aircraft in 2006] and we are coming to kill you." A Saudi, an Egyptian and a Chechen make similar threats.

The film is professionally made, and was probably shot somewhere in northern or eastern Syria. It is worth looking at carefully, and keeping in mind that these are not an isolated band hiding in desert wastes or mountain caves. ISIS and Jabhat al-Nusra, the official affiliate of al-Qa'ida, now control, or can easily operate in, a great swathe of territory from the Tigris to the Mediterranean, and from the Jordanian border to southern Turkey.

Threats, such as those made by the group burning their passports, are creating something near panic among Iraq's neighbours, who were slow to take on board last year that Syrian armed opposition had come to be dominated by al-Qa'ida or its clones. A report by the International Crisis Group (ICG), "The Rising Cost of Turkey's Syrian Quagmire", published last week, cites a Turkish official saying: "The armed al-Qa'ida element will be a problem for the Turks. As a secular country, we do not fit with their ideology. What happens if they can't get what they want in Syria? They will blame Turkey and attack it." Bear in mind that the thousands of foreign jihadis who have poured into Syria and Iraq mostly got there by crossing the 510-mile-long Turkish-Syrian border. The head of an influential Turkish think tank is quoted by ICG as saying that "When Turkey starts arresting them [jihadis], which it will do, we know what will happen. There will be bombs all over Turkey."

Jordan is also showing signs of extreme nervousness over support being given to the Syrian armed opposition, just across its border in southern Syria. American, Saudi and Jordanian intelligence have been working on creating a "southern front" around Daraa, the southern city where the Syrian revolt began, a front supposedly made up of moderate, secular fighters, who are both anti-Assad and anti-jihadi. This is deceptive, since an important force in such operations would be Jabhat al-Nusra which, on this front, is reportedly acting in coordination with a Jordanian, Saudi and US intelligence joint operations room in Amman.

But the Jordanians have got cold feet over the idea of a southern offensive launched from their territory. They are no longer as confident as they were in 2011 and 2012 that President Assad is bound to lose. They worry about an estimated 2,000 Jordanian jihadis in Syria, and what happens when they return to Jordan. There was a mysterious Jordanian airforce attack destroying vehicles entering Jordan from Syria on 16 April in which the Syrian government denied any involvement. The Jordanians also forbade an opposition offensive at Daraa timed to coincide with a rebel assault in Aleppo.

Even the US State Department's annual report on terrorism, issued last week, has noted that al-Qa'ida-type groups are getting stronger. Its image of al-Qa'ida in the past has been along the lines of a bureaucratic entity somewhat similar to the State Department itself. It therefore takes heart from the belief that because of organisational and leadership losses "AQ's core leadership has been degraded, limiting its ability to conduct attacks." The word "core" is useful here since it can mean either "a central command" or simply "at the centre of". In practice, al-Qa'ida since 2001 has primarily been an ideology and a method of operating, not a cohesive organisation.

The State Department has finally noted this, speaking of "the rise of increasingly aggressive and autonomous AQ affiliates and like-minded groups".

In reality, the situation is worse than the State Department admits, since over the last year ISIS has taken over much of Sunni Iraq. It levies taxes in cities such as Mosul and Tikrit and has substantial control in Fallujah and along the Euphrates valley, through western Iraq and eastern Syria up to the Turkish border. It has captured the Fallujah dam on the Euphrates, and can flood or deny water to areas further south; at Baiji on the Tigris, north of Baghdad, it has blown up an oil pipeline, polluting the river which had been used, after treatment, to supply drinking water to Baghdad. On the western outskirts of Baghdad at Abu Ghraib, ISIS has held a military parade and the famous prison was hastily evacuated. A comforting theory explaining the surge in ISIS's strength in Iraq is that Prime Minister Nouri al-Maliki exaggerated its power to frighten Shia voters before last Wednesday's parliamentary election. He thereby diverted attention from his administration's appalling record of corruption and incompetence by focusing on the danger of a Sunni counter-revolution. The outcome of the election will show if this strategy had worked.

Unfortunately, all the signs are that the political and military incapacity of the Iraqi government is all too real. Its armed forces are said in Baghdad to have suffered 5,000 casualties including 1,000 dead in fighting in Anbar province in the last four months. Whole battalions are reported to have melted away because the men were not being paid, or they have not received supplies of food and ammunition. According to one report, even the job of army divisional commander can be bought for $1m with the assumption that whoever takes the job can show a profit by making $50,000 a month through protection money and levies on vehicles passing checkpoints.

After the election the government may try to repeat the US strategy of successfully using the Sunni tribes against al-Qa'ida groups such as ISIS. The difficulty is that for the moment Sunni communities hate the Iraqi army and security forces more than they do al-Qa'ida.

Summer 2014

ISIS Takes Over

DEATH ZONE: THE SYRIAN INDUSTRIAL ESTATE TURNED INTO A SUICIDE FORTRESS BY AL-QA'IDA
By Robert Fisk
7 June 2014

Al-Qa'ida City was an industrial zone, a vast plain of concrete and stone factories, cattle sheds and homes, 10 miles north-east of Aleppo.

When Bashar al-Assad's army crashed up the main highway from Hama, lifting the rebel siege of Aleppo and careering on towards the Turkish border, the soldiers and tank crews were suddenly confronted by the biggest and most sophisticated fortress ever built by followers of the late Osama bin Laden.

Today, Syrian 155mm guns fire northbound shells from the olive and walnut orchards around what was one of the country's economic powerhouses, now reduced to square miles of smashed factories and burned chemical plants.

There, according to Syrian commanders who had to smash their way into this place of pulverised iron, rubble and ash, hundreds of Islamist suicide fighters blew themselves up rather than surrender.

Colonel Saleh, sunglasses wrapped round a burned, lean face, stared at one heap of sandwiched concrete in the middle of the grey wasteland and made a rare admission of loss for an officer of the Syrian army in this dangerous place. "The terrorists all blew themselves up with suicide belts," he said. "They brought the buildings down on top of them as we attacked. I lost 27 of my soldiers storming this one area."

Miles of tunnels still lace their way beneath what was the Sheikh Najjar Industrial Zone. Above them, men from al-Qa'ida, Jabhat el-Nusra, the al-Sham Brigade and remnants of the old "Free Syria Army" - all struggling to overthrow Assad's regime - had spent two years mining the buildings, hacking lorry-wide passageways between walls and cutting out sniper's nests in every street and every floor. What had been one of Syria's newest industrial estates was transformed into a place of death; food stores and grain mills were turned into arms depots, their basements into dormitories for the hundreds of rebels who lived here.

It should take seven minutes on the highway from Aleppo to reach this extraordinary city of ruins, but the front lines of the Islamist forces north- east of the city so encroach on the countryside that we had to drive 30 winding miles along earthen lanes and beneath the grass-covered tracks of the old railway line to Turkey, once the final stretch of track on Agatha Christie's famed Oriental Express to Aleppo.

But there is nothing romantic about this battlefield. Just outside the rooftop headquarters where Colonel Saleh sits, surrounded by squawking radio sets, is a blasted Syrian tank. Captured in the early months of the war, it was used by two suicide fighters in a vain attempt to smash the vehicle - packed with explosives - into the huge walls of Aleppo prison. The jail, in which hundreds of inmates are reported to have died of disease, hunger and ill-treatment over two years - and which was never taken by the rebel forces - was not breached. "There were two suiciders inside," Colonel Saleh says. "One was Syrian, the other Egyptian."

His colleagues are eager to talk of the huge number of foreign fighters who were based in this industrial complex - Chechens, they say, and Afghans and Egyptians, Saudis, Qataris, Algerians - and only rarely do they admit to the Syrians who also fought here against the government army. It is now a familiar format: Bashar al-Assad's army are fighting "foreign terrorists".

But this was not just a geopolitical battle for the land north of Aleppo. You only have to drive a few miles east of the ruins to find a deserted but undamaged motorway with its signposts to Raqqa, the one large Syrian city still totally under rebel control.

The colonel and his men led me through acres of crushed factories, all surrounded by deep trenches, most of them gouged out by shell-fire and explosives. A headquarters dormitory had been built beneath a towering cereal feed mill whose outer walls had been smashed down, apparently by air attack, although the colonel denied this.

Next to it was a factory for producing a spice called zaatar - piles of crushed grain still lay across the floor amid cartridge cases. Tunnels had been dug up to five metres deep beneath the surrounding buildings, shorn up by earthen sandbags made out of animal feed sacks.

There was one salient fact about this grim city of death: it was built and defended by technical men, by strategists, by experts in design and defence whose interests went deeper than Islam. Did they come from Turkey? Afghanistan? Pakistan? Or were they local men trained outside the Muslim world, perhaps originally aided by Western supplies, initially so promiscuously dispatched to anyone fighting the Assad regime?

For young men supposedly fixated by submission to God, the hundreds of Islamists who died here had been remarkably self-regarding about their own identity. "Abu Mohamed" and "Hassan of Raqqa" had spray-painted their names beside an empty sheep and cattle market. "The Heroes of Yasser" - a suburb of Damascus - had proudly painted their names next to a bunker. The Syrian army spoke only vaguely of survivors; there was no mention of prisons for those who may have surrendered - one must imagine that few did - and there is no final figure for the hundreds of al-Qa'ida dead. Colonel Saleh's 27 men were just a few of the Syrian soldiers who also perished. "Our sacrifice was very great," one man said bleakly.

ISIS MAKES ITS MOVE
By Patrick Cockburn
9 June 2014

Islamic fundamentalists have opened new fronts in their battle to establish an Islamic state across Iraq and Syria as they launch attacks in cities which were previously under the control of the Baghdad government.

A multi-pronged assault across central and northern Iraq in the past four days shows that the Islamic State of Iraq and the Levant (ISIS) has taken over from the al-Qa'ida organisation founded by Osama bin Laden as the most powerful and effective extreme jihadi group in the world.

ISIS now controls or can operate with impunity in a great stretch of territory in western Iraq and eastern Syria, making it militarily the most successful jihadi movement ever.

Led since 2010 by Abu Bakr al-Baghdadi, also known as Abu Dua, it has proved itself even more violent and sectarian than what US officials call the "core" al-Qa'ida, led by Ayman al-Zawahiri, who is based in Pakistan. ISIS is highly fanatical, killing Shia Muslims and Christians whenever possible, as well as militarily efficient and under tight direction by top leaders.

In Iraq in the past four days, it has fought its way into the northern capital of Mosul, sent a column of its fighters into the central city of Samarra and taken over Iraq's largest university at Ramadi, in the west of the country. In addition, it launched devastating bombings targeting Shia civilians in Baghdad that killed at least 52 people.

The creation of a sort of proto-Caliphate by extreme jihadis in northern Syria and Iraq is provoking fears in surrounding countries such as Jordan, Saudi Arabia and Turkey that they will become targets of battle-hardened Sunni fighters.

The well-coordinated attacks appear designed to keep the Iraqi security forces off balance, uncertain where the next attack will come. They started on Thursday when ISIS fighters in trucks with heavy machine guns stormed into the city of Samarra, which is mostly the city of Samarra, which is mostly Sunni but contains the golden-domed al-Askari shrine sacred to Shia.

Destruction of this shrine by al-Qa'ida bombers in 2006 led to wholesale massacres of Sunni by Shia.

The ISIS tactic is to make a surprise attack, inflict maximum casualties and spread fear before withdrawing without suffering heavy losses. On Friday, they attacked in Mosul, where their power is already strong enough to tax local businesses, from family groceries to mobile phone and construction companies. Some 200 people were killed in the fighting, according to local hospitals, though the government gives a figure of 59 dead, 21 of them policemen and 38 insurgents.

This assault was followed by an early-morning attack on Saturday on the University of Anbar at Ramadi that has 10,000 students. Ahmed al-Mehamdi, a student who was taken hostage, told a news agency that he was woken up by the sound of shots, looked out the window and saw armed men dressed in black running across the campus. They entered his dormitory, said they belonged to ISIS, told everybody to stay in their rooms but took others away.

One leader told female students: "We will teach you a lesson you'll never forget." They turned the science building into their headquarters, but may later have retreated. On the same day, seven bombs exploded in an hour in Baghdad, killing at least 52 people.

ISIS specialises in using militarily untrained foreign volunteers as suicide bombers either moving on foot wearing suicide vests, or driving vehicles packed with explosives. Often more than one suicide bomber is used, as happened yesterday when a vehicle exploded at the headquarters of a Kurdish party, the Patriotic Union of Kurdistan in the town of Jalawla in the divided and much fought-over province of Diyala, north-east of Baghdad. In the confusion caused by the blast, a second bomber on foot slipped into the office and blew himself up, killing some 18 people, including a senior police officer.

The swift rise of ISIS since Abu Bakr al-Baghdadi became its leader has come because the uprising of the Sunni in Syria in 2011 led the Iraqi Sunni to protest about their political and economic marginalisation since the fall of Saddam Hussein. Peaceful demonstrations from the end of 2012 won few concessions, with Iraq's Shia-dominated government convinced that the protesters wanted not reform but a revolution returning their community to power. The five or six million Iraqi Sunni became more alienated and sympathetic towards armed action by ISIS.

ISIS launched a well-planned campaign last year including a successful assault on Abu Ghraib prison last summer to free leaders and experienced fighters. This January, they took over Fallujah, 40 miles west of Baghdad, and have held it ever since in the face of artillery and air attack. The military sophistication of ISIS in Iraq is much greater than al-Qa'ida, the organisation out of which it grew, which reached the peak of its success in 2006-07 before the Americans turned many of the Sunni tribes against it.

ISIS has the great advantage of being able to operate on both sides of the Syrian-Iraq border, though in Syria it is engaged in an intra-jihadi civil war with Jabhat al-Nusra, Ahrar al-Sham and other groups. But ISIS controls Raqqa, the only provincial capital taken by the opposition, and much of eastern Syria outside enclaves held by the Kurds close to the Turkish border.

ISIS is today a little more circumspect in killing all who work for the government including rubbish collectors, something that alienated the Sunni population previously. But horrifically violent, though professionally made propaganda videos show ISIS forcing families with sons in the Iraqi army to dig their own graves before they are shot. The message is that their enemies can expect no mercy.

The violence continued yesterday as at least 18 people were killed in two explosions at the headquarters of a Kurdish political party in Iraq's ethnically mixed province of Diyala. ISIS claimed responsibility.

Most of the victims of Sunday's attack were members of the Kurdish security forces who were guarding the office of the Patriotic Union of Kurdistan (PUK) party in the town of Jalawla.

The explosions were the latest in a show of strength by militants who in recent days have overrun parts of two major cities, occupied a university campus in western Iraq and set off a dozen car bombs in Baghdad.

Jalawla lies in disputed territory, and is one of several towns where Iraqi troops and Kurdish peshmerga regional guards have previously faced off, asserting their claims over the area. Both are a target for Sunni Islamist insurgents.

THE SYRIAN 'MODERATES' WHO AREN'T SO MODERATE IN IRAQ
By Robert Fisk
28 June 2014

Well, God bless Barack Obama - he's found some "moderate" rebels in Syria. Enough to supply them with weapons and training worth $500m. Congress wants to arm these brave freedom fighters, you see. And Obama, having sent his 300 elite Spartan lads to Iraq to help Nouri al-Maliki fight the rebels there, needs to send help to the rebels in Syria - even though most of them are on the side of the rebels in Iraq whom Obama wants Maliki to defeat.

Confusing? You bet. So first steps first. Who are the "moderate" rebels whom Obama wants to train and arm? He doesn't name them - and he can't, because the original "moderates" whom America swore to arm (with the help of the CIA, the Brits, Saudi Arabia, Qatar and

Turkey) were the so-called "Free Syrian Army", mostly composed of deserters from Assad's government forces. But the FSA - briefly beloved of John McCain until he discovered a pro-al-Qa'ida fighter sharing a photo-op with him in northern Syria - has decomposed.

Its men have gone home, switched to the bearded Islamists of the Nusrah or ISIS - or Isil if we heed the latest acronym - or re-deserted to the government army and taken up arms for Assad again. Some freedom fighters! They weren't given enough weapons, we are told. Now they'll get more. And no doubt sell them - as they did the last lot. For it is a sad fact of war that whenever a gun crosses a border, it represents not loyalty but cash.

Give an FSA man - if you can find one - an anti-aircraft missile and it will be sold to the highest bidder. In all the civil wars I've covered, I've never seen a weapon in the hands of a militia which hasn't bought it from someone else. In a humiliating interview on Channel 4, our own Defence Secretary admitted that weapons given to Syrian rebels had fallen into the hands of the bad guys. How do you monitor all the guys whom you give a gun to? Send them off with a personal drone to make sure they don't sell it?

Besides, how do you actually find a "moderate" these days in Syria's war? The Islamist rebels fight to the death. No "moderates" they. And – accursed facts now intervene - these are the very same Islamist rebels now threatening the Iraqi state. And just to make things even more confusing, Maliki has just been thanking Assad's boys for air-raiding his own rebel enemies on the Iraqi-Syrian border on the grounds that Syria and Iraq are "friends".

So now to our own real friend, the Department of Home Truths. What's left of the FSA has been fighting the Islamist ISIS-Isil forces. So have the Kurdish militias in northern Syria. So have a few village militias. And the Syrians have a suspicion that this is Obama's half-baked plan: to arm the anti- Islamist Syrian rebels to fight the pro-al-Qa'ida rebels and thus - indirectly - keep both the Assad and Maliki regimes in power.

The problem is that Obama must do this without revealing that the Syrian- Iraqi battle against Sunni Wahabis is one and the same war, that Assad's Syrian army - using Russian jets - is struggling against exactly the same enemy as Maliki's Iraqi army, also soon to be augmented (if we are to believe Maliki's blather to the BBC Arabic Service) with Russian jets. In other words, Assad not only has the public support of Moscow; he has the private support of Washington (and therefore, of course, of Israel).

Why else would the White House say that the money for Syrian "moderates" would help "counter terrorist threats" - "terrorist" being Assad's description of his enemies. But of course, Obama must keep calling Assad a "brutal dictator". Difficult to explain all this on Fox News, of course. So just keep repeating the word "moderate". Over and over again.

ISIS MARCHES FURTHER INTO SYRIA
By Patrick Cockburn
16 July 2014

ISIS fighters have captured much of eastern Syria in the past few days while international attention has been focused on the Israeli bombardment of Gaza. Using tanks and artillery seized in Iraq, it has taken almost all of oil- rich Deir Ezzor province and is battling to crush the resistance of the Syrian Kurds.

ISIS is establishing dominance over the opposition to Syria's President, Bashar al-Assad, as other rebel groups flee or pledge allegiance to the caliphate declared by the ISIS leader, Abu Bakr al-Baghdadi, after the capture of Mosul on 10 June. On Monday, the jihadists took over the rebel-held half of Deir Ezzor on the Euphrates river, raising their black flag over the city and executing the rebel commander from Jabhat al-Nusra, the al-Qa'ida affiliate that was previously in control.

The recent ISIS advances in Syria, following victories in Iraq last month, are altering the balance of power in the whole region. The opposition military forces not aligned with the Syrian government or ISIS are being squeezed out of existence, making obsolete the US, British, Saudi and Turkish policy of backing groups hostile to both Assad and ISIS.

ISIS is seeking to capture the Syrian Kurdish enclave at Kobani, or Ayn al- Arab, where some 500,000 Kurds are concentrated, many of them refugees from other parts of northern Syria. "ISIS have about 5,000 fighters which have been attacking us for the past 13 days using tanks and rockets and American Humvees captured in Iraq," Idris

Naasan, a political activist in Kobani, told The Independent by telephone. "The fighting is very heavy and we have lost three villages we are trying to regain."

He said the normal population of Kobani region was 200,000 but this number is swollen by refugees from the border area and from Aleppo. Causing particular concern is the fate of 400 Kurdish hostages taken by ISIS, including 133 schoolchildren aged between 13 and 14. Mr Idris said negotiations with ISIS to exchange them for ISIS prisoners "took place three days ago but fell through because ISIS tried to take more hostages".

Maria Calivis, the UNICEF regional director for Middle East and Northern Africa, said in a statement at the start of the month that all of the children, with the exception of four who escaped, were still captive. "It has been over four weeks since the children were abducted as they returned to their home town of Ayn al-Arab [Kobani], after taking their junior high school final exams in Aleppo," she said.

There is no eyewitness information about the children but a report in the al- Quds al-Arabi newspaper said some of those abducted by ISIS may have been tortured. It added that they were being held in two schools and that families living nearby said they could not sleep because of the sound of children crying and screaming as they were tortured. They said they heard three shots from the direction of one of the schools, leading them to fear that children may have been killed.

The Kurdish enclave under attack at Kobani is one of several regions which are home to Syria's 2.5 million-strong Kurdish minority, most of whom live in the north and north-east of the country. The fate of Kobani has become a national cause for Kurds, particularly in Turkey just across the border. A statement from the Kurdish Democratic Union Party, whose "people's protection units" are doing most of the fighting to defend the enclave, says "all the Kurds should head towards Kobani and participate in the resistance". Mr Idris accuses the Turkish government of giving "logistical aid intelligence information to ISIS". Other Kurdish sources say this is unlikely, though they concede that Turkey has helped ISIS and Jabhat al-Nusra in the past.

The other main thrust of the ISIS offensive in eastern Syria has been towards Deir Ezzor, where it has defeated the Jabhat al-Nusra and Ahrar al-Sham groups. They say they are out-gunned and out-numbered by ISIS, which by one estimate has 10,000 fighters in Syria. Its morale is high, it is well financed through plundering banks and through the capture of oil wells in north-east Syria. ISIS has been successful in winning the allegiance of tribes, which are strong in Deir Ezzor and Raqqa provinces, by allocating to them oil production from different wells that can be sold on the black market.

ISIS has been engaged in a "civil war within the civil war" since the start of the year in which it battled the rest of the Syrian armed opposition, jihadi and non-jihadi. Up to 7,000 fighters may have been killed in this fighting. ISIS, which has always been well-led militarily, withdrew from Idlib province, Aleppo city and northern Aleppo province earlier in the year, a retreat misinterpreted as a sign of weakness by other rebel groups, but apparently a tactically astute manoeuvre to concentrate its forces.

Fresh from success in Iraq, ISIS is now counter-attacking strongly and, having taken Deir Ezzor, may seek to move back into Aleppo city from its base at al-Bab in east Aleppo province. Meanwhile, government forces in Aleppo city have been advancing against weakening rebel resistance and may soon have isolated the rebel-held districts. The Syrian army and ISIS may then confront each other as the only important players left in the civil war.

The Syrian opposition has always claimed that ISIS and Syrian government forces have had a sort of de facto ceasefire and hinted at undercover links. This was mostly propaganda, though regurgitated in Washington, London and Paris, but it is true that since ISIS helped to take Minnigh air base north of Aleppo last summer, it has mainly fought other rebel groups. When President Assad and al-Baghdadi do confront each other, the West and its allies will have to decide if they will go on trying to weaken the Syrian government.

AIR STRIKES? TALK OF GOD? OBAMA IS FOLLOWING THE JIHADISTS' SCRIPT
By Robert Fisk
22 August 2014

The "caliphate" has some pretty tough theatrical producers. They write a bleak and savage script. Our job is now to respond to each line, and they understand us well enough to know just what we'll say. So they beheaded James Foley and threatened to do the same to one of his colleagues, and what do we do? Exactly what I predicted 24 hours ago: turn Foley's murder into a further reason to go on bombing the ISIS "caliphate". And what else did they provoke from us - or at least from America's vacationing President? A battle on strictly religious terms, which is exactly what they wanted.

Yes, Barack Obama - before he headed back to the golf links - informed the world that "No just God would stand for what they [ISIS] did yesterday, and for what they do every single day." So there you have it: Obama turned the "caliphate's" savagery into an inter-religious battle of rival Gods, "ours" [ie the West's] against "theirs" [the Muslim God, of course]. This was the nearest Obama has yet come in rivalling George W Bush's gormless reaction to 9/11 in which he said that "we" are going to go on a "Crusade".

Now of course, Obama didn't mean the Muslim God, any more than Bush intended to send thousands of horse-mounted Christian warriors to the Biblical lands of the Middle East: indeed, Bush only sent tank-mounted and helicopter-borne warriors to those lands. No, Obama was also announcing that the "caliphate's" victims are "overwhelmingly Muslim" - ie that the "Caliphate" wasn't Muslim at all - although his enthusiasm to intervene earlier this month was not caused by his sympathy for these thousands of poor Muslims, but by the persecution of Christians and Yazidis. And of course the danger to potential American victims - a fact which Abu Bakr al- Baghdadi's men understood all too well.

That's why they slaughtered poor James Foley. Not because he was a journalist, but because he was an American, indeed one of the Americans Obama was promising to defend in Iraq. Whether or not Obama forgot about US hostages in Syria - the US military's attempt to rescue them at least proved they knew Foley was in Syria. But why is ISIS in Syria? To overthrow the Assad regime, of course, which is what we too are trying to do, is it not?

What on earth made Obama believe he could tell Muslims about what a "just God" would or would not do? For a President who regrets the Bush war in Iraq, does he not realise that millions of Muslims in Iraq believe that "no just God" would stand for the American invasion of Iraq in 2003, nor for the tens of thousands of Iraqis massacred because of the lies of Bush and Blair? I was amazed to hear Obama announce that "one thing we [sic] can all agree on" was that "a group like Isil has no place in the 21st century".

This is the same claptrap which that old scallywag Bill Clinton used when he addressed the Jordanian parliament after King Hussein's unpopular peace treaty with Israel: that those Muslim groups who opposed it were "yesterday's men". For some reason, we really think that the Muslims of the Middle East need us to tell them their history, what is good for them, what is bad for them. Muslims who agreed that Foley's murder was a revolting crime against humanity will have been insulted by being told by a Christian what a "just God" would approve or disapprove of. And those who supported such a crime will have been further convinced that America was a justified enemy of all Muslims.

As for the sinister British executioner "John", I rather think he may have lived in Newcastle-upon-Tyne or Gateshead, because - having spent time on Tyneside - I thought he seemed to have just a hint of the Geordie accent. But "John" could have been French or Russian or Spanish. It's not what went wrong in his mind, but what phenomena have afflicted so many other young men, in their thousands to do the same. How, for example, did an Australian apparently allow his young son to pose with the head of a decapitated Syrian soldier (a soldier serving, of course, in the army of the Assad regime we have all sworn to overthrow)?

And how have our security "services" responded to this? With the usual nonsense about how merely looking at such gruesome execution videotapes may be a terrorist crime. What is this tosh? Personally, I find it equally offensive to film - and show on television - the mass killing of human beings by US aircraft. But we do show them, don't we? We are repeatedly invited to observe on our television screens the targeting of supposed ISIS fighters and imagine their fate in the bubble of fire that consumes their pick-up trucks.

Because we can't see their faces doesn't make this any less obscene. Of course, their activities are the opposite of what James Foley stood for. But were they all actually fighters? We haven't yet heard that outrageous linguistic curse "collateral damage", but I bet we will.

So are our security bosses going to make the viewing of US military target videos a terrorist crime? I doubt it - unless, of course, the film shows us massacring lots of civilians. Then they could claim - rightly - that such viewing might encourage "terrorism". And we'd all have to give up covering the war.

Autumn 2014

Breeding ISIS

FROM DAMASCUS TO LATAKIA, A TOUR OF A NATION CONVULSED
By Robert Fisk
4 September 2014

Abdul Qadir al-Djezairi's palace is on the right, noble in spirit as well as architecture. He is the one who brought the Christians and Jews of Damascus to his home when they feared the Muslims in the 19th century.

He refused to countenance a Sunni-only city here; he was an ancestral enemy, I suppose, of the Daesh, as he would have called ISIS had they existed in his day, and as Arabs call it now. Below the walls at this moment are a row of minibuses at the local filling station. Their drivers queue for days for their diesel, ever more expensive, ever scarcer as an early winter burns up fuel for home heating.

In the coming days, I will see the alternative, truck after truck heading past me to Damascus, loaded with the chopped-up branches of great trees. The forests above Latakia are being denuded, the hillsides turned naked to warm the people of Syria's capital. Think Kabul. Or maybe Germany in the winter of 1944.

Of course there is no real comparison with that titanic tragedy. But drive north from Damascus and you cannot shrug off the Syrian war just because the first rains have washed the desert and the wind blows cold across the scrub. There to the west is Sidnaya. The Christians in their little towns here endured the taunts of those who said they "stood aside" in the war, hoping to escape the fury of the government's enemies.

In Homs, they tried to step aside, and when the Free Syrian Army - which existed then outside the Obama imagination - asked them to get Syrian checkpoints off their streets, the Christians obliged, only to find the rebels in their streets the next day.

Well, in Sidnaya, the Christians caught members of the Nusra Front and decided to change the narrative. They chopped off the heads of the Nusra and pushed them on to sticks because they didn't want the Christians to appear "soft" any more. Christians in Syria are traditionally very educated. They open restaurants, become doctors, engineers, make jewellery. A new picture now.

The road north is under repair - they are widening the dual carriageway to motorway proportions. Normality, you see. Just like it would have been four years and 200,000 lives ago. Nothing unusual. The government has confidence, does it not? So widen the roads! The industrial city of Adra glides by to the east, recaptured by the Syrian army last month, a place of horror for those who were massacred there and those few baked alive in the local bread ovens (courtesy of one Zahran Aloush of the Islamic Army).

Thousands were taken hostage, so many that they had to be freed and turned over to the Syrian army's Third Division, which witnessed this Biblical exodus, a replay of Palestine 1948 according to some soldiers who feared gunmen were among them - but who eventually overturned trucks carrying tuna so that they could feed the refugees. Vehicles in road accidents, you have to understand, become the responsibility of the security forces.

We drive past in silence. Empty highway. Not good news to any driver in a civil war. So we talk. My companion has a brother in the army and he was in the Aleppo military academy when the rebels surrounded it in July of 2012. Back in 1979 - 16 June, to be precise - Muslim Brotherhood rebels had stormed the academy and slaughtered 70 cadets. In 2012, my friend's brother - with his fellow undergraduates - waited amid the stench of corpses on the hillside around the school as his enemies shouted from below: "Remember the massacre of 1979? We're here to do it again!"

The Syrian military held out. The brother was saved. It's not always like that. In the Minegh airbase in Aleppo province, the Syrian army was overwhelmed by Islamist fighters, its last 130 soldiers attempting a final escape (having buried their dead comrades in the compound). The army claims it killed 1,300 rebels in the 15 months of siege (pinch of salt time, perhaps). Even their commander, Air Force

Major General Ali Selim Mahmoud, was killed in the final days of battle. Now Minegh is home to those famous gentlemen whose capital is in Raqqa, throat-cutting capital of the world, at least on video, certainly when journalists and Western NGO workers are to be dispatched.

Elsewhere in Syria, government soldiers are still surrounded, supplied by helicopter in their little fortresses, "festungs" that must not be surrendered - shades here of the German army on the Baltic coast in 1945 - as government-held territory slips and slides. There's a long, bleak stretch of road on the way to Homs which I don't like. Too few checkpoints. The Syrian Third Division fought twice to recapture this highway from the rebels last year.

Altogether, the Islamists held the road for 60 days. There are smashed restaurants, broken gas stations, a mosque tipping into a street. Turn left before Homs and there, far away beyond the trees is Krak de Chevaliers, Lawrence of Arabia's favourite Crusader castle, still standing, gleaming in the winter sun - too far for me to see its modern wounds - but blessed by a crescent of rainbows in far away rain.

And how suddenly we come to the brash money-belt of Tartous and Banias, landowners flourishing from the refugees flocking from the east of Syria. New apartment blocks of outrageous proportion above the Mediterranean, behind walls blossoming with death notices. If you doubt the 33,000 Syrian soldiers dead - or 46,000 as I suspect the real figure to be - then take a look at these black-and-white advertisements for war. The city flourishes as it loses its own sons in conflict.

There's a vile new shopping mall in Tartous that has appalled even Bashar al-Assad's supporters - you can't build a mall in Syria without someone giving you permission - and the death notices grow thicker as you drive north, even past the magnificent red-roofed villas of ex-vice president Abdul Halim Khaddam, defector and now Paris resident, but perhaps one day to return to his seaside home as a prodigal son of the regime - though I doubt it.

At Banias we turn east into the mountains, the Alawite hills, heimat of Bashar himself, his father Hafez and some of his warriors. Dreikish with its olives is home to "The Tiger", the general who freed the road from Hama to Aleppo, and some of these villages hold graves of men whom Baathist history books will record in years to come, supposing the party of the great Arab renaissance survives.

Sunnis are the backbone of the Syrian army - as they are of their enemies - but the Alawites, a minority of course, have paid a bloody cost for their own allegiance. Their soldiers fought in the Arab-Israeli war of 1973, the Israeli-Lebanon war of 1982, the town of Jibleh always a reservoir for the military. And now the mountain villages - the higher you go, the more breathtaking their beauty - are shadowed with crumbling Crusader keeps and waterfalls which shower down the rocks as flourishing and bountiful as the death notices on every wall.

This is the homeland of Hillal Assad, cousin of the president, head of National Defence in Latakia, felled by a mortar shell on the front line. There are squares named after the dead - the early casualties of this war were given whole streets named after them; but as the war gobbled up more casualties, there were not enough streets. A giant boot in Banias, planted with flowers - all soldiers supposedly know the suffering involved in wearing military boots -remembers the city's dead.

But above the Mediterranean, we come across the memorial to "Air Force Major General Ali Selim Mahmoud", born 25 July 1958, died 4 May 2013, commander of the Minegh air base in Aleppo province, a "Martyr Hero", or so it is written on the plinth, whose 130 surviving men made it home. Well, most of them, but that's another story). On top of the marble is a scale- model MiG fighter aircraft, any child's dream to take home as a toy.

And so we drive on, ever higher, till there is frost on the roofs. Opposite what the locals call the 'Spring of Esther' - yes, of course we drank the water - is a small garden of remembrance, and then wall after wall of the local dead. In some cases, their faces stare at us in monochrome photographs. Here is Corporal Amal Mohamed, killed in Aleppo, Major General Yassin Hassoun of the Syrian Army's 17th Division, killed in the Raqqa air base on 29 July 2014 before it collapsed to ISIS. "Considered dead," the poster says. In other words, his body never came home.

And here, too, are the death notices of - let us give them a little reality for a moment - Petty Officer Ayman Ibrahim, Private Ali Hafez Ahmed and Private Bashar Maon Aissa, Captain Murad Subah (killed 25 September 2012 at Quneitra, six months married), Captain Hassan Ali Mohamed (killed on the road to Aleppo,1 October 2013), Lieutenant Hassan Daboul and Private Samir Youssef Ahmed.

Yes, the Alawite villages have paid for all this. Beneath Private Aissa's death notice is printed a poem. "You will answer the call of the homeland/Our feet are firm on the ground./The mountains may move, but we won't/And God knows that our memory will live." Will it? Here in the village, perhaps. But remember, in the eyes of the world, these are the army of war criminals, the enemies of the West, of America - before Barack Obama decided that ISIS was even more horrible than the Syrian army.

But just one pause for thought. It was here in the mountains that I learnt of a unique Syrian military law. No family of brothers will serve in the army at the same time, even in war. There will always be a survivor. And a lone son does not have to serve in the military. In Syria, they don't have to save Private Ryan.

ASSAD'S LETTER TO AMERICA
By Robert Fisk
17 September 2014

Syria has asked Washington to engage in military and intelligence collaboration to defeat their mutual enemy ISIS, inviting US congressmen and senators to visit Damascus to discuss joint action against the jihadis who threaten both America and the regime of President Bashar al- Assad.

It's an offer that President Barack Obama will have to refuse - but not without some embarrassment. After deciding to bomb the forces of ISIS, which calls itself Islamic State, in Syria as well as Iraq, Mr Obama was confronted by Vladimir Putin's warning that any such unilateral action in Syria would be "an act of aggression".

The US President will now have to explain yet again why he cannot collaborate against America's "apocalyptic" enemies with a Syrian regime which he has also sworn to overthrow - even though this regime is fighting exactly the same enemies.

The letter to the US House of Representatives pointedly invites Congress and Senate members - who last year condemned the Syrian government for chemical attacks in the suburbs of Damascus - to collaborate "to save Syrian and American lives from a possible dirty bombing terror attack" by ISIS, Jabhat al-Nusra and other groups.

The Syrian offer, contained in a letter yesterday from Mohamed Jihad al-Laham, the Speaker of the tame Syrian parliament - addressed, among others, to John Boehner, the Speaker of the House of Representatives, and Nancy Pelosi, the House Minority Leader - also claims that the "moderate" Syrian opposition which the US has promised to aid and train is identical to the jihadi groups supporting ISIS, (or Isil as the Syrians prefer to call it, using another of the organisation's acronyms).

What was called the "moderate opposition", Mr Assad's parliamentary Speaker writes, "sold to Isil the innocent, beheaded US journalist. There is nothing to prevent those groups from selling US weapons to Isil as ... is their proven common practice." Arming "non-state Islamic jihadi individuals", the letter goes on, "is a clear violation of [UN] Security Council Resolution 2170 ... that any co-operation to combat terrorism should be among the member states".

Resolution 2170, passed last month, calls on member states "to suppress the flow of foreign fighters, financing and other support to Islamist extremist groups in Iraq and Syria" - identified in the UN document as ISIS and the al-Qaeda-linked Jabhat al-Nusra - and "to prevent fighters from travelling from their soil to join the groups".

Syria, of course, insists no "moderate" opposition now exists in the country, a statement which carries the mark of truth, and that all opponents of Mr Assad's rule were from the start Wahhabi-inspired Sunni jihadists - which was not in fact the case. Mr Laham's letter – which could not have been sent without the approval of the regime - accuses Saudi Arabia, which funds

Mr Assad's enemies, of sponsoring schools which are "teaching the ideology of hate, 'takfiri' [a Muslim accusing a fellow Muslim of apostasy] and jihad as holy duty".

Re-emphasising its own loathing of the Saudi regime, the Syrian letter says all "terrorists" are the product of "this Salafi, Wahhabi, jihadi ideology - from 9/11, to [the] Boston bombing, to the beheading of the two American journalists - beheading, which is a governmental legal practice in Saudi Arabia". Mr Obama should not form any coalition outside UN Resolution 2170, "especially with states that have a conflict of interest due to their practised ideology."

The letter may have been influenced by Khaled Mahjoub, a US citizen and Syrian businessman who is also a personal confidant of Bashar al-Assad, for it repeats Mr Mahjoub's oft-quoted observation that only re-education of "terrorists'" families and communities through "loving Sufism" can rehabilitate those who use violence. Sufism, with its mystical poetry and its desire to find divine love, is regarded by many Syrians as the very opposite of "jihadism"; Sufi missionaries spread Islam into Africa and central Asia as well as India.

All of which is a far cry from the titanic civil war in Syria where "moderate" schools of Sufism take third place to military hardware and the Russian-Iranian alliance in the regime's battle against ISIS. In truth, Western intelligence agents have for many months now been in contact with their Syrian opposite numbers to secure the kind of collaboration in secret which the regime is now offering in public - though without, it has to be said, much success.

Come into my parlour, says the spider to the fly. For the Syrian regime's web has proven far tougher than America and Europe imagined - and the principal fly has exhibited all the characteristics of weakness, fear and indecision which the Syrian spider understands. Only just over a year ago, the US was planning to smash the Syrian regime with bombs and missiles - and now that it wants to smash the ISIS regime with bombs and missiles, Syria will exact a price for any assistance Washington seeks.

SYRIAN ARMY LEADERS SLAUGHTERED
By Robert Fisk
28 October 2014

Syria almost lost its second city to the jihadists of ISIS and Jabhat al-Nusra last night when hundreds of fighters stormed into the provincial capital, Idlib, captured the newly installed governor's office and began beheading Syrian army officers. By the time government troops recaptured the building, at least 70 soldiers - many senior officers - had been executed, leaving one of the oldest cities in Syria in chaos. "They were slaughtered," a message to Damascus said before the army was able to declare Idlib saved.

The eastern city of Raqqa has been in the hands of ISIS for months, but Idlib lies strategically placed between Aleppo and the coastal city of Latakia - both of which are still held by President Bashar al-Assad's regime. Idlib's fall would have been a devastating blow to the government.

At one point, the Assad administration was told the city had fallen after police and security officers in the headquarters of governor Kheir Eddib Asayed defected to the rebels. Many did, in fact, surrender the building. But by chance soldiers on the city's perimeter did not receive this news and continued to fight hundreds of jihadis trying to break into Idlib. They were still holding off the attackers when the governor's office was recaptured.

Idlib lies scarcely 30 miles from Syria's largest city, Aleppo, and is home to more than 200,000 people. Its museum is well known to long-ago tourists wishing to see the treasures of the so- called Roman "dead cities" of northern Syria, and it has been in a virtual stage of siege for well over a year. But the shock at its near-collapse was palpable in the capital, Damascus, where the new governor - who was not in his office at the time - managed to call army headquarters just in time to prevent the announcement of Idlib's fall.

Although the attackers were identified as Jabhat al-Nusra rebels - the Syrian army regards all of its opponents as "terrorists" and part of ISIS - the assault was obviously intended to crown another shattering victory for the so-called Islamic caliphate which now stretches from eastern Aleppo to the outskirts of Baghdad in Iraq. The ferocity of the attack - some soldiers managed to call Damascus to alert the government to their imminent execution - shows just how hard-pressed the Syrian regime is in its battle against the same enemy that the US President, Barack Obama, has promised to "degrade and destroy". Degraded was the one thing the armed men who stormed Idlib appeared not to be.

When they arrived in the city centre, much as their comrades flooded into the Iraqi city of Mosul when the caliphate was first declared, the gunmen made sure to capture as many senior regime officers as possible. Their murder - by ritual beheading with a knife rather than shooting - was entirely in keeping with ISIS policy. Before they lost the centre of the city, Jabhat al-Nusra was boasting that its "victory" was "a second Raqqa" and that "soon, you will hear the screams of unbelievers". At Mushamah Hill outside the city, the jihadists captured two army tanks and 12 soldiers - their fate still unknown - while police in the city, apparently in league with would-be suicide bombers, opened the governor's office to the attackers.

It seems they were able to identify the senior regime soldiers for decapitation. They could not be saved. Government officials in Damascus would speak only of "many dead" when the first news of the assault reached the capital. The country's army has already lost at least 33,000 men - the real figure may well be above 46,000 - and the fall of Idlib would have marked a gruesome new stage in the Syrian war. Last night, the government's flag again flew over the governor's office. But for how long?

DESTROYED, THE SHRINE TO VICTIMS OF ARMENIAN GENOCIDE
By Robert Fisk
11 November 2014

In the most savage act of vandalism against Syria's Christians, Islamists have blown up the great Armenian church in Deir el-Zour, built in dedication to the one and a half million Armenians slaughtered by the Turks during the 1915 genocide.

All of the church archives, dating back to 1841 and containing thousands of documents on the Armenian holocaust, were burned to ashes, while the bones of hundreds of genocide victims, packed into the church's crypt in memory of the mass killings 99 years ago, were thrown into the street beside the ruins.

This act of sacrilege will cause huge pain among the Armenians scattered across the world - as well as in the rump state of Armenia which emerged after the 1914-1918 war, not least because many hundreds of thousands of victims died in death camps around the very same city of Deir el-Zour.

Jabhat al-Nusra rebels appear to have been the culprits this time, but since many Syrians believe that the group has received arms from Turkey, the destruction will be regarded by many Armenians as a further stage in their historical annihilation by the descendants of those who perpetrated the genocide 99 years ago.

Turkey, of course, miserably claims there was no genocide - the equivalent of modern day Germany denying the Jewish Holocaust - but hundreds of historians, including one prominent Turkish academic, have proved beyond any doubt that the Armenians were deliberately massacred on the orders of the Ottoman Turkish government across all of modern-day Turkey and inside the desert of what is now northern Syria - the very region where ISIS and its kindred ideological armed groups now hold. Even Israelis refer to the Armenian genocide with the same Hebrew word they use for their own destruction by Nazi Germany: "Shoah", which means "holocaust".

The Armenian priest responsible for the Deir el-Zour district, Monsignor Antranik Ayvazian, revealed to me that before the explosions tore the church apart towards the end of September, he received a message from the Islamists promising to spare the church archives if he acknowledged them as the legislative authority in that part of Syria. "I refused," he said. "And after I refused, they destroyed all our papers and endowments. The only genocide victims' bones left were further north in the Murgada sanctuary and I buried them before I left. They destroyed the church there, but now if I could go back, I don't even know if I could find where I put the bones."

Msr Ayvazian later received a photograph taken in secret and smuggled to him from the ISIS- controlled area, showing clearly that only part of the central tower of the Deir el-Zour church, built in 1846 and renovated 43 years later, remains. Every Armenian who has returned to then killing fields of the genocide has prayed at the church. Across these same lands, broken skulls and bones from 1915 still lie in the sand.

When I investigated the death marches in this same region 22 years ago with a French photographer, we uncovered dozens of skeletons in the crevasse of a hill at a point where so many Armenian dead were thrown into the waters of the Khabur that the river changed its course forever. I gave some of the skulls and bones we found to an Armenian friend who placed them in the crypt of the Deir el-Zour church - the very same building which now lies in ruins.

"During the Armenian genocide, the Turks entered the church and killed its priest, Father Petrus Terzibashian, in front of the congregation," Msr Ayvazian said. "Then they threw his body into the Euphrates. This time when the Islamists came, our priest there fled for his life." Msr Ayvazian suffered his own personal loss in the Syrian war when Islamist fighters broke into the Mediterranean town of Qassab on 22 April this year.

"They burned all my books and documents, many of them very old, and left my library with nothing but 60cm of ash on the floor." Msr

Ayvazian showed me a photograph of the Qassab church altar, upon which one of the Islamists had written in Arabic: "Thanks be to God for al- Qaeda, the Nusra Front and Bilal al-Sham" (another Islamist group). The town was retaken by Syrian government troops on 22 June.

Msr Ayvazian recounted his own extraordinary story of how he tried to prevent foreign Islamist fighters from taking over or destroying an Armenian-built hospital - how he drove to meet the Islamist gunmen and agreed to recover the corpses of some of their comrades killed in battle in return for a promise not to damage the hospital. "As I approached the hospital, a Syrian jet flew over me and dropped a bomb 40 metres from the building. I know the officer who sent the aircraft. He said it was his way of trying to warn the rebels not to harm me. They came out of the hospital like rats - but they did not harm me."

I spoke later to the local Syrian military air force dispatcher and he confirmed that he had indeed sent a MiG fighter-bomber to attack waste ground near the building. Msr Ayvazian subsequently went to the old battlefield with Syrian government permission and recovered several bodies, all in a state of advanced decay and one with a leg eaten off by dogs. But he bravely set off with trucks carrying the dead and handed the remains to the Islamists.

"They kept their word and later withdrew all their foreign fighters from the province of Hassake. I later received a letter from one of their emirs, very polite, telling me - and here the priest produced a copy of the note - that: "We vow to keep your property and your cherished possessions, which we also hold dear to us." Msr Ayvazian looked scornfully at the letter. "Look, here at the start," he said, "they have even made a mistake in their first quotation from the Koran! And then look what happened at Deir el-Zour. It was all for nothing."

Each year, thousands of Armenians have gathered at their church in Deir el-Zour on 25 April - the date they commemorate the start of the genocide, when Armenian lawyers, teachers and doctors were arrested and executed by the Turks outside Istanbul - to remember their million and a half dead. The 100th anniversary of the mass slaughter would have been a major event in Deir ez-Zour's history.

And although Syrian soldiers are still holding out in part of the town today, and Syrian authorities have promised to rebuild Armenian churches when their lands are retaken from the Islamists, there is little hope that any Armenians will be able to visit the ruins of their church in five months' time.

As for the Turks, they will do their best to stifle interest in the Armenian holocaust by holding their own commemorations next year - to mark their victory over Allied troops at the 1915 battle for Gallipoli.

'NO ONE IS BORN A TERRORIST. THE ISLAMIC COUNTRIES HAVE HELPED TO BREED ISIS'
By Robert Fisk
14 November 2014

The skies are grey-black from the oilfields and refineries at Rumeilan, a dingy, depressing cover that stretches from this Kurdish enclave far to the southern horizon where the Islamists of ISIS are sucking their own wealth out of the ground. Not that the Kurds have much money. Without refining chemicals, the "Democratic Self-Administration of Kurdistan West" - the wedge of territory that Syria allows the Kurds to hold between Qamishli and the Iraqi-Kurdish border - can only produce 30,000 barrels a day, and that's for their own use.

But this quaint little sub-state lives in a world almost as dark as the oil fires. Its "Self Protection Unit" militiamen lounge around the wells and beside the highway checkpoints, but no one can travel in or out of the enclave. Grass drifts over the old railway line to Mosul and all roads south lead to ISIS. Turkey won't open its border here and, half way into Qamishli, Syrian government forces control the land. The Kurds are in an enclave, reachable only by air. "Kurdistan East", by the way, is supposed to be Iraqi Kurdistan with its capital in Irbil - which has also closed its border to the "Democratic Self-Administration of Kurdistan West". All in all, a pretty pickle.

And there's no point in fooling yourself about where this would-be Ruritania searches for its ideological roots. Abdullah Ocalan's picture adorns street lamp-posts - the PKK leader still rots away in his Turkish prison - and there's a banner over the road 20 miles east of Qamishli which insists that "Kobani is the graveyard of ISIS" while avoiding the fact that Kobani has sent quite a few hundred Kurds to their grave as well.

But you've got to admire the Kurds, even though their history suggests they were born to be betrayed. They run a plucky little newspaper in Qamishli called Ronahi - "Light" - with 20 pages in Arabic, four in Kurdish, one of whose writers is 40-year old Mohamed Kamal who, in his world of websites, prefers to call himself a "media activist". "We are under a full economic siege," he says. "Everything is overpriced. Some traders even import at a price from ISIS and then sell at higher prices. We understand that the oil and wheat here belongs to all of Syria. But we should have a priority benefit from the wells in our area. We have no plans for independence from Syria, but we want self-administration and use our own resources here." Of the local 12,000 wells, the Kurds can operate only around 250, small affairs where the stink of oil and grit turns into dirty petroleum and asphalt.

Mr Kamal does not mince his words. "There has been a case of denial of the Kurdish people and their culture for the past 40 years, in fact ever since Syria's 'unity' with Egypt. Some people say the Assad family also have Kurdish roots, but it has made no difference. We were not even allowed to name a child with a Kurdish name. Yes, before we lived well but we had no freedom. Now we have freedom, but we don't live well."

Dream on, I thought to myself. I don't see a post-war Damascus government handing out oil concessions to these Kurds, especially when the Iraqi regime next door is a living example of what happens when you let a Kurdish federation take over some of your oil wealth. But Mr Kamal does dream on. "We have a diverse, democratic government here, based on ethnic and ideological plurality. Forty per cent of our administration officers are women. The two heads of administration are always one man and one woman. And if it were not for us, the rebels would have taken Hassake and Qamishli a long time ago."

This is not, I should add, the view of the army in Qamishli, which claims that without its tanks and air support, ISIS would have taken the Kurdish district a long time ago. But as we bump over the disused tracks of the Mosul railway, we enter the territory of the local Shumaa Arab tribe which is giving its support to the Self Protection Units. Some of these men rescued the Yazidi refugees on Sinjar mountain when ISIS attacked them. The Kurds - here and at Kobani - estimate they have already lost 1,000 "martyrs" in the battle with the Islamists in the last year. And of course, when I am about to meet the vice-president of the Energy Commission of the local Kurdish administration in the town of Makileh, I forget that this is Ocalan country and expect a middle-aged and verbose official to meet me. But Hivrine Khalaf is a 30-year old female civil engineer who knows all the senior oil workers by name and leads us to wells and refineries, reeling off statistics - Rumeilan at full capacity can produce 165,000 barrels-a-day rather than the measly 30,000 it provides for local consumption - and proving that these people really do believe in women's rights.

Hassan, an engineer, is running an ancient East German asphalt production plant - he says he was fired by the Syrian government on 27 May this year because he chose to work for the Kurdish self-administration here - and he's the first to suggest that ISIS must be receiving outside technical help to produce its oil. Another engineer was much more to the point. "We've talked to people - traitors - who sell oil for ISIS and they say that Turkish engineers are helping ISIS to operate the wells and refineries in their area, and they often see these Turkish engineers. We hear this all the time now - that the Turks are in the ISIS oilfields."

An intriguing remark. And if true, no wonder there exists a weird half-truce relationship between Turkey and the Islamists. Another member of the administration produced their own analysis of just why ISIS exists. "This has deep historical roots. They want to restore an Islamic state in this area. And this here is a culture that allows ISIS to prosper. No one is born a terrorist. The Islamic countries in particular have helped to breed this. Europe has overcome its history. But ISIS turned Syria into a rubbish pit where they send all their foreign fighters - and they arrive there from Turkey."

And of course, I asked Mr Kamal and Ms Khalaf about those well-known Middle Eastern characteristics - or at least the ones we Westerners like to graft onto the place - of patriarchy and chauvinism. "Our struggle is changing us," Mr Kamal said. "We have changed our view of the role of men and women. If our society is to evolve, women must have a bigger role." Ms Khalaf listens carefully to this. "Our struggle is a joint struggle," she replies. So maybe the Kurds do have a chance.

Winter 2015

ISIS Digs In

WEST IS WRONG AGAIN IN FIGHT AGAINST TERROR
By Patrick Cockburn
4 January 2015

Islamic State (IS) will remain at the centre of the escalating crisis in the Middle East this year as it was in 2014. The territories it conquered in a series of lightning campaigns last summer remain almost entirely under its control, even though it has lost some towns to the Kurds and Shia militias in recent weeks. United States air strikes in Iraq from 8 August and Syria from 23 September may have slowed up IS advances and inflicted heavy casualties on its forces in the Syrian Kurdish town of Kobani. But IS has its own state machinery and is conscripting tens of thousands of fighters to replace casualties, enabling it to fight on multiple fronts from Jalawla on Iraq's border with Iran to the outskirts of Aleppo in Syria. In western Syria, IS is a growing power as the Syrian government of President Bashar al-Assad loses its advantage of fighting a fragmented opposition, that is now uniting under the leadership of IS and Jabhat al-Nusra, the Syrian affiliate of al-Qaeda.

Yet it is only a year ago that President Obama dismissed the importance of IS, comparing it to a junior university basketball team. Speaking of IS last January, he said that "the analogy we use around here sometimes, and I think it is accurate, is if a JV [junior varsity] team puts on Lakers uniforms it doesn't make them Kobe Bryant [famed player for the Los Angeles Lakers basketball team]." A year later Obama's flip tone and disastrously inaccurate judgement jumps out at one from the page, but at the time it must have been the majority view of his national security staff.

Underrating the strength of IS was the third of three great mistakes made by the US and its Western allies in Syria since 2011, errors that fostered the explosive growth of IS. Between 2011 and 2013 they were convinced that Assad would fall in much the same way as Muammar Gaddafi had in Libya. Despite repeated warnings from the Iraqi government, Washington never took on board that the continuing war in Syria would upset the balance of forces in Iraq and lead to a resumption of the civil war there. Instead they blamed everything that was going wrong in Iraq on Prime Minister Nouri al-Maliki, who has a great deal to answer for but was not the root cause of Iraq's return to war. The Sunni monarchies of the Gulf were probably not so naïve and could see that aiding jihadi rebels in Syria would spill over and weaken the Shia government in Iraq.

How far has the political and military situation changed today? IS has many more enemies, but they remain divided. American political and military strategies point in different directions. US air strikes are only really decisive when they take place in close cooperation with troops on the ground. This happened at Kobani from mid-October when the White House decided at the last minute that it could not allow IS to humiliate it by winning another victory. Suddenly the Syrian Kurdish fighters battling IS shifted from being "terrorists" held at arm's length to being endangered allies. As in Afghanistan in 2001 and in northern Iraq in 2003, experienced personnel in the front line capable of directing the attacks of aircraft overhead are essential if those strikes are to be effective.

When the bombing of IS in Syria started, the government in Damascus felt that this was to its advantage. But while the US, Arab monarchies, Syrian rebels and Turkey may have overplayed their hands in Syria between 2011 and 2013, last year it was the Syrian government that did the same thing by seeking a solely military solution to the war. It has never seriously tried to broaden its political base at home by credible offers to share power, relying instead on its supporters to go on fighting because they believe that anything is better than a jihadi victory.

But these supporters are becoming worn out by the struggle because they see no end in sight. The government has always been short of combat troops, a weakness becoming more apparent as it calls up more reservists and diverts conscripts from entering the National Defence Force militia into the regular army. Government forces have made gains around Aleppo and Damascus, but they are losing ground south of the capital and in Idlib province. There have always been political advantages for Assad at home and abroad in having the Syrian rebels dominated by "terrorists" of whom the West is frightened. But the dominance of IS and Jabhat al-Nusra means that the Syrian army is losing its advantage of being a single force facing a disunited foe with 1,200 different factions. A sign of this underlying weakness is the failure of government troops to launch an expected offensive to retake rebel held parts of Aleppo.

IS won great victories in Iraq in the course of the year by taking advantage of the alienation of the Iraqi Sunni Arab community. This tied the Sunnis' fortunes to IS and, while they may regret the bargain, they probably have no alternative but to stick with it. The war has become a sectarian bloodbath. Where Iraqi army, Shia militia or Kurdish peshmerga have driven IS fighters out of Sunni villages and towns from which civilians have not already fled, any remaining Sunni have been expelled, killed or detained. Could IS launch another surprise attack as in June? This would be difficult outside Sunni-majority areas, though it could provoke an uprising in the Sunni enclaves in Baghdad, probably with disastrous results for the remaining Sunni in the capital. They were forced out of mixed areas in 2006 and 2007 and mostly confined to what a US diplomatic cable at the time called "islands of fear" in west Baghdad. IS could create mayhem in the capital, but the strength of the Shia militias is such that it would probably be at the price of the elimination of remaining Sunni enclaves.

Syria's two main foreign backers, Russia and Iran, are both suffering from the collapse in the oil price. This may make them more open to a power-sharing compromise in Syria, but it is by no means clear that they are being offered a deal by the West and its Arab allies. This may be a mistake since at the end of the day the great confrontation between Sunni and Shia across the Muslim world is not going to be decided by Iranian or Russian budgetary problems. Iraqi Shia militia units that withdrew from Syria to fight IS in Iraq can always be sent back and reinforced. The Iranians really do feel this is a war they cannot lose whatever the impact of economic sanctions imposed by the US. The balance of power between government and IS looks fairly even in Iraq at the moment, but this is not true in Syria where Sunni Arabs are 60 per cent of the population as opposed to 20 per cent in Iraq. Above all, IS is strengthened in Syria by the fact that the West,

Turkey and the Sunni Arab states are seeking the fall of Assad, IS's main opponent, as well as the overthrow of IS itself.

The mutual hatreds of its enemies remain IS's strongest card.

FOR CENTURIES, EVERY SYRIAN HAD A RIGHT OF PASSAGE TO LEBANON. NOT ANY MORE
By Robert Fisk
7 January 2015

ISIS is destroying the old Sykes-Picot border between Syria and Iraq, but Lebanon - its population diluted by refugees - is reinforcing its old French-created frontier with Syria. Not since 1943, when the French gave Lebanon its theoretical independence, has a Syrian citizen been forced to obtain a Lebanese visa to cross a border that for hundreds of years did not exist.

A quarter of Lebanon's population is now Syrian and although the refugee flow will continue - the Lebanese army can no more guard the smugglers' trails of misery leading from Syria's civil war than they can prevent ISIS from making forays into Lebanon - Syrian citizens arriving at the formal immigration post at Masnaa must now seek business, education, tourism or transit visas to enter. Tourist visas must be accompanied by a hotel reservation and proof that the traveller has £1,000. But permits will be given automatically to Syrians who own property in Lebanon. In other words, the rich - as usual - will pass more easily than the poor.

But none watch this influx of Syria's huddled masses with more social, political and historical interest than the Palestinian refugees who fled - or whose parents or grandparents fled - Palestine in 1948, victims of fear and massacre at the time of Israel's creation. Perhaps a quarter of the 750,000 refugees sought refuge in Lebanon then, believing - as many Syrians assume today - that they would be able to return "home" within days or months, if not years.

And since the Palestinians and their descendants in Lebanon - whose figures may have reached 350,000, and then diminished through further exile to nearer 200,000 - were treated with initial kindness, but then with suspicion, fear and ultimately hostility, one can only wonder how the 1.15 million registered Syrian refugees in Lebanon today will be regarded in future. Christian militias cruelly blamed the Palestinians for the 1975-90 civil war and feared that the country's minority Sunni community would become all-powerful if the Palestinian refugees, the majority of them also Sunnis, were to become citizens. UN refugee statistics suggest that 30 per cent of the world's refugees never return home. So how will Lebanon cope, even now, with perhaps 35 per cent of its occupants of Syrian nationality, most of them also Sunnis?

The figures are by nature vague. Besides 1.15 million UN-registered Syrian refugees, there are 12,500 waiting for registration in Lebanon, and perhaps another half million long-term Syrian residents or migrant workers - many of whom are children engaged in virtual slave labour in the fields of the Bekaa Valley. The total refugee population of Lebanon, including Syrians and Palestinians, might come close to 1,750,000.

Despite some outrageous rents, Christian-imposed curfews of poor Syrians living in mountain villages, and some intimidation of refugees in poorer areas of Beirut, the Lebanese have been remarkably kind to their Syrian brothers and sisters, perhaps mindful of the generosity of a peaceful Syria which received hundreds of thousands of Lebanese refugees during their civil war - and even more refugees from Iraq after America's 2003 invasion. Elaborate schemes have been introduced to educate Syrian children in Lebanese schools - taking into account the salient fact that Syrian educational standards are lower than those in Lebanon. Many Lebanese work without pay to help teach children in the UN-created tent refugee schools in the Bekaa Valley.

But there is no disguising the real - and, dare one say, understandable - anger directed at the Syrian rebel militias, who have used the Lebanese border as a sanctuary from Bashar al-Assad's army and also captured 29 Lebanese troops and police in the town of Arsal, three of whom they have murdered. The rest are now threatened with beheading. Weeks of street fighting between the army and Sunni militants in the northern Lebanese city of Tripoli have further damaged relations between Sunnis and Shia inside Lebanon - not least because the Shia Hezbollah militia is fighting alongside Assad's men inside Syria. Why, Lebanon's Sunnis have asked repeatedly, is the Lebanese army arresting armed Sunnis in Tripoli and imprisoning members of Sunni militias, yet allowing armed Shia Hezbollah members to patrol parts of Lebanon's border and to pass freely across the same frontier to fight for Assad?

The answer is painful: because Hezbollah largely leaves Lebanese Sunnis alone, but an armed Sunni community might go to war with Hezbollah. Assad's forces hold almost all the territory north and east of Damascus. A large-scale battle between Lebanese Sunnis and Assad's army, loyal to a Shia Alawite president, would bring Syria's civil war into Lebanon.

Unfortunately, history takes a back seat. Few outside Lebanon realise that before France partitioned Syria - a division opposed by a majority in the "new" Lebanon - Tripoli was the business hinterland of much of central Syria. Hundreds of thousands of Tripolitanians are related to Syrians who live in and around Homs. The French post-Great War border divided villages - as if by way of compensation, the French often built beautiful bridges between the two parts of each village, so that families could still cross the rivers that formed the new frontier.

Dreamers in the State Department may still demand strict sovereign adherence to these fraudulent borders; but that's not quite how the people who live there see the land around them, however many Syrian refugees are arriving in their midst.

'WE CANNOT PUT SOLDIERS EVERYWHERE ON THE SYRIAN BORDER'
By Patrick Cockburn
22 January 2015

President Barack Obama says that the US is to go on the offensive in Iraq, providing close air support to the Iraqi army when it attacks ISIS forces. But Iraqi sources say that the Iraqi army, badly beaten by ISIS last summer, is failing to reconstitute itself despite US efforts to retrain it. Even when supported by air strikes, it has made little headway and many of its combat units remain grossly understrength.

ISIS is likely to continue to rule most of the territory it has seized in Iraq and Syria because its many enemies are failing to unite and act decisively against it, according to those most familiar with the situation. Neither the Iraqi nor the Syrian army is capable of inflicting a decisive defeat on the self-declared caliphate.

The Turkish Prime Minister, Ahmet Davutoglu, who is visiting London, told The Independent that Turkey is unable to close its 510-mile-long border with Syria, which has been crossed by thousands of foreign jihadi volunteers. He said: "We cannot put soldiers everywhere on the border. In any case, there isn't any state on the other side [of the frontier]." Critics of Turkish policy say that much more could be done to hinder the flow of jihadis in and out of ISIS territory and into Turkey.

Mr Davutoglu said that Turkey opposes either ISIS or Syrian President Bashar al-Assad winning the war in Syria. He believes that if the international community is not going to send ground troops to Syria "the only alternative is to train and equip moderate opposition forces". Since such a force does not currently exist, and the armed opposition is increasingly dominated by ISIS and by the al-Qaeda affiliate Jabhat al-Nusra, Turkey evidently sees a long war with no obvious reason why it should end. The Syrian army is short of recruits and exhausted by four years of war while its three main allies, Russia, Iran and Hezbollah in Lebanon, have problems of their own.

American policy in Iraq and Syria continues to lack a credible strategy to defeat ISIS six months after it scored a series of victories over the Iraqi army that left it in control of northern and western Iraq. Mr Obama said that the first phase of a US-led campaign to defeat ISIS was over and had involved "getting an Iraqi government that was inclusive and credible - and we now have done that". In the next phase Mr Obama said that the US would provide close air support with air strikes clearing the way for an Iraqi army advance.

In reality, the political and military situation in Baghdad is by no means so rosy, despite Haider al-Abadi replacing the discredited Nouri al-Maliki as Prime Minister. For all Mr

Obama's optimism, US officials remain dubious about the real extent of Mr Abadi's authority.

The most significant failing in Iraq is its inability to build up an effective army after it disintegrated at the time of the fall of Mosul, Iraq's northern capital, on 10 June. "Ghost" soldiers abound. Divisions that are meant to have 4,000 combat troops may have only a few hundred men willing to fight.

The Iraqi army recaptured the refinery town of Baiji on the Tigris north of Baghdad at the end of last year in one of its few successes. But ISIS counter-attacked and recaptured the town which the army is once again trying to clear. ISIS said in a statement that a British jihadi, whom it called "Abu Sumayyah al-Britani" had blown himself up near Baijiin in a truck with eight tons of explosives, killing a police general, Faisalal-Zamili.

Contrary to Mr Obama's assertions, the most effective fighting forces of the Baghdad government are Shia militias that cleared ISIS-held towns south-west of Baghdad and won local victories in the mixed Sunni-Shia province of Diyala north-west of the capital. But the militias terrify Iraq's Sunni population and make it very difficult for the US to use its old strategy of splitting the Sunni community and turning the Sunni tribes against ISIS.

In Syria, ISIS is benefiting from the disarray and internecine hatreds of its opponents. Mr Davotoglu brushed aside reports that the US is no longer committed to ousting Mr Assad because it fears that, if he did go, ISIS, Jabhat al-Nusra and other al-Qaeda-type groups would be the main beneficiaries. Mr Davutoglu said he did not believe these reports and that the US had been saying openly and "telling us behind closed doors" that it still wants Assad to go.

Turkey plays a crucial role in the Syrian crisis because of its long border with Syria, part of which is now controlled by ISIS. Mr Davutoglu describes how Turkey's close relations with Mr Assad - "I visited there 62 times in 10 years" - soured in 2011 when "Assad started to kill his own people".

Mr Davutoglu makes no secret of his irritation at the way in which Turkey's motives and actions are misinterpreted as sympathy for ISIS. He points out that Turkey is looking after 1.5 million Syrian refugees who have fled Assad and 200,000 who have fled ISIS in Syria, in addition to 300,000 Iraqis who have been forced to flee because of ISIS advances.

With some justice, the Turkish Prime Minister says that ISIS was the creation of the war in Iraq and the US occupation after 2003 and Turkey had nothing to do with it.

Nevertheless, Turkey's policy in Syria has zig-zagged backwards and forwards, notably when ISIS attacked the Syrian Kurds at Kobani and almost captured the town in October. The Turkish President, Recep Tayyip Erdogan, denounced its defenders, the Syrian branch of the Kurdistan Workers' Party, as terrorists who were just as bad as ISIS. But

Turkey let Syrian Kurdish refugees into the country as well as allowing 150 Iraqi Kurdish Peshmerga to transit Turkey to reinforce Kobani.

The Americans find it easier to co-operate with the Iraqi Kurds than with the Iraqi army or the Shia militias. The Peshmerga has launched an offensive from the Mosul Dam near the town of Tal Afar that is held by ISIS, west of Mosul. Advancing with the aid of US air strikes - there were at least 23 on Tuesday and yesterday in Iraq and Syria - in this largely open landscape, the Peshmerga wants to cut ISIS road communications between Mosul and Syria.

But the politics of war in Iraq and Syria are very much shaped by sectarian and ethnic allegiances. Thus, though the Kurds may advance successfully, they probably will not try to storm Sunni Arab cities such as Tal Afar or Mosul itself.

The only force that might be acceptable to Sunni Arabs, if Mosul was to be attacked, would be the Iraqi army which is seen as less the monopoly of a single community than the Shia militias or the Kurds. That is why the failure to rebuild the Iraqi army is such an obstacle to a successful counter-offensive against ISIS.

HOW SYRIA LOST ITS HUMANITY
By Kim Sengupta
12 February 2015

Three years ago, when President Bashar al-Assad's position in Syria looked less secure, Abu Sakkar was among those the West regarded as a "moderate" rebel and a highly effective one at that. Omar al-Farouq - his khatiba, or brigade - was praised for confronting Islamic extremists. They had even arrested and executed the leader of a group of foreign jihadists who were then a new presence in the increasingly bitter strife. Khalid al-Hammad, which was his real name, was a jovial character. Any squeamishness we may have had being in the company of a killer was tempered by the fact that the man he had executed, Mohammed al-Absi, was himself a murderer and believed to be responsible for the kidnapping of the journalists John Cantlie and Jeroen Oerlemans - one British, one Dutch - who were subsequently rescued.

In the autumn of 2012, Cantlie went back to Syria with an American colleague, Jim Foley. In November, he was kidnapped again, as was Foley, and both ended up in the hands of ISIS.

Foley, who was a friend to many of us, was beheaded; Cantlie now appears in ISIS promotional videos - coerced, it is believed, into taking part. First seeing them came as a shock.

But a video featuring Sakkar - which appeared in May 2013, seven months after we had first met him - led to an even bigger shock: shock and disgust, which was expressed around the world.

Sakkar was filmed eating the freshly cut lungs of a dead government soldier, shouting, while mutilating a corpse: "I swear to God we will eat your hearts and your livers, you soldiers of Bashar the dog..." A gunman alongside grinned: "It looks like you're carving him a Valentine's heart."

A few of us journalists phoned each other: "Was that really him? Sakkar? What happened?" The man himself sought to explain to the BBC's Paul Wood in an interview a little later: "Put yourself in my shoes. They took your father and mother and insulted them. They slaughtered your brothers, they murdered your uncle and aunt. They slaughter your neighbours," he said. "We have to terrify the enemy, humiliate them, just as they do us. I didn't want to do this; I had to.

Now, they don't dare be wherever Abu Sakkar is."

The violence in Syria has since then continued relentlessly, with an ever rising body count. Even by the vicious standards of this conflict, the burning alive of the Jordanian pilot Moath al- Kasasba was stunning in its savagery. But it followed all manner of horrific executions - by beheading, stoning and being thrown off high buildings - charted in "snuff" videos coming out of Syria and Iraq; they generate expressions of horror, if little expectation of the atrocities ending.

But those carrying out these acts have not suddenly appeared out of nowhere. What we are seeing is people who would have been in our realm of normality not so long ago, now embracing extreme violence. This, of course, has happened in many conflicts in recent history, but in the carnage of Syria, the descent into barbarity has been remarkably swift.

The latest Cantlie video, released this week, had scenes from the town of Al-Bab, and I studied the brief footage with curiosity. Having spent some time in the town since the uprising began, I recall the friendship and protectiveness shown by the people at times of great danger.

By the summer of 2012, Al-Bab had become a focal point of protest against Bashar al-Assad. I was with a crowd, many of them unarmed, when they stormed a government military base from which artillery rounds were being lobbed on to the population. I also accompanied their fighters during the ferocious battle for Aleppo later that year, when the town provided the largest contingent on the rebel side.

The town was later taken over by Jabhat al-Nusra, an al-Qaeda affiliate, and then by ISIS - and both these groups started off by taking over the military barracks and bombarding the population, just as the regime forces had done. Then, on each occasion, they occupied the town. Local fighters drove off the extremists a number times, but were ultimately overwhelmed by numbers.

The harshest Islamic rule was then imposed on an already conservative society. A shisha café where we relaxed after a day of air strikes and tank fire in Aleppo - with its ever-hospitable young owner, Mohammed, who would laughingly talk about opening up branches in London - was closed down.

But this was a minor act in a process of purification compared with the introduction of whipping, amputations and hangings that followed. The young activists, the students, lawyers and doctors who used to debate about the future democratic shape of Syria late into the night in Mohammed's café disappeared. Some were killed or imprisoned, others fled across the border into Turkey. But not all of them; a very few joined the persecutors.

One, 26 year-old Abdulhamid, a shop assistant, made the jihadist journey through increasingly hard-line groups. I met him in the Aleppo province in the autumn of 2013, when the US was threatening to bomb the regime after the chemical attack on Al-Ghouta. (This was dropped after the Russians brokered a deal under which President Assad was supposedly giving up his WMD arsenal.)

Abdulhamid had fought with a small band under the black banner of al-Nusra, which was then in the process of merging with a then little known group coming out of Iraq called ISIS. (They were to have a violent split later.) Now, at a village near the town of Mara, Abdulhamid described in detail how he had executed rafidis, a pejorative term used by Sunnis for both the Shias and their offshoot, the Alawites, from which Syria's ruling elite is drawn.

When I reminded him of his past views - how there should be room for all denominations and political persuasions in his country - there was righteous indignation. He was furious at the American failure to act over the chemical attacks, a constant complaint in opposition-held areas at the time, and at the hypocrisy of the West, including its media.

"People in Europe and America want us to fight Bashar, but where is the help? How many people have died waiting for them to help? You have seen what Bashar's people have been doing. Then people come and lecture us.

" The rafidis I killed were dogs. I am proud to have killed them. It is easy to kill a man when you hate him so much. Others used their knives. I shot them; some of them I shot several times to make them suffer. I have no regrets, no regrets," he declared, glaring around the roadside shack. The others in there looked away.

Abdulhamid and his men took us to a row of five graves. "Spies. One of them was quite young, maybe 12. But a baby snake grows up to be a big snake, so better to kill when it's young," said one of the fighters with a shrug.

Four little boys, playing nearby, came over and started shouting revolutionary slogans, eagerly waiting in line for a chance to hold the men's Kalashnikovs, which were almost as big as they were. My translator asked what they thought of the boy buried there.

"He was a traitor. He deserved to be killed," piped up one. Later, out of earshot, the translator whispered: "What have we done to these kids?"

I met Abdulhamid again early last year in the Turkish border town of Gaziantep. His long beard had been trimmed and he had changed his combat fatigues for jeans and a T-shirt.

Accompanying him was another young man - Yusuf, from Idlib City - also in civilian clothes. Both of them claimed they were disillusioned with the fighting and wanted to focus on the civic struggle instead.

By then, I had already spent the afternoon listening to the harrowing story of a female activist who had been assaulted by the Mukhabarat, the Syrian regime's secret police, in the city of Hama. On being released she had fled to Turkey - but then her sister was arrested and gang raped, having her jaw, ribs and a hand broken in repeated beatings.

"I still cannot believe all these things happened; that things like these are happening now," she said. "Our Hama will never be the same again. Our country will never be the same again.

Everything has now been crushed."

I told Abdulhamid and Yusuf that I could, perhaps, understand how the rage sparked by such abuse had led to the excesses committed by the rebels. But Abdulhamid was distracted, twisting a paper napkin in his hand. According to his account, he had joined ISIS and then left of his own volition. According to others, he had been chased out for transgressions.

He didn't want to talk much about what he had done with ISIS, only saying that he had seen some "really bad things".

Yusuf, a 20-year-old student, shook his head: "If I was the brother and husband of those women, for sure I would kill Assad's soldiers, the Shabiha [Alawite militia]. But I would not torture them and I certainly would not kill civilians just because they were Alawites."

There had been reports by then that Abu Sakkar had been killed: gory photographs had appeared of his supposed death.

"Of course what he did with the body was haram [unlawful in Islam]. But you heard that female members of his family were raped and murdered? That affected him -and in this war, a lot of people have done bad things," Abdulhamid wanted to stress this.

Yusuf pointed out "When the protests first started, Khalid al-Hamad [Abu Sakkar] was in Baba Amr, and was just taking part in marches like the others. It is when Assad's people started shooting the peaceful people that he began to fight. What was right or wrong in fighting in the past is not so clear now."

In the end, Abdulhamid went back to Syria, unable to resist the lure of combat. Yusuf remains in Turkey, trying to get to another country. He says he won't go back to Syria even if the war ends.

"There'll be no real peace," he said. "Families will try to take revenge on each other. Too much has already been done in blood."

Spring 2015

Defeating ISIS

'THE BEATING WENT ON AND ON. I KNEW I MUST FIGHT BUT I BEGAN TO PASS OUT'
By Kim Sengupta
2 May 2015

Rayan was smashed in the face with a rifle butt and flung head first down concrete steps. Then he was hung from the ceiling by his wrists and beaten. Even then, the torture was not over: it stopped only when he fainted from the excruciating pain of being placed in a tyre while his legs were twisted and wrenched with a stick.

The 37-year-old interior decorator and judo trainer had been among the first to join the protest movement against Syria's President, Bashar al-Assad. But the torture inflicted on him was not by the regime. It was by rebels supposedly on his side - another grim example of how Syria's revolution is now consuming its own children.

Rayan is the nickname of Mohammed Oun, a well-known civil rights campaigner in northern Syria. He was held captive by Islamist extremists after taking part in the first large-scale demonstration inside rebel-held Syria against groups like ISIS and Jabhat al-Nusra, held by people protesting against their vicious rule in the city of Aleppo.

Speaking in the safety of a town just across the Turkish border, Rayan described how the extremists attacked that brave demonstration, held in the first week of April. He told me of the mounting despair among those who had seen their revolution against the Assad regime hijacked, with the ideals for which they had sacrificed so much now lost. He also spoke of his intention to go back to Aleppo, despite the risks this would entail.

I had first met Rayan in Aleppo during the fierce battle in the summer of 2012 for the country's richest and largest city. Two Syrian activists and I had gone to pick up Jim Foley and Nicole Tong, friends and fellow journalists, who were staying with Rayan at his home in the Bustan al-Qasr district, an area taken over by regime forces.

I had worked alongside Foley and Tong, covering a number of wars. Foley was kidnapped and murdered on a subsequent visit to Syria, the first of six foreign hostages to be beheaded by "Jhadi John" - the Londoner, Mohammed Emwazi, who has become the grotesque star of the organisation's slick "snuff" videos. Foley had been kidnapped along with the British photographer, John Cantlie, in Autumn 2012. A little later, Tong visited Rayan in Aleppo and told him what had happened.

Rayan, softly spoken and good humoured, recalled his own concerns about Foley. "Criminal gangs were kidnapping people and selling them to groups like Daesh [ISIS] who were lookingfor Western people," he said.

"We knew how violent they were, what they might do. At the time we thought - we hoped - something will be done and Jim will be freed. We were very grateful for foreign journalists coming to the free part of Syria to show the terrible things going on. It was shocking thatthey and aid workers were being taken prisoner. We were protesting against the way some ofthese extremist groups were behaving."

Rayan searched long and hard for Foley but he, along with Cantlie, had been passed repeatedly from one group to another. Later Rayan saw the video of Foley's death. "It showed what had happened to our revolution. The only foreigners the extremists wanted here were those who would take part in their jihad. Local people in Aleppo were also suffering badly in the hands of these people and we felt we must keep speaking up - we mustprotest."

But that came at a cost. Rayan had previously been abducted by the al-Qaeda affiliate, Jabhat al- Nusra - the first time, in November 2013, after he and others objected to their treatment of anyone questioning their version of sharia law. He was subjected to one of their favourite forms of torture, the "aeroplane", in which victims are suspended from the ceiling and beaten.

The activist was released after a few days with a warning. At the time the hardliners did not worry about liberals like Rayan too much: they were on a roll, extending their fiefdom as the Western-backed Free Syrian Army lost ground, men and influence. Al-Nusra and ISIS were sometimes in alliance, sometimes fighting each other.

By the beginning of this year, most moderate activists in opposition areas had been forced to flee, been imprisoned or killed. But those who remained decided they must take a stand for the original values of the revolution before it was too late. A demonstration was to be staged in Aleppo, with the organisers declaring that all the differing groups of the revolution would be welcome.

Bari, another activist, said: "The aim was to re-establish the ideal of the revolution - democracy, equality and a united Syria. We could not let this continue, the extremists oppressing the people while Bashar continues to do his own oppression. We wanted there to be a debate about the course of the revolution."

Bari's own home town, al-Bab, around 20 miles from Aleppo, was a microcosm of what happened. The moderate rebels took control first; then al-Nusra, which is allied to al-Qaeda, established a presence, and finally came occupation by ISIS, and with it a savage regime of shooting, hanging and flogging.

Rayan said that at the Aleppo demonstration at first, there was laughter, camaraderie and cries of "freedom" from the crowd of around 300, just like the early days of the revolution. But then al-Nusra men appeared in trucks, along with some of their supporters. These included members of Hizb ut-Tahrir, a radical Islamic group with an extensive network in the UK. The organisation in the UK has denied any links with Al-Nusra.

Al-Nusra responded to calls for tolerance with their swords, chopping down the green, white and black flags of the revolution. They then turned their swords on the protesters. One of their leaders who tried to calm the situation was screamed at by one of his own fighters, waving a Kalashnikov assault rifle: "You have become an atheist!"

The activists decided to complain about the attacks to the sharia court and Rayan was chosen as their spokesman. As he left court the next day, he was ambushed by three masked men and knocked down with rifle butts. Blindfolded, he was taken to what he thought was a warehouse an hour's drive away.

Rayan was put in a tiny cell. He then heard a whisper, the prisoner next door had gouged a hole in the wall and desperately wanted to get a message to the outside. He was an officer in the Farouq Brigade, a moderate group which had been accused of killing a leader of a Salafist faction, Dawa al-Islamiyah.

Here was another strand of the web linking Islamist rebels with hostage taking. Dawa was suspected of being behind the kidnap in 2012 of Cantlie, along with a Dutch photographer, Jeroen Oerlemans.

The two men were rescued by moderate fighters; the execution of the Dawa leader, Abo Mohammed al-Shami, was seen as retribution for the abductions.

Since his second kidnapping, Cantlie remains the last known Western hostage of ISIS. He has been appearing, under duress, to appear in the group's propaganda videos.

Rayan decided there was no point in being apologetic during his interrogation. "They knew my views, they wouldn't have believed if I had told them that I had suddenly changed my mind and agreed with them. In any case they brought along an informer who accused me of spying on al-Nusra, being a kuffir [an unbeliever], all kinds of things. So, I was found guilty very quickly.

"At that point the man questioning me took off his mask. Now, I began to feel frightened: if he was willing to show his face to me, I thought for the first time that I wasn't going to get out alive. There was a tremendous feeling of hopelessness, but I knew I must fight against it."

Guards were called and ordered that the "kuffir" be punished. Rayan was thrown down the stairs, his head bouncing on the steps. Then the vicious ritual began: he was strapped to a bed and whipped with a length of cable. Then came the "aeroplane", more beating. "It went on and on, but it was probably about two hours," he said. "I tried to shut my mind, but the pain gets through; when I thought it was over, I realised they had other plans for me."

Rayan was placed inside a tyre and a stick was used to twist his legs. "This was worse than anything before, and I began to pass [out]. As I was fading away I could hear one of them complaining that I was fainting too soon."

He was awakened with water thrown over him, and then driven back to Aleppo in a van, his face forced down on the floor with a boot on his head. He was produced before a sharia court. But if al-Nusra had expected a swift sentence of judicial killing they were disappointed: fighters from moderate rebel militias were there, having heard what had happened.

When al-Nusra officials accused Rayan of inventing his torture account, he took off his shirt to show the marks of whipping on his body, and then his trousers to reveal horrific injuries to his legs. "The judge was a good judge, and he said I must be freed immediately. That shows there are still people who will stand up to extremists - it is something we can build on," he insisted.

Now Rayan says he will be going back to Aleppo soon. The dangers are obvious, but he says: "We need to continue fighting back. These people have gained so much power because other people have been afraid to speak up. But the protest march showed people are prepared to stand up for the revolution despite the dangers: we have no other choice."

THE KURDISH FORCES WITH A LESSON IN HOW TO DEFEAT ISIS
By Patrick Cockburn
23 May 2015

In a room in a house on the slopes of Mount Abdulaziz, five ISIS fighters were under siege by Syrian Kurdish fighters. "They can't get out," says a voice cutting through the crackle on the field radio. "But one of those bastards just shot and wounded one of our men."

This was a mopping-up operation, a day after a major battle for Mount Abdulaziz had ended with the defeat of some 1,000 ISIS fighters who had been besieged. The mountain was one of the jihadists' strongholds in this corner of north-east Syria, from which they could fire artillery into the nearby Kurdish city of al-Hasakah and menace a fertile Kurdish enclave with a population of one million.

ISIS fighters did not leave much behind in their retreat. There remain a few freshly painted slogans in praise of ISIS, and some burned-out hulks of cars that had been used as bombs. Crisp new cards lie discarded on the floor of one building, saying "Office of Zakat (obligatory tax for the benefit of the poor) and Insurance", which appear to be ration cards requiring the listing of names, numbers and other details. The cards underline the extent to which ISIS is well organised - and confirm that its leaders have renamed the Syrian provinces, changing al-Hasakah to Barakat.

The defeat of ISIS in the battle which started on 6 May is in sharp contrast to the jihadist group's victories over the Iraqi army at Ramadi and the Syrian army at Palmyra over the last week. An explanation for the difference in the outcome of the three battles is that the Syrian Kurdish forces are highly motivated, disciplined and come from the area in which they are fighting. The Kurdish commander General Garzan Gerer, interviewed by The Independent beside a pine forest just below the mountain, said "We fight better than the Syrian army at Palmyra because we have strong beliefs and we are defending our own land."

There is another more material reason why the Kurds won and ISIS lost. Young Kurdish fighters resting in a captured ISIS command post, painted in green, cream and brown camouflage colours, are open about how much they benefit from US air strikes. Botan Damhat, a smooth-faced squad commander aged only 18, said: "Without the American planes, it would have been much harder to take the mountain. We would have won in the end, but we would have lost a lot more men."

Kurdish commanders were unclear yesterday about casualties, saying they had buried 300 bodies of ISIS fighters but many more had been carried away. They put their own fatalities at between 25 and 30, the disparity perhaps being explained by the effectiveness of American airstrikes. Asked why some ISIS headquarters had not been bombed, Botan Damhat said that on the whole ISIS had hidden in the pine forests on the slopes of the mountain "and the Americans knew that so they did not destroy the buildings". In some cases, ISIS set fire to its buildings before retreating.

General Gerer said the two main problems in capturing the mountain were the terrain and the fact that "many of the local villages are Arab and they often supported Daesh", using the invariable name in Iraq and Syria for ISIS. He said that there were also 25 Assyrian Christian villages where the jihadists had prevented people from leaving so they could be used as hostages in the event of a Kurdish attack. He did not think more than a few of the Arabs who had supported ISIS would come back. As we left, we saw a party of Arabs with their belongings returning to their house in a village. They waved rather frantically as we drove past in a military vehicle, as if uncertain about how they would be treated by the victorious Kurds.

Who were the ISIS fighters holding Mount Abdulaziz? The Kurds insisted their opponents were Muslims from all over the world, one of three of those captured turning out to be Chinese. In one building, they had found neat little notebooks with translations of different words into a variety of languages, and drawings of a desk and chair with their names in tiny handwriting.

Yalmaz Shahid, 25, another squad leader, said that ISIS had fought well. "We were particularly afraid of their suicide bombers and booby traps." Another fighter, who gave his name as Ernesto, said "they are very professional snipers".

The victory at Mount Abdulaziz is the biggest Kurdish success since the four-and-a-half month siege of the town of Kobani on the Turkish border which ended earlier this year. In the town of Amuda, where I am staying, a few miles from the Kurdish city of al-Qamishli, there was the rattle of festive gunfire well into the night and parties of children patrolled the streets singing patriotic songs in celebration.

But not all the news this week is good for the Kurds. With the fall of Palmyra, ISIS now holds half of Syria and part of the rest is held by Jabhat al-Nusra, the Syrian affiliate of al-Qaeda that has fought the Kurds in the past. Overall, ISIS is much stronger than it was pre-Ramadi and Palmyra in terms of morale and prestige among the Sunni Arabs, not to mention captured equipment.

In an interview with The Independent, Amina Osse, the deputy foreign affairs manager for what Kurds call Rojava, said that she feared that ISIS was now expanding fast "and may soon threaten to take all of Aleppo", Syria's largest city. She added that, as with the fall of Mosul last year, ISIS had captured a lot of arms and ammunition. This would enable them to renew their assault on the Syrian Kurds when they want to.

She did not have much confidence in President Bashar al-Assad's Syrian army, saying it was exhausted and suffered from the old Baath party tradition of having few links with, and thus little support from, the people of the local area. She recalled that in one battle last year, the Syrian army had abandoned 35 tanks after rejecting offers of Kurdish help against ISIS.

The problem for the Syrian Kurds is that, although their discipline, backed by US air power, has been effective, they number only about 2.2 million or 10 per cent of the Syrian population. They will have difficulty holding off an ISIS able to draw on resources in Syria and Iraq and having recently defeated the regular armies of both countries. The Kurdish cantons strung along the Turkish border are isolated and economically besieged from all sides.

The region is fertile with wheat fields, and the roads are full of vehicles with harvesting machinery. There are also over 1,000 "nodding donkeys", the pumps which once produced oil but are now almost all unused and rusting. Some oil is produced locally, but it is of poor quality, causing damage to vehicle engines.

The outcome of the battle for Mount Abdulaziz shows the Syrian Kurds are militarily strong and can hold their own against ISIS in a way that Syrian and Iraqi soldiers cannot. But in the long term, their de facto independent enclaves, ruling themselves for the first time in history, are very vulnerable to whoever turns out to be the winner in the Syrian civil war.

KURDS COUNT THE COST OF BATTLING ISIS
By Patrick Cockburn
24 May 2015

A squad of Syrian Kurdish fighters was ambushed as it advanced through a grove on the outskirts of a village held by Islamic State (IS) fighters near al-Hasakah in the Kurdish enclave in north-east Syria. Azad Judy, an 18-year-old Kurd, recalls: "We had divided into three groups that were trying to attack the village when we were hit by intense fire from behind and from the trees on each side of us."

Azad, who comes from Nusaybin just across the border in Turkey, was hit by a single bullet in the spine. He says: "After being wounded, I tried to crawl away and then another fighter came and gave me first aid and an injection." Azad is now lying in bed in the Shahid Khavat military hospital in the Syrian Kurdish city of al-Qamishli with a despairing look on his face because he may suspect that his legs are paralysed for ever and he will never walk again.

In a week during which the Syrian and Iraqi regular armies were defeated by IS at Palmyra and Ramadi, the lightly armed Syrian Kurdish militia, known as the YPG, won an important victory. It captured a strategically placed mountain known as Abdulaziz in Arabic and Kazwan in Kurdish, which had been a heavily defended IS stronghold. Supported by US air strikes, 1,000 YPG fighters surrounded the mountain whose lower slopes are covered by pine woods. The battle started on 6 May and ended last Wednesday when the remaining IS forces withdrew after suffering heavy losses. The Kurds say they buried 300 bodies of IS fighters and believe more were carried away.

A military hospital is a good place to hear eyewitness accounts of the warfare that laps around this isolated area of Syria where it borders Turkey and Iraq. It is part of Rojava, the de facto independent Kurdish state-let where several million Kurds live in three separate cantons on the Turkish border. Though 10 per cent of the Syrian population of 22 million, the Kurds were a persecuted minority up to the moment that the Syrian army withdrew in 2012. Discrimination was so intense that everything from babies to mountains had to be referred to by an Arabic rather than a Kurdish name.

Ignored by the outside world, the Syrian Kurds unexpectedly achieved international notoriety when they successfully defended their city of Kobani against IS assault in a 134-day-long siege that ended earlier this year. This is the most serious defeat that IS has suffered since the fall of Mosul and creation of Islamic State in June 2014.

Among the wounded fighters in the military hospital is a man who says he would like to be referred to only by his Kurdish name of Shiyar, but turns out to be from West Yorkshire. I have always had something of a prejudice against volunteer soldiers in war in the Middle East, suspecting them of indulging in martial fantasies and bigger on bravado than military effectiveness. But Shiyar, 33, turns out to be modest and self-deprecating, giving a compelling account of recent fighting and saying that his wound from shrapnel that had hit him in the back of the head was not as serious as he had feared.

Shiyar says he was born in Halifax and joined the British Army when he was 18, but otherwise he had worked as a roofer and a driver and had lived for five years in Portugal. He had come to this part of Syria to fight IS because "nobody else seemed to be doing anything". Smuggled across the border from Iraqi Kurdistan, he was part of a rapid reaction force to retrieve wounded and make counterattacks. He speaks highly of his Kurdish commander, Hebal Saram, and says other members of his unit were foreigners who had been members of regular armies, or Kurds.

He himself had been wounded in confused fighting when attacking some IS fighters who exploded an IED behind him. He looks gaunt and unsteady on his feet, but he says that his worst long-term injury is deafness in one ear because another fighter was firing his machine gun a few inches from him as he lay on the ground.

Of the Syrian Kurds as fighters, he had nothing but praise saying: "I have never met a braver bunch of soldiers in my life." He added that they were armed only with old Kalashnikovs and some Russian light machine guns, while IS had the latest Humvees and machine guns captured from the Iraqi army. He said he seldom saw enemy fighters though they had launched a vehicle packed with 5,000lb of explosives at them, which they fired at until it blew up. He was intending to return to the front when the doctors let him out of hospital.

The Syrian Kurdish fighters may be brave, but they are also isolated by IS whom they are fighting on one side, a hostile Turkey to the north and Iraqi Kurdistan (known as the Kurdistan Regional Government) which sees the PYD, the ruling party of Rojava, as a possible rival. The PYD is effectively the Syrian branch of the Kurdistan Workers' Party or PKK of Turkey, which has periodically tense relations with the KRG.

These complex Kurdish rivalries can have unfortunate consequences for Kurds living on the front line. One of the beds in the military hospital is occupied by Jinda, a 20-year-old woman who had been shot through the right side of the chest, but this had happened in Shingal, a Kurdish-controlled area in Iraq. Jinda says proudly that she was one of the first women to join protection units of Shingal and had been wounded during a sudden IS attack She believes she might be arrested if she went to a KRG hospital, though she had been allowed across the border from KRG to hospital in al-Qamishli. She speaks scathingly of the Iraqi Kurdish Peshmerga failure to defend Shingal last August, "when they withdrew and left our women to be taken as captives and our men massacred".

The Syrian Kurdish experience is that IS can be defeated when an effective light infantry on the ground is matched with US air power overhead. In the case of the YPG, they simply send co-ordinates of IS positions back to the US-Kurdish operations room in Irbil, the Kurdish capital, which directs air strikes. But a notable feature of the past week in Syria is that the US air force did not bomb IS forces when they were advancing on Palmyra. The Americans avoided doing this because they did not want to be accused of doing anything that might lead them to be accused of helping the Syrian army or President Bashar al-Assad. Likewise in Iraq, they did not want the Shia militias deployed to defend Ramadi and refused to supply air cover and intelligence if this did happen.

But the IS victories of the past week mean that the US may now have no alternative but to give air support to all enemies of IS regardless of their identity.

THE ROAD TO RAQQA
By Patrick Cockburn
26 May 2015

The Kurdish soldiers relax half a mile behind the front line where they have been battling ISIS forces west of the Syrian town of Ras al-Ayn. The women are in no doubt about why they are fighting.

Nujaan, who is 27 and has been a soldier for four years, says that ISIS's "target is women". She says: "Look at Shingal [in Iraq] where they raped the women and massacred the men. It is a matter of honour to defend ourselves first, and then our families and lands." Sitting beside her is Zenya, 22, who adds that she also "is fighting for myself and my family".

Overhead, the drone of US aircraft is clearly audible and Nujaan reports that there have been several air strikes that morning, as well as ground fighting.

She says that several Kurdish soldiers have been killed and wounded, though she does not know the details. She adds that the YPJ Kurdish women's militia, to which she belongs, is gradually driving ISIS towards the west. She and the other women appear remote and detached from what they are saying, possibly because they are exhausted from days on the front line.

In fact, the push westwards mentioned by Nujaan is of great military and possibly political significance because the Syrian Kurdish armed forces are closing in on a crucial ISIS-controlled border crossing point from Syria into Turkey at Tal Abyad. The Syrian Kurds note bitterly that Turkey has closed the crossing points into Kurdish-held territory, but has kept open those used by ISIS.

But now Tal Abyad, the northern end of the road that leads straight to Raqqa, the ISIS Syrian capital, is threatened by a pincer movement by Kurds advancing from both the east and west. Some are coming from the battered town of Ras al-Ayn in the main Kurdish canton of al-Jazeera and, from the west, forces are advancing from Kobani, which withstood a four-and-a-half-month ISIS siege.

Sehanok Dibo, adviser to Saleh Muslim and Asya Abdullah, the leaders of the PYD (Democratic Union Party), the ruling party in the three Kurdish cantons on the Turkish border that make up the statelet of Rojava, told The Independent in an interview that Tal Abyad is the next Kurdish military target. "We are 18km from Tal Abyad in the east and 20km [from Tal Abyad] in the west," he said. "We hope to liberate it soon." If this happens, it will be a serious blow to ISIS, and also to Turkey, which will see even more of the Syrian side of its southern frontier controlled by Kurds. Mr Dibo takes it as a matter of proven fact that "Turkey supports Daesh [the Arabic acronym for ISIS used in Iraq and Syria]".

He stresses that he is not part of the Syrian Kurdish military command structure, but his opinion about ISIS's future strategy is significant because the Syrian Kurds are the only military force in Iraq and Syria consistently to defeat the jihadis. He says: "I think their next target will be Dayr Az Zawr [the provincial capital on the Euphrates which is partly held by Syrian government forces] because the people in the city are Sunni Arabs and tribal. ISIS will get support there."

In the longer term, Mr Dibo expects ISIS and other jihadist groups, such as Jabhat al-Nusra, to try to capture the half of Aleppo that is still held by President Bashar al-Assad and the Syrian army. He sees Mr Assad's military strength ebbing by the day. Despite savage rivalries between ISIS and Jabhat al-Nusra, he believes that in most respects they are just the same. "They are the children of al-Qaeda," he says.

The leaders of the Syrian Kurds are jubilant at the moment because of their victory over ISIS at Mount Abdulaziz last week. Trucks full of cheering soldiers are returning from the front. The Kurds in this north-east corner of Syria know, somewhat to their own surprise, that, encircled by enemies though they may be, they are living in the safest part of Syria. The territory behind the front line where Nujaan and Zenya are fighting is full of farmers bringing in the wheat harvest and without the undercurrent of terror you find in the rest ofSyria.

Of course, the greater safety in this triangular-shaped Kurdish enclave only stands out because of the contrast with everywhere else on the borders of the "Islamic State". But, for the moment, there are no car bombs, kidnappings, bandit gangs at check points or fear of massacre. The PYD and its armed wing, the YPG (People's Defence Units), have an effective monopoly of power here, as it does in the two other Kurdish cantons on the Turkish frontier that gained de facto autonomy when the Syrian army withdrew in July 2012. Though its militarised rule is not popular with all Kurds, its militiamen and women do provide genuine protection - unlike the Syrian or Iraqi armies.

It may not last and it has not come easily. Ras al-Ayn, a town of about 30,000 people, still looks shattered by heavy fighting in 2012 and 2013 when it was at the centre of clashes between the Kurds and extreme jihadists led by Jabhat al-Nusra, then the Syrian branch of ISIS and now the official affiliate of al-Qaeda in Syria. Everywhere in this shabby little town, there are bombed- out ruins and surviving walls peppered with the pockmarks made by machine-gun bullets.

Ibrahim and Jamil, two middle-aged PYD representatives, give a guided tour of their town, pointing to the border crossing with Turkey across which Jabhat al-Nusra-led forces poured on 11 November 2012. They say that "at first we welcomed them because they were against the Assad regime and then we were shocked to find they were all jihadis".

They enforced compulsory attendance at the mosque, stole Christian houses and attacked and killed all who opposed them. Captured officers from the ruling Allawi sect were massacred and the regime in Damascus responded with random bombing that killed many civilians and levelled rows of houses.

The battle for Ras al-Ayn went on from November 2012 to July 2013 and has similarities with the struggle within the opposition to the regime between the jihadis and secular forces. The difference is that, here in Ras al-Ayn, the anti-jihadis were well armed and militarily experienced, since the PYD is effectively the Syrian branch of the Kurdistan Workers Party (PKK) that has been fighting the Turkish army since 1984.

Ibrahim says the final stage of this complex battle, which had many ceasefires interrupted by new bouts of street fighting, came on 16 July 2013. Rojna, leader of the YPJ women's fighters, was buying material for uniforms in the bazaar, when she and her guards were attacked by al- Nusra militants infuriated by the sight of a female military leader. "It was then we decided to finally drive them out," says Ibrahim.

The Kurdish canton of al-Jazeera is a well- defended island in a sea full of sharks. Turkey has demanded a "buffer zone" in Syria that would conveniently allow it to occupy the Kurdish enclaves along the border. Mr Dibo says that it is difficult to predict what will happen next as "the balance of power in the war in Syria can be changed abruptly at any moment by the actions of one of the outside powers".

Summer 2015

No End To The Slaughter

MY SOLDIER'S BROTHER WAS BEHEADED FAR AWAY IN IDLIB. THEY VIDEOED IT AND SENT THE RECORDING TO HIS PHONE HERE
By Robert Fisk
2 June 2015

Above us, white clouds graze the top of Tel Moussa, 9,400 feet of red rock above foothills of granite and valleys of innocent-looking cherry orchards. Colonel Median of the Syrian army's 3rd Armoured Division stands on the dry, cold earth below, sun-shades above his stubble beard; he does not know the identity of the ancient Moussa who blessed this mountain with his name, but he knows how to curse him. "If I could catch him, I would hang him because he is the source of torture for me and many of my men."

Across the gaunt peaks and caves of the Qalamoun range, east of the Lebanese border, a kind of victory has been celebrated by the Syrian army after the sudden collapse of Palmyra to ISIS, a loss which - as they both admit freely - deeply shocked Col Median and his senior officer, General Ghassan. Months of fighting west of the town of Yabroud have freed a 25-mile front from the Nusra Islamists right up to the Lebanese frontier, and Gen Ghassan's 130mm artillery are now dug in on the Syrian side of the border, scarcely 12 miles from the Lebanese city of Baalbek.

It has been a personal war for these soldiers: infantrymen along with paratroopers from the Syrian Republican Guard and the locally raised "National Defence" militias - whose original creator was Gen Ghassan himself - and the hundreds of Lebanese Hezbollah fighters who also fought and died to the north of them on this same, bleak mountain range. In one small village, al-Sarkha, Col Median lost 25 men, and another 10 died climbing the slopes of Tel Moussa. Two were cut down by mortar fragments, three by mine explosions and five by sniper fire. He claims - with a flip of the hand to take account of the obvious exaggerations of war - that an "estimated" 300 Nusra men were killed in the Syrian artillery, MiG fighter and helicopter rocket attacks which took back this land.

At a jolly reunion in his headquarters at a marble-tiled villa in Yabroud, Gen Ghassan enthusiastically points to the local Syrian militia commander, a bespectacled, slim young man with short, dark hair, and then hands me a mobile phone. On the screen can be seen the bodies of several bearded, half-naked, equally young men, their stomachs covered in blood. An army boot is placed firmly on the face of one of the dead men. When I examine the face of the boot's owner on the screen, I realise it is the same bespectacled militia officer standing next to me. Yes, there were Syrians among the dead rebels, the soldiers agree, but there were also Chechens and Algerians and Saudis. Their list of foreign "jihadis" embraces much of the world.

They all debate the ferocious, throat-slitting executions of their Islamist enemies - a Saudi practice, they all agree, which has nothing to do with the Muslim religion and much to do with money, warped ideology, and the deliberate intention to put fear into their antagonists. "Of course, our soldiers are scared," Gen Ghassan says. "There is a saying in Syria, that a man who does not feel fear is a donkey. But that does not mean he is a coward. We see the videos of the execution of our soldiers, yes, we know some of them personally, we know their families."

And then Gen Ghassan speaks more quietly. "We have a soldier, his brother was murdered with a knife far away in Idlib. They videoed themselves as they cut off his head and a man then put his foot on the head and they sent the video to the dead man's brother, my soldier.

"And my soldier, he climbed Tel Moussa with us in the attack and as he climbed under rifle fire, he all the time kept looking at his mobile phone and the picture of his brother's head on the screen. And he wanted to capture a rebel and kill him for revenge, and when he reached the top, he captured a rebel. But he did not kill him."

Much silence follows these words, and the horror of this terrifying war begins to fill the military village headquarters, with its tables of slowly cooling tea and coffee cups. The general hands me another mobile phone image. It shows a row of Syrian soldiers kneeling on the ground, bearded after days in captivity, a "jihadi" executioner standing behind the man nearest the camera, a pistol pointed at the doomed man's head.

"There was a garrison of 40 of our men in one battle in Idlib province, and 14 were killed in the fighting and the other 26 were captured," Gen Ghassan says. "They executed them one by one, going from one man to the next to shoot him in the back of the head so that the others in the row would know what was about to happen to them. The question that haunts me to this day is what each soldier thought as death closed in on him, when he was three shots away, then two shots... It's the same with all these prisoners, the Egyptian Christians in Libya who had their throats cut, the blood - do you remember how they said: 'We are coming, Rome'?"

The soldiers believe there is a trained corps of "head choppers" who become mentally unhinged by their executions, although the Syrian officers dispute whether the "jihadis" they fight are motivated by money or by a failed ideology. Listening to these soldiers - regularly interrupted by visiting militiamen, an intelligence officer, even the local female Syrian MP for Qalamoun - it's easy to see how the war has changed them. They insist they will not stoop to the tactics of their enemies, but when I ask Col Median what happens to the bodies of his antagonists, he looks at me coldly and asks: "What else do you want to know?"

During the battles, the colonel said, his men would have achieved victory far more quickly if they possessed the advanced American-made missiles which were in the hands of the Islamists.

The Syrian soldiers listen to their enemies over their radios, noting how Nusra fighters identify themselves by nicknames. "They will call themselves by the names of birds," Gen Ghassan says. "They will say: 'This is the robin', or 'This is the falcon'. But the men from 'Daesh' [the acronym used for ISIS] use a first name, like 'Abu Ali' [father of Ali] followed by his country, like 'Abu Ali of Morocco' or 'Abu Ali the Frenchman'."

When originally driving Nusra out of Yabroud last year, Col Median called the rebels by mobile phone and gave them 24 hours to leave, to avoid casualties. Gen Ghassan tells a darker story of the last few weeks. "There was a local Nusra man called Tahar Zeidan, and I persuaded him to give up and come across to us, with 700 men, and hand over his weapons and trucks. But Col Median told me he was 'a son of a dog' and he was right. Before he came across, the so-called Nusra 'governor' of Damascus, Abu Ayub al-Iraqi, sent to him a Palestinian 'emir' called Abu

Abdullah and said that in future Tahar Zeidan would be regarded as a local emir. So Zeidan broke his word and did not come to us - just for a title!"

The checkpoints on the roads to al-Jibeh sprout yellow Hezbollah banners as well as the red, black and white flag of Syria, and Col Median proclaims that "we and the Hezbollah are one in Qalamoun". The way in which Hezbollah trucks speed through Syrian checkpoints in a cloud of dust does not betoken much brotherly love. But both must soon face a greater conflict further north of Tel Moussa , against ISIS rather than Nusra forces. And after Palmyra, it's a battle they need to win.

SLAUGHTER IN THE SACRED CITY OF PALMYRA: THE STORIES OF THE SURVIVORS
By Robert Fisk
5 June 2015

When the black-cowled gunmen of ISIS infiltrated the suburbs of Palmyra on 20 May, half of Assad Sulieman's oil and gas processing plant crews - 50 men in all - were working their 12- hour shift at the Hayan oil field 28 miles away. They were the lucky ones.

Their 50 off-duty colleagues were sleeping at their homes next to the ancient Roman city. Twenty-five of them would soon be dead, among up to 400 civilians - including women and children - who would be killed in the coming hours at the hands of the Islamist militia which every Syrian now calls by its self-styled acronym Daesh.

Oil engineer "Ahmed" - he chose this name to protect his family in Palmyra - was, by chance, completing a course at Damascus University on the fatal day when Palmyra fell. "I was appalled," he says. "I tried calling my family. It was still possible to get through on the phone. They said Daesh wasn't allowing anyone to leave their home. My brother later went on to the street. He took pictures of bodies. They had been decapitated. All men.

"He managed to send the photographs out to me from [the ISIS-controlled city of] Raqqa on the internet which is the only communications working there."

Some of the photographs are too terrible to publish. They show heads lying several feet from torsos, blood running in streams across a city street. In one, a body lies on a roadway while two men cycle past. So soon after the capture of Palmyra were the men slaughtered that shop-fronts can still be seen in the photographs. They are painted in the two stars and the red, white and black of the Syrian government's flag.

"Daesh forced the people to leave the bodies in the streets for three days," Ahmed continues. "They were not allowed to pick up the bodies or bury them without permission. The corpses were all over the city. My family said Daesh came to our house, two foreign men - one appeared to be an Afghan, the other from Tunisia or Morocco because he had a very heavy accent - and then they left.

"They killed three female nurses. One was killed in her home, another in her uncle's house, a third on the street. Perhaps it was because they helped the army. Some said they were beheaded but my brother said they were shot in the head."

In the panic to flee Palmyra, others perished when their cars drove over explosives planted by the Islamists. One was a retired Syrian general from the al-Daas family whose 40-year-old pharmacist wife and 12-year-old son were killed with him when their car's wheels touched the explosives. Later reports spoke of executions in the old Roman theatre amid the Palmyra ruins.

The director of the Hayan gas and oil processing plant, Assad Sulieman, shakes his head in near- disbelief as he recounts how word reached him of the murders of his off-duty staff. Some were, he believes, imprisoned in the gas fields which had fallen into the hands of ISIS. Others were taken from their homes and murdered because they were government employees. For months prior to the fall of Palmyra, he had received a series of terrifying phone calls from the Islamists, one of them when gunmen were besieging a neighbouring gas plant.

He says: "They came on my own phone, here in my office, and said: 'We are coming for you.' I said to them: 'I will be waiting'. The army drove them off but my staff also received these phone calls and they were very frightened. The army protected three of our fields then and drove them off."

Since the fall of Palmyra, the threatening phone calls have continued, even though Daesh has cut all mobile and landlines in the newly occupied city.

Another young engineer at Hayan was in Palmyra when ISIS arrived. So fearful is he that he refuses to volunteer a name for himself. "I had gone back to Palmyra two days before and everything seemed all right," he says. "When my family told me they had arrived, I stayed at home and so did my mother and brother and sisters and we did not go out.

"Everyone knew that when these men come things are not good. The electricity stopped for two days and then the gunmen restored it. We had plenty of food - we were a well-off family. We stayed there a week, we had to sort out our affairs and they never searched our home."

The man's evidence proved the almost haphazard nature of ISIS rule. A week after the occupation, the family made its way out of the house - the women in full Islamic covering - and caught a bus to the occupied city of Raqqa and from there to Damascus. "They looked at my ID but didn't ask my job," the man says. "The bus trip was normal. No one stopped us leaving."

Like Ahmed, the young oil worker was a Sunni Muslim - the same religion as ISIS's followers - but he had no doubts about the nature of Palmyra's occupiers. "When they arrive anywhere", he says, "there is no more life."

Syria's own oil and gas lifeline now stretches across 100 miles of desert from Homs in the midlands to the strategic oil fields across the broiling desert outside Palmyra. It takes two hours to reach a point 28 miles from Palmyra; the last Syrian troops are stationed eight miles closer to the city.

To the west lies the great Syrian air base of Tiyas - codenamed T-4, after the old fourth pumping station of the Iraq-Palestine oil pipeline - where I can see grey-painted twin-tailed MiG fighter bombers taking off into the dusk and settling back on to the runways.

A canopy of radar dishes and concrete bunkers protects the base and Syrian troops can be seen inside a series of earthen fortresses on each side of the main road to Palmyra, defending their redoubts with heavy machine guns, long-range artillery and missiles.

Syrian troops patrol the highway every few minutes on pick-up trucks - and make no secret of their precautions. They point out the site of an improvised explosive device found a few hours earlier - more than 30 miles west of Palmyra. Further down the road is the wreckage of trucks which had been hit by Syrian rocket-fire.

Assad Sulieman declares his father named him after President Bashar al-Asasad's father Hafez. He describes how Islamist rebels had totally destroyed one gas plant close to Hayan last year, and how his crews had totally restored it to production within months by using cannibalised equipment from other facilities. His plant's production capacity has been restored to three million cubic metres of gas per day for the country's power stations and 6,000 barrels of oil for the Homs refinery.

But the man who understands military risks is General Fouad - like everyone else in Palmyra, he prefers to use only his first name - a professional officer whose greatest victory over the rebels on a nearby mountain range came at the moment his soldier-son was killed in battle in Homs.

He makes no secret of "the big shock" he felt when Palmyra fell. He thinks the soldiers had been fighting for a long time in defence of the city and did not expect the mass attack. Other military men say that ISIS advanced on a 50-mile front, overwhelming the army at the time.

"They will get no further," General Fouad says. "We fought them off when they attacked three fields last year. Our soldiers stormed some of their local headquarters on the Shaer mountain. We found documents about our production facilities, we found religious books of Takfiri ideas. And we found lingerie."

What on earth, I asked, would ISIS be doing with lingerie? The general is not smiling. "We think that maybe they kept captured Yazidi women with them, the ones who were kidnapped in Iraq. When our soldiers reached their headquarters, we saw some of their senior men running away with some women."

But the general, like almost every other Syrian officer I meet on this visit to the desert - and every other civilian - had a thought on his mind: if the Americans were so keen to destroy ISIS, did they not know from satellites that thousands of gunmen were massing to strike at Palmyra?

Certainly they did not tell the Syrians of this. And they did not bomb them, either - though there must have been targets aplenty for the US air force in the days before the Palmyra attack, even if Washington does not like the Assad regime. A question, then, that still has to be answered.

NUSRA PLAYS THE NICE GUY, BUT IS AS NASTY AS ISIS
By Patrick Cockburn
14 June 2015

Last week fighters from Jabhat al-Nusra, the al-Qaeda affiliate in Syria, entered a village in Idlib province in the north-west of the country and shot dead at least 20 villagers from the Druze community. They had earlier forcibly converted hundreds of Druze to their fundamentalist variant of Sunni Islam.

The incident happened in the Druze village of Qalb Lawzeh in the Jabal al-Summaq region, a place where al-Nusra fighters have dug up historic graves and destroyed shrines in recent months, according to the pro-opposition Syrian Observatory for Human Rights. It says Nusra first tried to confiscate the house of a Druze government official and shot one villager dead. Another villager then seized a fighter's weapon and killed him. Nusra then sent reinforcements into the village and they opened fire.

It was just one more massacre in a land that has seen thousands of atrocities by government and rebels over the past four years. But what gives the Qalb Lawzeh killings peculiar significance is that they happened at a moment when Nusra, and the rebel coalition it leads, had inflicted a series of defeats on the Syrian army in the north, leading to speculation that the regime of President Bashar al-Assad might be starting to crumble under multiple pressures. It has recently lost Idlib province in the north, Palmyra in the east, and is on the retreat in the south.

A reason why Nusra and Ahrar al-Sham, another hard-line jihadi group, were able to break the military stalemate is the greater support they are getting from Turkey, Saudi Arabia and Qatar. Since succeeding to the throne in January, Saudi King Salman, along with other Sunni leaders, has pursued a more aggressive policy in backing extreme jihadi rebels in Syria.

Alongside this military offensive is an effort by Nusra and its supporters to rebrand itself as a completely different and more moderate entity than Islamic State. This is not easy to do. Nusra was created by IS in 2012 and split from it in 2013, since when the two movements have been fierce rivals who share the same fanatical beliefs and hatreds. The US regards both as terrorist organisations and periodically bombs Nusra, though not with the same intensity as it attacks IS. The Saudis and the others are not looking for the US to end its hostility to Nusra, but they do want Washington to continue to turn a blind eye to support for it from America's main Sunni allies.

The rebranding of Nusra is being energetically pursued. A dramatic if somewhat ludicrous episode in this campaign was a 47-minute interview with Abu Mohammed al-Golani, the leader of al-Nusra, broadcast by Al Jazeera television network on 27 May. Golani was to demonstrate to a Syrian and international audience how much more reasonable and less murderous his organisation was compared with IS when it came to Syria's minorities and to stress that it would not be launching terrorist operations against western targets.

The interview did not entirely succeed in conveying a comforting sense of restraint and moderation. This is not because Golani came under much pressure from the sympathetic Al Jazeera interviewer. "It was not Frost/Nixon, more like a high-school date," says the Syria expert Aron Lund, editor of Syria in Crisis, in the online newsletter Syria Comment. The softball approach, he says, "may well have been intentional. Many assume that Qatar, which owns and controls Al Jazeera, is eager to see the group show its gentler side, now that it and other rebels are capturing territory in north-western Syria."

Golani expressed his new-found moderation by saying that it would be safe for a member of the Allawite sect - to which President Assad and much of Syria's ruling elite belong - to surrender to Nusra fighters "even if he killed a thousand of us". But any Allawite considering taking advantage of Golami's kind offer must meet certain conditions. They must not only stop supporting Assad, but they must convert to Nusra's brand of extreme Sunni Islam or, in other words, stop being Allawites. Christians will be given a grace period before they have to start pay jizya, a special tax, and Golani takes for granted that Sharia will be implemented. "The basics remain the same," says Lund, "and they're extreme enough to be borderline genocidal even when sugar-coated by Al Jazeera."

What gives this interview such significance is that Golani leads a movement which might, if the Assad regime falls, form part of Syria's next government. Assad's military opposition is dominated by IS in the east, holding half the country, and Nusra, leading a coalition of al-Qaeda type jihadis in the north and centre.

"We have to deal with reality as it is," said Robert Ford, the former US ambassador to Syria in an interview with Hannah Allam of McClatchy news service earlier this year. "The people we have backed [moderate Syrian rebels] have not been strong enough to hold their ground against the Nusra Front."

What made Mr Ford's assertion that Nusra dominated the non-IS armed opposition so shocking for many was that he was the man who had resigned from the US government, accusing it of not giving enough support to the moderate rebels. Not so long ago he had been maintaining that the moderates were still a real force. But now Mr Ford was quoted as complaining that the rebels, as well as their patrons in Turkey and Qatar, were legitimising Nusra as an integral part of the anti- Assad opposition when, in reality, it was the same as IS. "Nusra Front is just as dangerous, and yet they keep pretending they're nice guys, they're Syrians," he said. Another problem was that weapons supplied by the US to more moderate groups were ending up in the hands of Nusra.

It is not just that Nusra is sectarian, violent and true to its al-Qaeda roots. Its presence at the heart of the armed opposition gives the rebels greater military strength, but politically it is a tremendous liability.

Mr Ford defends the moderates, saying that their alliance with Nusra is only tactical and the result of their weakness and disunity. But in a further interview with Middle East Monitor, Mr Ford makes an important point, warning that "with this cooperation [between moderates and Nusra], they have made it impossible to get a negotiated political deal, because the people in the regime who do not like Assad, and there are lots who don't like Assad, look at the opposition and say we cannot negotiate with an opposition that supports Nusra".

The presence of Nusra prevents any chance of a negotiated settlement, but will not be enough to win an outright military victory. Syria is being torn apart by a genuine civil war in which neither side can afford to let the other win. Members of the regime in Damascus know that getting rid of Assad is not going to do them any good and, if they lose, they may well end up dead, like the Druze villagers of Qalb Lawzeh.

TURKEY DUPED THE US, AND ISIS REAPS REWARDS
By Patrick Cockburn
30 August 2015

The disastrous miscalculation made by the United States in signing a military agreement with Turkey at the expense of the Kurds becomes daily more apparent. In return for the use of Incirlik Air Base just north of the Syrian border, the US betrayed the Syrian Kurds who have so far been its most effective ally against Islamic State (IS, also known as Daesh). In return for this deal signed on 22 July, the US got greater military cooperation from Turkey, but it swiftly emerged that Ankara's real target was the Kurds in Turkey, Syria and Iraq. Action against IS was almost an afterthought, and it was hit by only three Turkish airstrikes, compared to 300 against the bases of the Kurdistan Workers' Party (PKK).

President Barack Obama has assembled a grand coalition of 60 states, supposedly committed to combating IS, but the only forces on the ground to win successive victories against the jihadis over the past year are the ruling Syrian-Kurdish Party (PYD) and its People's Protection Units (YPG). Supported by US air power, the YPG heroically defeated the IS attempt to capture the border city of Kobani during a four-and-a-half month siege that ended in January, and seized the IS crossing point into Turkey at Tal Abyad in June.

The advance of the Syrian Kurds, who now hold half of the 550-mile Syrian-Kurdish border, was the main external reason why Turkish President Recep Tayyip Erdogan offered the US closer cooperation, including the use of Incirlik, which had previously been denied. The domestic impulse for an offensive by the Turkish state against the Kurds also took place in June when the pro-Kurdish People's Democratic Party (HDP) won 13 per cent of the vote in the Turkish general election, denying Mr Erdogan's Justice and Development Party (AKP) a majority for the first time since 2002. By strongly playing the Turkish nationalist and anti-Kurdish card, Mr Erdogan hopes to win back that majority in a second election on 1 November.

There are signs of a growing understanding in Washington that the US was duped by the Turks, or at best its negotiators deceived themselves when they agreed their bargain with Ankara.

Senior US military officers are anonymously protesting in the US media they did not know that Turkey was pretending to be going after

IS when in practice it was planning an offensive against its 18 million-strong Kurdish minority.

Further evidence of misgivings in Washington came last week with an article in The New York Times entitled "America's Dangerous Bargain with Turkey" by Eric S Edelman, former US ambassador to Turkey and under-secretary for defence policy, who is normally regarded as a neo-con of good standing. He accuses Mr Erdogan of unleashing "a new wave of repression aimed at Kurds in Turkey, which risks plunging the country into civil war" and he goes on to suggest that this might help the AKP win back its majority, but will certainly undermine the fight against IS. He says: "By disrupting logistics and communications between the PKK in Iraq and the PYD in Syria, Turkey is weakening the most effective ground force fighting the Islamic State in Syria: the Kurds."

In fact, there is growing evidence that the Turkish government has gone even further than that in weakening US allies opposing IS in Syria, Arab as well as Kurd. For several years the US has been trying to build up a moderate force of Syrian rebels who are able to fight both IS and the Syrian government in Damascus. The CIA-run initiative has not been going well because the Syrian military opposition these days is almost entirely dominated by IS, which holds half Syria, the al-Qaeda affiliate Jabhat al-Nusra, and the equally sectarian Sunni Ahrar al-Sham.

But in July, the US plan to create such a moderate force was humiliatingly knocked on the head when Jabhat al-Nusra attacked and kidnapped many of this US-trained force as they entered Syria from Turkey. It now seems certain that Nusra had been tipped off by Turkish intelligence about the movements of the US-backed unit known as "Division 30". Turkey apparently did this because it does not want the US to have its own surrogate in Syria. According to an investigation by Mitchell Prothero of the McClatchy news organisation, citing many Syrian sources in Turkey, the Turkish motive was to destroy the US-run movement, which was intended to number 15,000 fighters targeting IS. Its disintegration would leave the US with no alternative but to train Turkish-sponsored rebel groups whose primary aim is to topple Syria's President Bashar al-Assad. The article quotes a Syrian rebel commander in the Turkish city of Sanliurfa, 30 miles north of the Syrian border, as saying that the Turks "don't want anything bad to happen to their allies - Nusra and Ahrar al-Sham - along the border, and they know that both the Americans and the Syrian people will eventually recognise that there's no difference between groups such as Nusra, Ahrar and Daesh."

How does IS itself assess the new US-Turkish accord? Its fighters may find it more difficult to cross the Syrian-Turkish border, though even this is uncertain. But it will be relieved that its most effective enemy in Syria, the PYD, will in future be restrained by Turkish pressure. Its PKK parent organisation is coming under sustained attack from Turkish forces in south-east Turkey and in the Qandil Mountains of Iraq.

The destruction of one of the most famous temples at Palmyra by IS last week, and the decapitation of the site's most famous archaeologist a few days earlier, are a show of strength and acts of defiance very much in the tradition of the Islamic State. The aim is to dominate the news agenda, which can easily be done by some spectacular atrocity, and thereby say, in effect, "you may hate what you are seeing, but there is nothing you can do to stop it".

And this is demonstrably the case not just in Syria but in Iraq. IS captured Ramadi, the capital of Anbar province in Iraq on 17 May and Palmyra five days later on 22 May. In neither case has there been an effective counter-attack. IS is still winning victories where it counts, and faces no real threat to its existence.

The US campaign against IS is failing and the US-Turkish deal will not reverse that failure and may make it more complete. Why did US negotiators allow themselves to be deceived, if that is what happened. No doubt the US air force was over-eager for the use of Incirlik so it would not have to fly its planes from Jordan, Bahrain or carriers in the Gulf.

But there is a deeper reason for America's inability to confront IS successfully. Ever since 9/11, the US has wanted to combat al-Qaeda-type movements, but without disturbing its close relations with Sunni states such as Turkey, Saudi Arabia, Pakistan and the Gulf monarchies. But it is these same allies that have fostered, tolerated or failed to act against the al-Qaeda clones, which explains their continuing success.

Autumn 2015

No Good Guys Left

DESOLATION, RUINS, DANGER: SYRIA'S KURDS HAVE LITTLE CHOICE BUT TO FLEE
By Patrick Cockburn
4 September 2015

The Kurdish enclave of Kobani in north-east Syria, once the home of Aylan al-Kurdi and his family, is largely in ruins after a four-and-a-half month siege by ISIS fighters that ended in January. It was one of the greatest victories in Kurdish history, but a Pyrrhic one that saw 300,000 Syrian Kurds flee into Turkey from Kobani, a city just south of the Turkish border, and from the 250 villages surrounding it.

ISIS may have been driven back, but the Kobani enclave remains a desolate, ruined and very dangerous place. Some 70 per cent of the city was destroyed in the fighting, by ISIS suicide bombs and mortars, Kurdish counter-fire, and US air strikes using 500lb and 2,000lb bombs to smash ISIS positions. At one point, ISIS set fire to buildings in order to create a smokescreen to protect them from US aircraft.

In most of Kobani city there is no water or electricity supply and retreating ISIS forces booby- trapped many of the shattered buildings, so these cannot be easily cleared. The fighting was more intense and went on longer than any recent battle in Iraq or Syria, with ISIS - which calls itself Islamic State - losing an estimated 2,000 fighters and the Kurdish YPG militia some 560.

After January there was a trickle of Kurdish refugees returning from Turkey to Kobani because life among the ruins was better than in the squalid refugee camps. But the Syrian Kurdish authorities turned out to be tragically over-confident that ISIS was incapable of a counter-attack. On 25 June some 100 ISIS fighters disguised in YPG uniforms entered Kobani and a village 20km to the south of the city and began a massacre that left between 223 and 233 men, women and children butchered, along with 35 YPG militiamen. Syrian Kurdish refugees in Turkey will have got the message that it is not safe to go home even when their forces are advancing with the help of US air strikes and ISIS is retreating.

Kobani is one of three Kurdish enclaves just south of the Turkish border that have created their own quasi-state since the Syrian army withdrew in the summer of 2012. The 2.2 million Syrian Kurds, long discriminated against by the Damascus government, became a surprisingly important player in the Syrian civil war. Their enclaves, which they call cantons, are in strategically valuable places, controlling crossing points on the 550-mile border with Turkey.

Half this frontier is now held by the YPG, denying ISIS important crossing points between Turkey and Syria.

The Syrian Kurds have a political significance out of proportion to their numbers in the region's civil wars. They have achieved a real measure of practical independence in the de facto Kurdish state called Rojava under the control of the Democratic Union Party (PYD) and its well-disciplined YPG militia. Since last October, the YPG has been the only effective ground force in Syria co-operating with US airpower against ISIS. But the enhanced influence of the Syrian Kurds has made them a target for their many enemies. Turkey has been dismayed at finding what amounts to a Kurdish statelet controlling 250 miles of its southern frontier. Worse, the PYD and the YPG are the Syrian branch of the Kurdistan Workers' Party (PKK), a powerful guerrilla organisation that has been fighting the Turkish army since 1984.

This summer, Rojava, a fertile wedge of territory full of wheat fields and dotted with oil industry "nodding donkeys", looked idyllic and peaceful compared with the rest of Syria. But for Syrian Kurds the future is full of menaces in the shape of a hostile Turkey to the north and ISIS to the south. Moreover, any potential winner of the civil war in Syria may swiftly move to extinguish the Kurdish independent entity. In the face of these dangers, it is no wonder that Syrian Kurds will take any risk to escape to Europe or anywhere else where they might find safety.

IF JIHADIST FORCES CAPTURE THIS VITAL HIGHWAY, MORE AND MORE DESPERATE PEOPLE WILL FLEE SYRIA
By Patrick Cockburn
6 September 2015

Islamic State forces in Syria are threatening to capture a crucial road, the loss of which could touch off a panic and the exodus of several million refugees from government areas, in addition to the four million who have already fled. IS fighters have advanced recently to within 22 miles of the M5 highway, the only major route connecting government-held territory in Damascus to the north and west of the country.

The beginnings of the latest crisis for the government of President Bashar al-Assad came with the capture by IS on 6 August of the strategically placed, largely Christian town of al-Qaryatain, north-east of Damascus. Since then, Islamist units have advanced further west, capturing two villages closer to the M5. The Syrian Army has so far failed to retake Qaryatain, where IS has demolished the St Elian monastery, parts of which were 1,500 years old.

The four million Syrians who are already refugees mostly came from opposition or contested areas that have been systematically bombarded by government aircraft and artillery, making them uninhabitable. But the majority of the 17 million Syrians still in the country live in government-controlled areas now threatened by IS. These people are terrified of IS occupying their cities, towns and villages because of its reputation for mass executions, ritual mutilation and rape against those not obedient to its extreme variant of Sunni Islam.

Half the Syrian population has already been displaced inside or outside the country, so accurate figures are hard to estimate, but among those particularly at risk are the Alawites (2.6 million), the Shia heterodox sect that has provided the ruling elite of Syria since the 1960s, the Christians (two million), the Syrian Kurds (2.2 million), and Druze (650,000) in addition to millions of Sunni Arabs associated with the Syrian government and its army. The forced flight of these communities could swiftly double the total number of refugees to eight million.

Government forces are showing signs of being fought out after four years of war and have recently suffered a series of defeats at the hands of IS, which captured Palmyra in May, and by a coalition led by the al-Qaeda affiliate, Jabhat al-Nusra, which took Idlib city in March. But it would be a far more serious defeat for President Assad if IS cuts the M5, which is seen as "the spinal column of the regime". The government has never lost control of it for an extended period, though the road has been closed to civilian traffic by snipers hiding in the ruins of north Damascus, where whole districts have been blown up or bulldozed by the government. On two occasions, Nusra fighters seized the ancient Christian village of Maaloula, just off the M5, forcing inhabitants to escape to Damascus.

Governments and people in the EU have had to pay horrified attention to the plight of refugees in the past few days because of pictures of the drowned body of Aylan al-Kurdi. But there is scant attention to the deteriorating security situation in Syria that could produce millions more migrants fleeing for their lives.

The UNHCR says that Syria has "become the world's top source country of refugees, overtaking Afghanistan, which had held this position for more than three decades". Out of every four new refugees in the world today, one will be a Syrian. Commenting on this exodus, and the likelihood that it will be exacerbated if IS cuts the M5 highway, the online humanitarian news and analysis publication, IRIN, says that "Europe's current migration crisis is essentially the arrival of the Syrian crisis on European shores."

Unfortunately, European concern about ending the refugee crisis has not energised efforts to end the war in Syria which shows every sign of getting worse. Assad's forces are getting weaker and he admits to a shortage of troops, but territory lost by him is usually occupied by IS, Jabhat al-Nusra or Ahrar al-Sham, all Salafi-jihadi movements with the same violent and intolerant ideology.

Even former advocates of the "moderate" Syrian rebels, say that today the armed opposition is dominated by extreme fundamentalists. Their dominance makes it impossible to create any power-sharing government in Damascus that would be key to ending the war.

The Damascus government and its army are unlikely to implode as happened in Libya or northern Iraq, but people in government areas are understandably frightened by recent military reverses. Many argue that they and their families should get out while they can. Living in government areas does not always mean that they are in favour of Assad remaining in power, but they fear that the alternative to the present regime will be far worse. IS deliberately foments terror by showing videos of its atrocities to create panic among soldiers and civilians, and there is also the knowledge that the Syrian Army will bombard any place from which it retreats.

David Cameron said last week: "We think that the most important thing is to try to bring peace and stability to that part of the world." But in practice, Britain, the US, Gulf monarchies and Turkey have exacerbated the Syrian conflict by supporting an armed opposition that from an early stage was led by extreme jihadis. As early as August 2012 a Defense Intelligence Agency report states that "the Salafist, the Muslim Brotherhood, and AQI [Al- Qaeda in Iraq] are the major forces driving the insurgency in Syria."

Likely British participation in the US-led air campaign against IS in Syria will make little difference unless it is directed against IS when it is attacking the Syrian Army and is co- ordinated with its ground forces. These tactics worked effectively when the US collaborated with the Syrian Kurdish YPG militia to win battles at Kobani and Hassakah, but the US is so far opposed to doing anything that will be seen as helping the Assad government. A price for such aid might be an insistence that the Syrian air force stop barrel bombing civilian areas.

Surprisingly, even the fall of Mosul in Iraq to IS in the summer of 2014 and the seizure of more than half of Syria by IS over the past year, has not prevented US and European leaders underestimating IS. They have claimed that it is past its peak, wishful thinking that should have been deflated in May when IS took Ramadi, the capital of Anbar province in Iraq, and Palmyra in Syria five days later. So far neither the Syrian nor the Iraqi armies have launched counter- attacks capable of retaking either city.

The Assad government will not necessarily collapse overnight, but any sign that it is weakening will convince millions of Syrians that it is time to leave the country. Despite the deepening refugee crisis brought about by the continuing civil war in Syria, governments in Britain, the US,

France and elsewhere are doing little to help end it. Half the Syrian people have already been displaced from their homes and millions more may soon be desperately trying to flee their country. The Syrian war and European refugee crisis are part and parcel of the same thing.

RUSSIAN AIR STRIKES DESTROY ISIS TARGETS, BUT REBELS CLAIM MANY CIVILIAN DEATHS
By Kim Sengupta
3 October 2015

Russia's first sustained air strikes against ISIS have destroyed command centres and training camps, with the Kremlin stating that more attacks on the group are imminent in its new military campaign - its first in the Middle East since the Second World War.

The raids centred on Raqaa, the capital of the ISIS "caliphate" in Syria and Iraq, with Taqba military airport and locations in the villages of Maddan Jadid and Kasrat Faraj also targeted. Around a dozen fighters were killed, according to the British-based Syrian Observatory for Human Rights.

Russian military officials announced strikes on an ISIS communications centre in Daret Ezza in northern Aleppo; bunkers and weapons complexes in Maarat al-Numan and Habeet in Idlib; and a command post in Hama.

However, Syrian opposition activists maintained that the areas targeted in Aleppo, Idlib and Hama were not in ISIS hands, but instead were controlled by the al-Qaeda-affiliated Jabhat al- Nusra. They also claimed that a missile strike at al-Qarytain, a Christian town in Homs which had been overrun by ISIS, had resulted in civilian casualties.

Doubts about the air strikes deepened last night as President Barack Obama announced that the US will not co-operate with the Russian military forces and described the campaign as a self- defeating exercise that would prolong the conflict in Syria. He also raised concerns that the Russian attacks are failing to distinguish between ISIS and other anti-Assad forces.

There had been mounting accusations by the West, Turkey and the Gulf States that Moscow was using the pretext of striking ISIS to eliminate all rebel groups, including moderate ones, opposed to the regime of Bashar al-Assad. ISIS responded to yesterday's bombings by tweeting, "Death to Putin: we are coming soon", accompanied by an image showing St Basil's Cathedral in Moscow in flames.

The initial waves of Russian air strikes were aimed at the rebel groups that pose the greatest immediate threat to the regime. The main targets have been Jaysh al-Fateh, or the Army of Conquest, a coalition of Islamist groups ranging in extremism from al-Nusra to Ahrar al-Sham, which is backed by Turkey and Saudi Arabia.

The Russians insist that they have only targeted terrorists. The Foreign Minister, Sergei Lavrov, said that the Free Syrian Army (FSA), the military arm of the Western-backed Syrian opposition, was not considered by Russia to be terrorists and "should be part of the political process".

However, an FSA communications centre in Aleppo was destroyed late on Thursday night and when Vladimir Putin's spokesman, Dmitry Peskov, was asked about the FSA, he responded:

"Does it exist? Haven't most of them switched to ISIS? It existed, but whether it does now nobody knows for sure."

The expeditionary force that Moscow has dispatched has between 1,500 and 2,000 personnel, but the campaign will be primarily from the air. Forward air controllers, to guide strikes, may be deployed on the ground in the future.

The aircraft, missiles and bombs used in the mission are a mixture of old, going back to the Soviet era, and relatively new. There are 34 fixed-wing aircraft based at Latakia - 12 Su-25 and four Su-30SMs fighter-bombers; 12 Su-24M2 and six Su-34 bombers. There are also 16 Mi-24 helicopter gunships and Mi-8 multi-role helicopters, plus an unspecified number of unmanned drones.

The most advanced of these are the Su-34s, codenamed Fullbacks by NATO, which can carry out bombings and missile strikes and have never before been used in combat. The Su-25 is a veteran of the wars in Chechnya and Georgia, and vulnerable to Manpads (shoulder-fired surface-to-air missiles) of which there are many in Syria and Iraq.

The Kremlin has claimed that only precision strikes have been used, to minimise collateral damage. However, civilians have been killed and injured and video footage reveals intended targets being missed on several occasions.

The reality is that, compared with its major Western counterparts, the Russian air force lacks sophisticated precision weapons and targeting systems. Douglas Barrie, a senior fellow at the International Institute for Strategic Studies, said: "This is not a new problem... This issue was exposed during the Georgian War in 2008. The problem originated with the collapse of the Soviet Union and decades of very little investment in developing advanced weapons systems."

Mr Barrie added that the Russian military industry had "reinvigorated efforts" in an attempt to match the West. But while the Kremlin's forces now have laser and electro-optically guided bombs and missile systems, they have not deployed the targeting pods used by advanced Western aircraft to guide weapons.

Meanwhile, there are continued reports that Assad regime and Iranian troops are massing alongside Hezbollah fighters to carry out a ground offensive against the rebels following the air strikes.

SYRIA'S 'MODERATES' HAVE DISAPPEARED... AND THERE ARE NO GOOD GUYS LEFT
By Robert Fisk
5 October 2015

The Russian air force in Syria has flown straight into the West's fantasy air space. The Russians, we are now informed, are bombing the "moderates" in Syria - "moderates" whom even the Americans admitted two months ago, no longer existed.

It's rather like the ISIS fighters who left Europe to fight for the "Caliphate".Remember them? Scarcely two months ago, our political leaders - and leader writers - were warning us all of the enormous danger posed by "home-grown" Islamists who were leaving Britain and other European countries and America to fight for the monsters of ISIS. Then the hundreds of thousands of Muslim refugees began trekking up the Balkans towards Europe after risking death in the Mediterranean - and we were all told by the same political leaders to be fearful that ISIS killers were among them.

It's amazing how European Muslim fighters fly to Turkey to join ISIS, and a few weeks later, they're drowning in leaky boats or tramping back again and taking trains from Hungary to Germany. But if this nonsense was true, where did they get the time for all the terrorist training they need in order to attack us when they get back to Europe?

It is possible, of course, that this was mere storytelling. By contrast, the chorus of horror that has accompanied Russia's cruel air strikes this past week has gone beyond sanity.

Let's start with a reality check. The Russian military are killers who go for the jugular. They slaughtered the innocent of Chechnya to crush the Islamist uprising there, and they will cut down the innocent of Syria as they try to crush a new army of Islamists and save the ruthless regime of Bashar al-Assad. The Syrian army, some of whose members are war criminals, have struggled ferociously to preserve the state - and used barrel bombs to do it. They have also fought to the death.

"American officials" - those creatures beloved of The New York Times - claim that the Syrian army does not fight ISIS. If true, who on earth killed the 56,000 Syrian soldiers - the statistic an official secret, but nonetheless true - who have so far died in the Syrian war? The preposterous Free Syrian Army (FSA)?

This rubbish has reached its crescendo in the on-again off-again saga of the Syrian "moderates". These men were originally military defectors to the FSA, which America and European countries regarded as a possible pro-Western force to be used against the Syrian government army. But the FSA fell to pieces, corrupted, and the "moderates" defected all over again, this time to the Islamist Nusrah Front or to ISIS, selling their American-supplied weapons to the highest bidder or merely retiring quietly - and wisely - to the countryside where they maintained a few scattered checkpoints.

Washington admitted their disappearance, bemoaned their fate, concluded that new "moderates" were required, persuaded the CIA to arm and train 70 fighters, and this summer packed them off across the Turkish border to fight - whereupon all but 10 were captured by Nusrah and at least two of them were executed by their captors. Just two weeks ago, I heard in person one of the most senior ex-US officers in Iraq - David Petraeus's former No 2 in Baghdad - announce that the "moderates" had collapsed long ago. Now you see them - now you don't.

But within hours of Russia's air assaults last weekend, Washington, The New York Times, CNN, the poor old BBC and just about every newspaper in the Western world resurrected these ghosts and told us that the Russkies were bombing the brave "moderates" fighting Bashar's army in Syria - the very "moderates" who, according to the same storyline from the very same sources a few weeks earlier, no longer existed. Our finest commentators and experts - always a dodgy phrase - joined in the same chorus line.

So now a few harsh factoids. The Syrian army are drawing up the operational target lists for the Russian air force. But Vladimir Putin has his own enemies in Syria.

The first strikes - far from being aimed at the "moderates" whom the US had long ago dismissed - were directed at the large number of Turkmen villages in the far north-west of Syria which have for many months been occupied by hundreds of Chechen fighters - the very same Chechens whom Putin had been trying to liquidate in Chechnya itself. These Chechen forces assaulted and destroyed Syria's strategic hilltop military Position 451 north of Latakia last year. No wonder Bashar's army put them on the target list.

Other strikes were directed not at ISIS but at Islamist Jaish al-Shams force targets in the same area. But in the first 24 hours, Russian bombs were also dropped on the ISIS supply line through the mountains above Palmyra.

The Russians specifically attacked desert roads around the town of Salamia - the same tracks used by ISIS suicide convoys to defeat Syrian troops in the ancient Roman city of Palmyra last May.

They also bombed areas around Hassakeh and the ISIS-held Raqqa air base where Syrian troops have fought Islamists over the past year (and were beheaded when they surrendered).

Russian ground troops, however, are in Syria only to guard their bases. These are symbolic boots on the ground - but the idea that those boots are there to fight ISIS is a lie. The Russians intend to let the Syrian ground troops do the dying for them.

No, there are no good guys and bad guys in the Syrian war. The Russians don't care about the innocents they kill any more than do the Syrian army or NATO. Any movie of the Syrian war should be entitled War Criminals Galore!

But for heaven's sake, let's stop fantasising. A few days ago, a White House spokesman even told us that Russian bombing "drives moderate elements... into the hands of extremists".

Who's writing this fiction? "Moderate elements" indeed...

ALSO AVAILABLE FROM THE INDEPENDENT